THE CAMBRIDGE COMPANION TO
WAR WRITING

War writing is an ancient genre that continues to be of vital importance. Times of crisis push literature to its limits, requiring writers to exploit their expressive resources to the maximum in response to extreme events. This *Companion* focuses on British and American war writing, from *Beowulf* and Shakespeare to bloggers on the "war on terror." Thirteen period-based chapters are complemented by five thematic chapters and two chapters charting influences. This uniquely wide range facilitates both local and comparative study. Each chapter is written by an expert in the field and includes suggestions for further reading. A chronology illustrates how key texts relate to major conflicts. The *Companion* also explores the latest theoretical thinking on war representation to give access to this developing area and to suggest new directions for research. In addition to students of literature, the volume will interest those working in war studies, history, and cultural studies.

A complete list of books in the series is at the back of this book

D0223016

THE CAMBRIDGE
COMPANION TO
WAR WRITING

EDITED BY
KATE McLOUGHLIN

CAMBRIDGE
UNIVERSITY PRESS

CAMBRIDGE UNIVERSITY PRESS
Cambridge, New York, Melbourne, Madrid, Cape Town, Singapore, São Paulo, Delhi

Cambridge University Press
The Edinburgh Building, Cambridge CB2 8RU, UK

Published in the United States of America by Cambridge University Press, New York

www.cambridge.org
Information on this title: www.cambridge.org/9780521720045

© Cambridge University Press 2009

First published 2009

Printed in the United Kingdom at the University Press, Cambridge

A catalogue record for this publication is available from the British Library

Library of Congress Cataloguing in Publication data
The Cambridge companion to war writing / ed., Kate McLoughlin.
p.   cm.
Includes index.
ISBN 978-0-521-89568-2 – ISBN 978-0-521-72004-5
1. War stories, English – History and criticism.   2. War stories, American – History and
criticism.   3. War and literature – Great Britain.   4. War and literature – United States.
5. War in literature.   I. McLoughlin, Catherine Mary, 1970–   II. Title.
PR408.W37C36   2009
820.9'3581–dc22
2009005858

ISBN 978-0-521-89568-2 hardback
ISBN 978-0-521-72004-5 paperback

CONTENTS

CONTENTS

CONTENTS

CONTRIBUTORS

SARAH COLE is an Associate Professor in the Department of English and Comparative Literature at Columbia University, New York, USA. Her first book, *Modernism, Male Friendship, and the First World War*, was published in 2003. She has articles published or forthcoming in *PMLA*, *Modernism/Modernity*, *ELH*, *Modern Fiction Studies*, and several edited collections.

VALENTINE CUNNINGHAM, Professor of English Language and Literature at the University of Oxford, UK, and Fellow of Corpus Christi College, is the author of *British Writers of the Thirties* (1989), *In the Reading Gaol: Postmodernity, Texts, and History* (1994), and *Reading After Theory* (2002), and editor of *The Penguin Book of Spanish Civil War Verse* (1980), *Spanish Front: Writers on the Civil War* (1986), and *Cinco Escritores Británicos* (1990).

WALTER W. HÖLBLING is Professor of American Studies at Karl-Franzens-Universität, Graz, Austria. He is the author of *Fiktionen vom Krieg im neueren amerikanischen Roman (Fictions of War in the Recent American Novel)* (1987) and co-editor of *"Nature's Nation" Revisited: American Concepts of Nature from Wonder to Ecological Crisis* (2003), *What Is American?: New Identities in US Culture* (2004), *US Icons and Iconicity* (2006), and *Theories and Texts. For Students By Students* (2007).

DAVID JASPER is Professor of Literature and Theology in the University of Glasgow, UK, and the founding editor of the journal *Literature and Theology*. He is the author of *The Sacred Desert* (2004) and *The Sacred Body* (2008), and a co-editor of *The Oxford Handbook of English Literature and Theology* (2007).

WILL KAUFMAN is Professor of American Literature and Culture at the University of Central Lancashire, UK, and the author of *The Civil War in American Culture* (2006). His other publications include *The Comedian as Confidence Man: Studies in Irony Fatigue* (1997), *American Culture in the 1970s* (2009), and the co-edited encyclopedia, *Britain and the Americas: Culture, Politics and History* (2005).

EDWARD LARKIN is Assistant Professor of English at the University of Delaware, USA. He is the author of *Thomas Paine and the Literature of Revolution* (2005), as well as the Broadview Press edition of Paine's *Common Sense*. Recently, he has contributed essays to *Novel: A Forum on Fiction*, *Common-place.org*, and *Modern Intellectual History*.

KATE McLOUGHLIN is Lecturer in English Literature at the University of Glasgow, UK. Her first book, *Martha Gellhorn: The War Writer in the Field and in the Text*, was published in 2007.

DAVID PASCOE is Professor of English Literature and Culture at Utrecht University, The Netherlands. He specializes in the relations between culture and post-Enlightenment technologies, and his recent publications include *Airspaces* (2001) and *Aircraft* (2003).

ADAM PIETTE is Professor of Modern Literature at the University of Sheffield, UK. He is the author of *Remembering and the Sound of Words: Mallarmé, Proust, Joyce, Beckett* (1996) and *Imagination at War: British Fiction and Poetry, 1939–1945* (1995).

L.V. PITCHER is Lecturer in the Department of Classics and Ancient History at the University of Durham, UK. His publications include articles on classical historiography, biography, and epigram, and he has produced commentaries on three fragmentary Greek historians for Brill's New Jacoby. He is currently completing an introduction to history writing in the ancient world.

PATRICK QUINN is the Chair of the Department of English Literature at the University of Mississippi, USA. He has written a number of studies on both British and American literature of the Great War and is the general editor of the Robert Graves Program for Carcanet Press. He has recently co-edited a volume of post-colonial short stories and is currently working on a study of American Decadent Literature, 1880–1925.

MARK RAWLINSON is the author of *British Writing of the Second World War* (2000). He has written widely on the literature and culture of war in twentieth-century Britain, and is currently finishing a monograph on Pat Barker and editing the Norton Critical Edition of *A Clockwork Orange*. Future work includes a *Companion to Twentieth-Century War Literature* (with Adam Piette), the completion of a book on narratives of the Second World War after 1945, and further investigation of camouflage.

JOHN R. REED is Distinguished Professor of English at Wayne State University in Detroit, Michigan, USA. His books include *Victorian Conventions* (1975), *The Natural History of H. G. Wells* (1982), *Decadent Style* (1985), *Victorian Will*

(1989), and *Dickens and Thackeray: Punishment and Forgiveness* (1995). His study of the army and navy in nineteenth-century England is forthcoming from AMS Press.

GILLIAN RUSSELL is Reader in English in the School of Humanities, Australian National University, Canberra. She is the author of *The Theatres of War: Performance, Politics and Society, 1793–1915* (1995) and, most recently, *Women, Sociability and Theatre in Georgian London* (2007).

CORINNE SAUNDERS is Professor of English Literature at the University of Durham, UK. She specializes in medieval literature and the history of ideas. Her publications include *The Forest of Medieval Romance* (1993), *Rape and Ravishment in the Literature of Medieval England* (2001), a Blackwell Critical Guide to *Chaucer* (2001), and *A Companion to Romance* (2004). Her monograph *Magic and the Supernatural in Medieval Romance* is forthcoming with D. S. Brewer. With Françoise le Saux and Neil Thomas, she is the editor of *Writing War: Medieval Literary Responses* (2004).

HEW STRACHAN is Chichele Professor of the History of War at the University of Oxford and Fellow of All Souls College. His books include *European Armies and the Conduct of War* (1983), *Wellington's Legacy: The Reform of the British Army 1830–54* (1984), *From Waterloo to Balaclava: Tactics, Technology and the British Army 1815–1854* (1985) (awarded the Templer Medal), *The Politics of the British Army* (1997) (awarded the Westminster Medal), the first volume of his three-volume, *The First World War (To Arms)* (2001) (awarded two American military history prizes), *The First World War: A New Illustrated History* (2003), and *Carl von Clausewitz's On War: A Biography* (2007).

TRUDI TATE is a Fellow of Clare Hall, University of Cambridge, UK. Her publications include *Modernism, History and the First World War* (1998), *Women's Fiction and the Great War* (edited with Suzanne Raitt) (1997), *Literature, Science, Psychoanalysis, 1830–1970: Essays in Honour of Gillian Beer* (edited with Helen Small) (2003), and *Women, Men and the Great War: An Anthology of Stories* (1995).

JEFFREY WALSH taught at Manchester Metropolitan University, UK, where he published a range of books and articles, including *American War Literature: 1914 to Vietnam* (1982) and *The Gulf War Did Not Happen* (1995). His most recent publications are a chapter considering gender adaptations in modern war films in *Gender and Warfare in the Twentieth Century*, edited by Angela K. Smith (2004), and two poetry collections, *River Changes* (2006) and *Tall Ships Returning* (2008).

PHILIP WEST is Fellow and Tutor in English at Somerville College, University of Oxford, UK. He is the author of *Henry Vaughan's* Silex Scintillans: *Scripture Uses* (2001) and is currently editing the works of James Shirley.

ACKNOWLEDGMENTS

My thanks to all the contributors to this volume, to the readers of the original proposal and draft, and to Ray Ryan and the team at Cambridge University Press; to Muireann O'Cinneide, Kirstie Blair, and Hester Schadee ("the Crusades"); and, above all, to my true co-editor, Nick Trefethen. I should like to remember my grandfather, Sgt Jack Shipman, veteran of both the First and the Second World Wars, who died fifty years ago last year.

CHRONOLOGY

(Wars and major texts discussed in the volume)

BCE

11th or 12th century	Song of Moses in *Exodus*
c.750	Homer, *Iliad*
490	Battle of Marathon
mid-5th century	Herodotus, *Histories*
431	Start of the Peloponnesian War
415	Euripides, *The Trojan Women*
late 5th century	Thucydides, *History of the Peloponnesian War*
404	End of the Peloponnesian War
4th century	Sun-tzu, *The Art of War*
218–201	Second Punic War (the Hannibalic War)
58–52	Julius Caesar, *Commentaries on the Gallic War*
49–45	Civil War between Julius Caesar and Pompey
late 1st century	Vergil, *The Aeneid*

CE

c.61	Lucan begins *On the Civil War*
75	Plutarch, *Parallel Lives of the Greeks and Romans*

416–22	St. Augustine, *Concerning the City of God*
?7th century	*Dream of the Rood*
?late 8th century	*Beowulf* *The Wanderer*
10th century	*The Battle of Brunanburgh*
late 10th century	*The Battle of Maldon*
1095	Pope Urban II launches the First Crusade
mid-12th century	*La Chanson de Roland*
c.1225	*King Horn*
c.1270	St. Thomas Aquinas, *Summa Theologiae*
1271–2	Ninth and final Crusade
c.1275	*Havelok the Dane*
14th century	Alliterative *Morte Arthure*, Stanzaic *Morte Arthure* Auchinleck Manuscript (including *Guy of Warwick* and *Beves of Hampton*) *Gawain and the Green Knight*
1337	Start of the Hundred Years War
?1382–6	Geoffrey Chaucer, *Troilus and Criseyde*
late 14th century	Geoffrey Chaucer, *The Knight's Tale*
1413	Battle of Flodden
1415	Battle of Agincourt
1428–9	Siege of Orleans
1453	Battle of Castillon: end of the Hundred Years War Conquest of Constantinople by Mehmed II
1455	Start of the Wars of the Roses

1650	Andrew Marvell, "An Horatian Ode upon Cromwell's Return from Ireland" Henry Vaughan, "Peace"
1651	Andrew Marvell, "Upon Appleton House, To My Lord Fairfax" Thomas Hobbes, *Leviathan*
1652	End of the British Civil Wars Fulke Greville, *The Life of the Renowned Sir Philip Sidney* (written by 1612)
1667	John Milton, *Paradise Lost* (reissued in twelve books in 1674)
1678	John Bunyan, *The Pilgrim's Progress*
1682	John Bunyan, *The Holy War*
1688	Glorious Revolution
1689	Start of the French and Indian Wars
1700	Start of the War of the Spanish Succession
1702–4	Edward Hyde, First Earl of Clarendon, *History of the Rebellion and Civil Wars in England*
1704	Battle of Blenheim
1705	Joseph Addison, *The Campaign* John Philips, "Blenheim: A Poem"
1706	George Farquhar, *The Recruiting Officer*
1713	End of the War of the Spanish Succession
1715	First Jacobite Rebellion
1720	Daniel Defoe, *Memoirs of a Cavalier*
1740	Start of the War of the Austrian Succession
1745	Second Jacobite Rebellion
1748	End of the War of the Austrian Succession Samuel Richardson, *Clarissa*
1756	Start of the Seven Years War
1759–69	Laurence Sterne, *Tristram Shandy*

1763	End of the French and Indian Wars End of the Seven Years War
1773	Phillis Wheatley, "On Slavery"
1775	Start of the American Revolutionary War
1776	American Declaration of Independence (4 July)
1781	Anna Seward, *Monody on Major Andrè*
1782	Abbé Raynal, *The Revolution in America* Thomas Paine, *Letter to the Abbé Raynal*
1783	Treaty of Paris: end of the American Revolutionary War
1789	Start of the French Revolution; storming of the Bastille (14 July)
1791	Thomas Paine, *Rights of Man*
1792	Start of the French Revolutionary Wars
1793	Britain joins the French Revolutionary Wars
1794	Susanna Rowson, *Charlotte Temple*
1798	Samuel Taylor Coleridge, "Fears in Solitude"
1799	End of the French Revolution: Napoleon's *coup* of 18 Brumaire
1800	Mason Locke Weems, *Life of Washington*
1802	End of the French Revolutionary Wars Phillis Wheatley, "To the Earl of Dartmouth"
1803	Start of the Napoleonic Wars
1805	Battle of Trafalgar
1807	Start of the Peninsular War
1812	Anna Laetitia Barbauld, *Eighteen Hundred and Eleven*
1814	End of the Peninsular War
1815	Battle of Waterloo: end of the Napoleonic Wars
1825	G. R. Gleig, *The Subaltern*
1828	Sir William Napier, *History of the War in the Peninsula* (final volume published in 1840)

1830	The Belgian Revolution. The July Revolution in France
1832	Carl von Clausewitz, *On War*
1839	Start of the First Afghan War Stendhal, *The Charterhouse of Parma*
1842	End of the First Afghan War
1846	Start of the Mexican War
1848	Revolutions in Sicily, the Italian states, France, the German states, Hungary, Switzerland, Greater Poland, Wallachia, and Brazil End of the Mexican War
1854	Start of the Crimean War William Howard Russell begins coverage of the Crimean War for the London *Times* Alfred, Lord Tennyson, "The Charge of the Light Brigade"
1855	Robert Browning, "Childe Roland to the Dark Tower Came" Alfred, Lord Tennyson, "Maud"
1856	End of the Crimean War
1857	The Indian Mutiny Charles Dickens and Wilkie Collins, "The Perils of Certain English Prisoners" Mary Seacole, *Wonderful Adventures of Mrs. Seacole in Many Lands*
1858	Alfred, Lord Tennyson, "Havelock"
1859	Alfred, Lord Tennyson, *Idylls of the King* (completed 1885)
1861	Start of the American Civil War "John Brown's Body"
1862	Julia Ward Howe, "The Battle Hymn of the Republic" Christina Rossetti, "In the Round Tower at Jhansi"
1864	First Geneva Convention (revised 1949)
1865	End of the American Civil War Assassination of Abraham Lincoln John Ruskin gives lecture "On War" Leo Tolstoy, *War and Peace* (final volume published 1869)

Walt Whitman, *Drum-Taps* (incorporated into the 1867 edition of *Leaves of Grass*)

1866	Sir Francis Hastings Doyle, "The Red Thread of Honour" Herman Melville, *Battle-Pieces*
1867	William Wells Brown, *Clotelle; or, The Colored Heroine. A Tale of Southern States* John W. De Forest, *Miss Ravenel's Conversion from Secession to Loyalty* Ouida, *Under Two Flags*
1870–1	Franco-Prussian War
1878	Start of the Second Afghan War
1879	Anglo-Zulu War Alfred, Lord Tennyson, "The Defence of Lucknow"
1880–1	First Boer War
1881	End of the Second Afghan War
1882	Start of British occupation of Egypt
1884–5	Siege of Khartoum
1887	Walt Whitman, *Specimen Days in America*
1891	Ambrose Bierce, *Tales of Soldiers and Civilians*
1892	Rudyard Kipling, *Barrack-Room Ballads* (second series in 1896)
1895	Stephen Crane, *The Red Badge of Courage*
1897	Greco-Turkish War Henry Newbolt, "Vitaï Lampada"
1898	Spanish-American War Mahdist Rebellion Thomas Hardy, *Wessex Poems*
1899	Start of the Second ("Great") Boer War
1901	Thomas Hardy, *Poems of the Past and the Present*
1902	End of the Second ("Great") Boer War

1914	Start of the First World War (Britain declares war on Germany on 4 August) Rupert Brooke, "Peace," "The Soldier" Richard Harding Davis, *With the Allies*
1915	Sinking of the *Lusitania* Joyce Kilmer, "The White Ships and the Red" Siegfried Sassoon, "A Night Attack" Alan Seeger, "The Aisne"
1916	Battle of the Somme Henri Barbusse, *Under Fire* Alan Seeger, "I Have A Rendezvous With Death"
1917	USA enters the First World War (declares war on Germany on 6 April) Ivor Gurney, "Strange Hells" Wilfred Owen, "Dulce et Decorum Est" Isaac Rosenberg, "Dead Man's Dump" Siegfried Sassoon, *The Old Huntsman*
1918	End of the First World War (11 November) Enid Bagnold, *A Diary Without Dates* Joyce Kilmer, "Rouge Bouquet" Wilfred Owen, "Strange Meeting," "Mental Cases," "The Parable of the Old Man and the Young" Siegfried Sassoon, *Counter-Attack and Other Poems* Rebecca West, *The Return of the Soldier* Edith Wharton, *The Marne*
1919	Third Afghan War Rudyard Kipling, "Epitaphs of the War"
1920	John Dos Passos, *One Man's Initiation: 1917* Ernst Jünger, *Storm of Steel* Ezra Pound, "Hugh Selwyn Mauberley"
1921	John Dos Passos, *Three Soldiers*
1922	e. e. cummings, *The Enormous Room*
1923	Thomas Boyd, *Through the Wheat*
1924	Ford Madox Ford, *Parade's End* tetralogy (final volume published 1928)

R. H. Mottram, *The Spanish Farm Trilogy* (final volume published 1926)
Laurence Stallings, *Plumes*

1925   Edmund Blunden, "The Ancre at Hamel: Afterwards"
Ivor Gurney, "War Books"

1926   e. e. cummings, "my sweet old etcetera"
William Faulkner, *Soldier's Pay*
Allen Tate, "Ode to the Confederate Dead"

1928   Stephen Vincent Benét, *John Brown's Body*
Edmund Blunden, *Undertones of War*
R. C. Sherriff, *Journey's End*

1929   Richard Aldington, *Death of a Hero*
Mary Borden, *The Forbidden Zone*
Robert Graves, *Goodbye to All That*
Ernest Hemingway, *A Farewell to Arms*
Frederic Manning, *The Middle Parts of Fortune*
Erich Maria Remarque, *All Quiet on the Western Front*

1930   Siegfried Sassoon, *Memoirs of an Infantry Officer*
Helen Zenna Smith, *Not So Quiet: Stepdaughters of War*

1933   John Peale Bishop, "In the Dordogne"
Vera Brittain, *Testament of Youth*
William March, *Company K*

1936   Start of the Spanish Civil War
John Cornford, "Heart of the heartless world"
Margaret Mitchell, *Gone with the Wind*

1937   Bombing of Guernica
W. H. Auden, "Spain" (revised as "Spain 1937" [1940])
Authors Take Sides on the Spanish War
Franz Borkenau, *The Spanish Cockpit*
Margot Heinemann, "Grieve in a New Way for New Losses"
David Jones, *In Parenthesis*
Arthur Koestler, *Spanish Testament*
Wyndham Lewis, *Blasting and Bombardiering*
André Malraux, *Days of Hope*
John Sommerfield, *Volunteer in Spain*

1938   Georges Bernanos, *A Diary of My Times*

William Faulkner, *The Unvanquished*
Ernest Hemingway, *The Fifth Column*
Antonio Machado, "The Crime Took Place in Granada"
George Orwell, *Homage to Catalonia*
G. L. Steer, *The Tree of Gernika*
Evelyn Waugh, *Scoop*
Virginia Woolf, *Three Guineas*

1939   End of the Spanish Civil War
        Start of the Second World War (Britain declares war on
        Germany on 3 September)
        Louis MacNeice, *Autumn Journal*
        Dalton Trumbo, *Johnny Got His Gun*

1940   Battle of Britain
        Start of the Blitz
        Ernest Hemingway, *For Whom the Bell Tolls*
        Arthur Koestler, *Darkness at Noon*
        Gustav Regler, *The Great Crusade*

1941   Japanese attack on Pearl Harbor (7 December). USA enters the
        Second World War (declares war on Japan on 8 December, and
        on Germany and Italy on 11 December)
        Final attacks of the Blitz
        Lillian Hellman, *Watch on the Rhine*

1942   Richard Hillary, *The Last Enemy*

1943   Keith Douglas, "Desert Flowers," "Landscape with Figures"
        David Gascoyne, "Ecce Homo"
        Graham Green, *Ministry of Fear*
        Henry Green, *Caught*

1944   Operation Overlord (D-Day invasions) (6 June)
        Henry V (dir. Laurence Olivier)
        Harry Brown, *A Walk in the Sun*
        John Hersey, *A Bell for Adano*

1945   Bombing of Dresden (February)
        Dropping of atomic bombs on Hiroshima (6 August) and
        Nagasaki (9 August)
        End of the Second World War (VE Day 8 May; VJ Day 16 August)
        Richard Eberhart, "The Fury of Aerial Bombardment"
        Randall Jarrell, "The Death of the Ball Turret Gunner"

?1945   Start of the Cold War

1946   Keith Douglas, *Alamein to Zem Zem*
        John Hersey, *Hiroshima*
        Henry Reed, "Lessons of the War" (completed 1970)

1947   John Horne Burns, *The Gallery*
        Arthur Miller, *All My Sons*

1948   James Gould Cozzens, *Guard of Honor*
        Norman Mailer, *The Naked and the Dead*
        Irwin Shaw, *The Young Lions*

1949   Fourth Geneva Convention
        Elizabeth Bowen, *The Heat of the Day*
        Alfred Hayes, *The Girl on the Via Flaminea*
        George Orwell, *Nineteen Eighty-Four*
        Louis Simpson, "Carentan O Carentan"

1950   Start of the Korean War
        e. e. cummings, "whose are these (wraith a clinging with a wraith)"

1951   James Jones, *From Here to Eternity*
        Herman Wouk, *The Caine Mutiny*

1952   Evelyn Waugh, *Sword of Honour* trilogy (final volume published 1961)

1953   End of the Korean War
        James Michener, *The Bridges at Toko-Ri*

1956   Ian Fleming, *From Russia with Love*
        Primo Levi, *If This Is A Man* (written by 1946)

1960   Robert Lowell, "For the Union Dead"
        Elie Wiesel, *Night*

1961   Joseph Heller, *Catch-22*
        Kurt Vonnegut, *Mother Night*

1962   Len Deighton, *The Ipcress File*
        James Jones, *The Thin Red Line*
        Peter Porter, "Your Attention Please"

1964   Len Deighton, *Funeral in Berlin*

1965	Start of the Vietnam War
	James Dickey, "The Firebombing"
	William Eastlake, *Castle Keep*

1965 Start of the Vietnam War
      James Dickey, "The Firebombing"
      William Eastlake, *Castle Keep*

1967 David Halberstam, *One Very Hot Day*
      Norman Mailer, *Why Are We In Vietnam?*
      Mary McCarthy, *Vietnam*

1968 Richard Hooker, *M*A*S*H*
      Norman Mailer, *Armies of the Night*
      Navarre Scott Momaday, *House Made of Dawn*

1969 Kurt Vonnegut, *Slaughterhouse-Five*

1972 Frederick Forsyth, *The Odessa File*
      Larry Rottmann, Jan Barry, and Basil T. Paquet (eds.), *Winning Hearts and Minds*
      Art Spiegelman begins comic strip, *Maus* (ended in 1977)

1973 End of the Vietnam War
      Tim O'Brien, *If I Die in a Combat Zone*
      Thomas Pynchon, *Gravity's Rainbow*

1976 Jan Barry and W. D. Ehrhart (eds.), *Demilitarized Zones*

1977 Philip Caputo, *A Rumor of War*
      Larry Heinemann, *Close Quarters*
      Michael Herr, *Dispatches*
      Leslie Marmon Silko, *Ceremony*

1978 Graham Greene, *The Human Factor*
      Tim O'Brien, *Going After Cacciato*
      James Webb, *Fields of Fire*

1979 William Styron, *Sophie's Choice*

1981 Claude Simon, *Les Géorgiques*

1982 Falklands War
      John del Vecchio, *The 13th Valley*

1986 Larry Heinemann, *Paco's Story*

1990 Start of the First Gulf War
      Gustav Hasford, *The Phantom Blooper*
      Tim O'Brien, *The Things They Carried*

1991	Dissolution of the USSR: end of the Cold War
	End of the First Gulf War
	Pat Barker, *Regeneration* trilogy (final volume published 1995)
	Don DeLillo, *Mao II*
	Norman Mailer, *Harlot's Ghost*
1994	Jean Baudrillard, *The Gulf War Did Not Take Place*
	Sebastian Faulks, *Birdsong*
1997	Don DeLillo, *Underworld*
	Robert Edric, *Desolate Heaven*
	W. D. Ehrhart (ed.), *I Remember: Soldier Poets of the Korean War*
	Charles Frazier, *Cold Mountain*
1999	NATO bombing of the Federal Republic of Yugoslavia
	W. D. Ehrhart and Philip K. Jason (eds.), *Retrieving Bones: Stories and Poems of the Korean War*
2001	Al-Qaeda attacks on the World Trade Center and the Pentagon (11 September)
	Declaration of the "war on terror"
	Start of the war in Afghanistan
	Ian McEwan, *Atonement*
	Alice Randall, *The Wind Done Gone*
2002	Tom Paulin, *The Invasion Handbook*
2003	Start of the Second Gulf War
2004	John le Carré, *Absolute Friends*
2005	Jonathan Safran Foer, *Extremely Loud and Incredibly Close*
2007	Don DeLillo, *Falling Man*
2008	Martin Amis, *The Second Plane*

KATE McLOUGHLIN

Introduction

How war is written about concerns every individual. It is vital that techniques and tools are found to represent war accurately: such representation might not stop future wars, but it can at least keep the record straight. It is equally vital that techniques and tools are found to dismantle accounts of war that are distorting or deceitful: the process of dismantling might do nothing to prevent conflict, but it can at least lay bare the nature of what is at stake. In identifying these techniques and tools, literary scholarship has a unique opportunity – that of constituting an act of good citizenship.

Less grandiosely, the study of war writing is a source of enhanced literary insight. War reverberates through literature. It is, Ernest Hemingway wrote in a letter to F. Scott Fitzgerald, the writer's "best subject," as it "groups the maximum of material and speeds up the action and brings out all sorts of stuff that normally you have to wait a lifetime to get."[1] War demands the writer's best skills at evocation, not least because of duties owed to the wounded and the dead. Certain literary movements and genres cannot be understood without reference to conflict – modernism and the First World War, romanticism and the French Revolution, epic and the wars of antiquity, to give a few examples – and appreciating the workings of war literature is also a matter of comprehending their wider literary context.

A principle underlying this *Companion* is that all wars are different and also the same. Wars, and writings about them, function a little like the literary canon: influences work backwards as well as forwards; omissions are both inevitable and intriguing; predecessors and successors have to be read – but within reasonable limits. What makes wars differ from one another are factors such as historical moment, *casus belli*, political and cultural disposition of the sides involved, type of terrain, professional or conscripted armies, weapons technology, and so on. These variables ensure that each conflict has its own poesis (and, potentially, genre: in the twentieth and twenty-first centuries, think of the First World War and the lyric poem, the Second World War and the epic novel, Vietnam and the movie, the "war on terror" and the blog). The chapters listed under "Poetics" are period-based and attempt to show what is distinct about the war writing of that time. Further divisions could be made – premodern, modern, and postmodern; pre- and postindustrial, for instance – and, indeed, these and other categories emerge in the course of the "Poetics" chapters. These chapters are confined to British and American war writing ("British," pre- and even post-1707, is a problematic term, but is intended here to refer to the island of Great Britain; "American" is equally sensitive, but is intended to refer to the United States and her preceding colonies). In an ideal world, the scope would be even greater, but addressing war writing from every nation and culture would make for a cumbersome *Companion* and the body of literature that *is* included here has both the centripetal cohesion and the centrifugal outreach to foster fruitful study.

The chapters listed under "Themes" and "Influences" reflect the fact that wars and writings about wars all share common features. "The idea of war" is important to consider as a term-defining starting point. There follow chapters on the words, people, and places of war – categories that must be considered every time conflict is represented. The chapter on war in print journalism identifies the issues that come into play whenever news is brought of war: how closely involved should the war reporter be? How is credibility established? Can and should "objectivity" be achieved? What difference can journalism make? The role of women in war is another hugely important subject. Instead of being confined to a single chapter, women's war writing is addressed throughout the volume, as is writing about women and their lot in wartime. The two "Influences" chapters are biblical and classical. The Judeo-Christian Bible is not the only religious text and Greece and Rome are not the only ancient cultures to influence British and American writing about conflict. But they are the major ancient influences and it is important to be able to identify their traces. Where other religious discourses permeate the representation of war, this is noted in the course of the volume.

The *Companion*'s principle of "different and the same" means that a student of any war writer or war literature will have immediate access to an authoritative account of the war writing of the relevant period *and* will also be able to read lucid and manageable essays about preceding and succeeding periods and applicable themes and influences. A student working on a Victorian war writer, for instance, may quickly turn to the chapter on medieval war writing to find out about chivalry in its original context and then to the chapters on First World War writings to discover what happened to chivalric notions after 1914. And, while it forms a "one-stop-shop" for a student working on any aspect of British or American war writing, the volume also provides more advanced scholars and specialists with instant recourse to the latest thinking by leading experts on war representation, period-based or otherwise, and stimuli for further research.

From what has already been said in this Introduction, it should be evident that writing about war, and writing about that writing, is fraught with possibilities of offending sensibilities, whether by omission or inclusion, and particularly by nomenclature. Every attempt has been made in this volume to avoid such offence, most often by remarking and explaining the nature of any controversy. But, even at the risk of offending, war, for the reasons given at the start, must be written about – and that writing must be written about. Discomfort is only to be expected. Every student of war writing, too, must be aware of the larger-than-usual gap between representation and referent. Five minutes in battle could teach more than any number of texts. Whenever war is written or read about, it is also actually happening and this must give both urgency and humility to our reading and writing.

NOTES

1. Ernest Hemingway, *Ernest Hemingway Selected Letters 1917–1961*, ed. Carlos Baker (London: Granada, 1981), 176.

PART ONE

Themes

I

HEW STRACHAN

The idea of war

The most sustained attempt to understand the nature of war, Carl von Clausewitz's *On War*, posthumously published in 1832, opens with a chapter entitled "What is war?" It immediately proceeds to a normative definition. Having described war as a duel, albeit on a larger scale, Clausewitz (1780–1831) concludes with a sentence which in most editions of the text is italicized: "War is thus an act of force to compel our enemy to do our will."[1]

For Clausewitz, therefore, the central elements of war are reciprocity and the use of force. It takes at least two to wage a war. The one-sided application of violence is not war, and the coercion of another without the use of force is also not war. In practice there may be qualifications to these norms. NATO's attack on Serbia during the Kosovo campaign in 1999 was, to all intents and purposes, a one-sided use of force, with minimal – if any – reciprocity, and the Cold War was waged by threatening the use of force, not by its actual employment (and that may be a very good reason for concluding that it was not in fact a war).

Significantly, nothing in this characterization of war is "Clausewitzian" in the sense used by contemporary journalism. So used, the epithet refers to a view of war as an instrument of policy, a view which refers to war's potential utility, not to its nature. Of course, if a state has recourse to war, its reasons can be called political. That is true even when the decision to fight is more instinctive than deliberative – for example, a response to invasion – and the war not one of choice but of survival. But once a war has begun, its capacity to deliver on the declared objectives of one side or the other is constrained by the progression of the war itself. That is particularly likely to be the case when the war is protracted, and when the original parties to the conflict are joined by others with differing objectives. So policy becomes more often the tool of war, or at least its reflection, than its guiding instrument. In the English-language tradition these self-evident truths lost their purchase in the age of so-called "total war."

Towards the end of the First World War, the French government, inspired by Georges Clemenceau, appointed prime minister in November 1917, deployed the rhetoric of the French Revolution to reject any talk of compromise with the enemy and to remobilize the nation in its pursuit of victory. After the war was over the phrase "total war" acquired a currency in English and German as well as French. It was a language of warning as well as of commitment – a reminder in the interwar years of how destructive European warfare had become. The Second World War proved that the admonition was warranted. Furthermore, that war revealed more starkly than its predecessor the corollary of true national mobilization. If war required the sustained effort of the nation's entire population, civilian as well as military, then those who had hitherto been regarded as noncombatants could no longer be exempted from attack (a corollary which increased the number of potential war writers with first-hand experience). The principle of reciprocity, as well as the justification of military necessity, demanded the bombing of cities and the coercion of labor. The Nazis' extermination camps and the Soviet gulags needed the background of total war to rationalize the horrors of their genocidal policies, even to their perpetrators. The result was a war of appalling destructiveness, particularly for Germany, the Soviet Union, and Japan.

In 1945, the dropping of the atomic bombs on Hiroshima and Nagasaki suggested that any future war would be shaped by similar considerations, by full national mobilization, intellectual and cultural as well as economic and social. Moreover, the air forces of the United States imagined that they now had the weapon to guarantee the effectiveness of aerial bombardment as an independent war-winner. But some civilian strategists argued that the atomic bomb represented not a continuity but a revolution. The threat of total war had now reached its culmination and they contended that the function of strategy was less the waging of war, and more the use of the fear of its being waged to deter war. Thus thinking about war became shaped less by its conduct and more by its political utility, not least because that seemed to be the best way to limit it, and even to prevent it altogether.

The subordination of war to policy brought the destructiveness of war back under control, by setting limits which would be observed not because of moral or legal constraints, but because they would reflect the self-interest of the belligerents. And so a narrative was constructed which made sense of war by defining it as a state activity pursued to fulfill the ends of policy. It was a construction put together by modern historians, certainly with one eye cocked to current agendas, but who were able to trace its intellectual origins to Machiavelli and Hobbes. Niccolò Machiavelli (1469–1527) linked changes in military organization and tactics (both subjects which he addressed in their own right) to political development. "A ruler," he wrote in *The Prince* (1532), "should have no other objective and no other concern, nor occupy himself with anything else except war and its methods and practices." And, he went on, "if rulers concern themselves more with the refinements of life than with military matters, they lose power. The main reason why they lose it is their neglect of the art of war; and being proficient in this art is what enables one to gain power."[2] Clausewitz read Machiavelli and was profoundly influenced by him. It is not clear whether he ever read the work of Thomas Hobbes (1588–1679), although in the English-language tradition Hobbes – thanks not only to his arguments but also to his prose style – has had a far greater influence on thinking about the relationship between war and the state.

Hobbes's *Leviathan*, published in 1651, was a product of what international relations theorists have come to call the pre-Westphalian order. In the first half of the seventeenth century, Europe was ravaged by wars waged not only to define the state and the power of its government, but also to determine its religious confession. Hobbes lived through the British Civil Wars (1638–52), interlinked conflicts in England, Ireland, and Scotland, which collectively resulted in a loss of life in relation to the population comparable with that of the First World War. But the suffering of the British Isles was secondary to that of central Europe in the Thirty Years War (1618–48), a war, or rather a sequence of wars, which for Germans defined the awfulness of war until the First World War. The peace of Westphalia, which ended the war in 1648, did not mark such a neat break between wars of religion and wars waged solely by sovereign states as standard generalizations suggest, but the point remains that for Hobbes, the wars of his own lifetime, fought by weak states and sustained by private military companies, supported his construct that man in a state of nature was predisposed to violence. By ceding power to a sovereign government, and conferring on it the monopoly of force, man gave himself the best chance of living in a state of domestic peace.

The view that the resort to war is the monopoly of the state, and that warfare is therefore solely a feature of international relations, leaves far too much out of the account. In particular it neglects the fact that many wars before 1648, and not a few since, can best be characterized as civil wars. Conflicts conducted to define the state, whether in terms of religion, ethnicity, or governmental structure, have tended to be fought with a brutality and perseverance even greater than those evident in the interstate wars of early modern and modern Europe, at least until the wars of the first half of the twentieth century. But once the definition of war encompasses civil war, it encounters challenges sufficiently great to generate doubts about what the idea of war is.

The British Civil Wars created a legacy for war writing in Britain, not just through Hobbes but also through constitutionalist fears of military government, manifested in Cromwell's use of major generals to administer the country in 1655. It was a legacy shared by the colonials of North America. But for them, too, civil war defined the nation, first through their rebellion against the British government in 1775, and then through the war between the Union and the Confederate states (1861–65). The American Civil War was waged in accordance with the expectations of morality and customary law established for interstate war in Europe. In 1863, the Union adopted the Lieber Code to ensure that the conventions observed with respect to the enemy conformed to the principles of the just war tradition. The Confederate states were rebels, and could have been treated as such, for all that their armies wore a recognizable uniform and their government provided a recognizable political authority. By contrast, in Europe the revolutions of 1848, like those of 1830, were not treated as wars. The revolutionaries produced lists of political demands; they formed assemblies to articulate and debate those demands; and they created uniformed and organized bodies to keep order. In some cases, as in Hungary and Piedmont, the revolutions also contained a clear cultural, linguistic, and national framework. But when the sovereigns of Europe sent in their armies to reimpose order, they used them quite explicitly as counterrevolutionary forces. The viciousness of the repression was prompted by fear, a mood wonderfully captured by Stendhal in *The Charterhouse of Parma* (1839). The monarchs knew, from the experience of France in 1789, that revolution in one country could lead not just to terror within its own frontiers, but also to more general war throughout Europe. The conflation of war and revolution was precisely what had made the Napoleonic Wars approximate to what Clausewitz (in another normative statement) called "absolute war."

It suited nineteenth-century governments, at least within Europe, to work with narrow definitions of war: indeed British military commentators used the phrase "civilized warfare" to distinguish war between recognized nation states from war outside Europe in the pursuit of colonial objectives. To be sure, the latter could fit into a romantic image of war, a combination of travelogue, big-game hunting, and exploration, with a little fighting to spice up the tale, but the reality was often much more brutal than its more fanciful depictions. The native Americans on the western frontier of the United States or the Pathans of the north-west frontier of India did not obey the conventions of war as embodied in the Lieber Code. The refusal to take prisoners and the ritualized mutilation of bodies were capable of generating a cycle of atrocity that was anything but "civilized." The deaths of British women and children at the hands of the sepoys during the "Indian Mutiny" of 1857, luridly reported in the press, were matched by the degradation of captured muti-neers, who were then executed by being blown away by artillery. Punitive expeditions conducted against those reluctant to accept colonial rule had the trappings of later "total war," as they targeted the economic infrastructures of tribal societies and rejected distinctions between warriors and the families whose economic contributions sustained them in the field.

In other words, wars were fought, not only outside Europe and not only in the nineteenth century, which did not obey the customary conventions of war, and which were often not dignified with the name of war. Terrorism and violence could prevail in situations which, while not exactly peaceful, would still be deemed not to be wars in any normative sense. This is not the case today. Since the end of the Cold War in 1989, and even more since the attacks on the twin towers in New York on September 11, 2001, the term "war" has been broadened to embrace many more levels of violence, including its use for purposes that are not strictly political. The United States's adoption of the "global war on terror" is one such oxymoronic usage – a war waged against a means of fighting rather than for an identifiable purpose. Significantly, inter-national lawyers have preferred to drop the word "war" altogether, and to speak of "armed conflict."

For the idea of war to have purchase, war cannot be defined just by the use of force. It is important, for example, to sustain the distinction between war and crime. War is not the same as murder, for all the radical slogans to the contrary. Crime, like revolution, can exploit the opportunity that war creates: by weakening government or by channeling governmental efforts into areas other than policing, war provides criminals with an invitation to profiteer or pillage, or to murder or rape, with greater impunity. But that does not mean that war and crime are synonymous (or that war is a crime). To be sure, the use of violence is a characteristic of war. But so too is the fact that war is engaged in by groups, not by individuals. Groups that are not nations or states can engage in something that we can recognize to be a war, not least because their objectives may still be political. Insurgents committed to ejecting an invader or a colonial occupier are cases in point, and the 1977 additional protocols of the Geneva Convention acknowledged as much.

Identifying the purpose in fighting is therefore one of the ways in which we give coherence to the idea of war, and it needs to go beyond the needs of the individual, unless that individual is a monarch claiming to represent the nation over which he or she is sovereign. However, for most of those engaged in war, including the soldiers of a despot fighting solely because they are acting in conformity with his or her will, war has an inwardness that can elude international relations theory. It has its own dynamic and is best understood as a free-standing phenomenon.

War understood in this way, free of utilitarian assumptions, has two contrasting ideas at its heart. The first derives precisely from the notion of reciprocity, and the unpredictability that that injects into its course. This nonlinear progression is the consequence of the interaction of human agency, but war is also subject to changes in weather, the effect of topography, and the function of luck and chance. Clausewitz spoke of the "friction" of war;[3] others have used words like "fog" and "chaos." The word "war" itself captures these elements. It is derived from the old Germanic term *werra* (confusion, strife), a word which also gives *guerre* in French and *guerra* in Spanish and Italian.

The challenge for commanders is to master this chaotic environment, not to be overwhelmed by the bloodiness of the battlefield, and still to try to impose order and direction – a challenge also encountered by any writer attempting to describe war. The Latin word for war, *bellum*, carries these connotations of order, and significantly also belongs in the realm of law. The tool which the general uses to direct the war is strategy, which Clausewitz described as the use of the battle for the purposes of the war. For him and his generation, the word "strategy" was a comparatively recent coining – the product of the Enlightenment rather than of any classical inheritance, for all its Greek derivation. Today, strategy is used much more loosely and much more widely, often denoting policy itself. But it was strategy that gave us the key concepts by which we understand action in war, and by which victory, at least in the circumscribed sense of military victory, could be defined. Napoleon tried to engage and so pin his opponents from the front and sent forces to envelop their flanks and even encircle their main force. This use of maneuver to achieve decisive battle remained the gold standard of operational excellence at least until the First Gulf War of 1990–91. But many critics, including Clausewitz and his equally influential contemporary, Antoine-Henri Jomini (1779–1869), were doubtful – firstly, because the strategy of envelopment was risky as it required the division, not the concentration, of forces, and secondly, because most commanders lacked the qualities of Napoleon. Clausewitz noticed the similarities between the organized armies of the great powers and the tendency of battles to become prolonged firefights between evenly matched forces – a phenomenon which in the First World War would be called attrition, where success came to be measured not by the effects of maneuver but by the balance of manpower and relative losses.

Jomini's influence in the nineteenth century was greater than Clausewitz's precisely because he set out less to understand war than to provide a guide for commanders as to how to wage it. That didactic purpose has motivated the bulk of writing on war: the dominant aim in the theoretical literature on war has been to provide a shortcut to victory. Sun-tzu's *The Art of War*, a product of warring states in China in the fourth century BCE, is a case in point, albeit one whose impact in the West was remarkably limited until late in the twentieth century. Succinct and even dogmatic, Sun-tzu puts less stress on battle than on deception. This has led some recent critics to see the former as a particularly Western approach to war, derived from the hoplites of ancient Greece and sustained by the Romans. Although this is a tendentious and selective argument, it is one that another well-known didactic writer on war, Basil Liddell Hart (1895–1970), who urged commanders to adopt "the line of least expectation," or what he called the "indirect approach," would probably have endorsed.[4]

What is striking about the idea of war when considered in the context of Britain and America is how much it is in fact dependent on a continental European tradition, and so bound by land warfare. Both countries have relied far more on maritime power than on territorial forces for their own defense and for their prosperity and growth. The latter may be part of the explanation for the low profile of war at sea: maritime power is not exclusively military, but relies on a seafaring people and the use of the sea in peace as well as in war. However, these explanations are insufficient. The English defeat of the Spanish Armada in 1588 and Nelson's victory over the French and Spanish fleets at Trafalgar in 1805, while not without resonance in English literature, did not produce contemporary sustained prose of the quality and passion evident in General Sir William Napier's *History of the War in the Peninsula* (1828–40), arguably the foundation stone of military historical writing in the English language.

NOTES

1. Carl von Clausewitz, *On War*, ed. and trans. Michael Howard and Peter Paret (New Jersey: Princeton University Press, 1976), 75.
2. Niccolò Machiavelli, *The Prince*, ed. Quentin Skinner and Russell Price (Cambridge University Press, 1988), 51–2.
3. Clausewitz, *On War*, 119.
4. B. H. Liddell Hart, *Strategy: The Indirect Approach* (London: Faber, 1967).

FURTHER READING

Gérard Chaliand (ed.), *The Art of War in World History from Antiquity to the Nuclear Age* (Berkeley: University of California Press, 1994).
Azar Gat, *War in Human Civilization* (Oxford University Press, 2006).
Michael Howard, *War in European History* (Oxford University Press, 1976).
John Keegan, *The Face of Battle* (London: Jonathan Cape, 1976).
Brian McAllister Linn, *The Echo of Battle: The Army's Way of War* (Boston, MA: Harvard University Press, 2007).

Jay Luvaas, *The Education of an Army: British Military Thought 1815–1914* (London: Cassell, 1965).

Peter Paret (ed.), *Makers of Modern Strategy from Machiavelli to the Nuclear Age* (Oxford University Press, 1986).

Hew Strachan, *Carl von Clausewitz's* On War: *A Biography* (London: Atlantic, 2007).

Russell F. Weigley, *The American Way of War: A History of United States Military Strategy and Policy* (New York: Macmillan, 1973).

2

KATE McLOUGHLIN

War and words

War literature constantly advertises its own inadequacy. "How can I picture it all? It would take a god to tell the tale," despairs Homer in the *Iliad*[1] – and this in what is perhaps the greatest of all representations of war. Homer's disclaimer is an example of the classical rhetorical trope adynaton (in Latin, *impossibilia*), which can be defined as the expression of "the impossibility of addressing oneself adequately to the topic."[2] It is easy to suggest why this topos proliferates in war writing – but is it anything other than an expression of (false) modesty? This chapter considers why it is difficult to find words to convey war; why, nevertheless, words must be found, and what happens when war and words are brought together.

Why is it difficult to find words for war?

War is a massive and complex phenomenon. The Second World War lasted six years, ranged over the globe, and killed some fifty million people.[3] War reconfigures nations, displaces populations, devastates land. Difficulties in finding words for all this arise immediately. Here is Shakespeare on the particular problems faced by the theater:

> [P]ardon, gentles all,
> The flat unraised spirits that hath dared
> On this unworthy scaffold to bring forth
> So great an object. Can this cockpit hold
> The vasty fields of France? Or may we cram
> Within this wooden O the very casques
> That did affright the air at Agincourt?[4]

Acknowledging that full-scale military conflict can hardly be enacted on-stage, Shakespeare petitions audience members to marshal their "imaginary forces."[5] A link is therefore established between representative disclaimer and imaginative freedom – a key technique in conveying war that will be returned to.

In addition to these practical and logistical problems, other difficulties beset the war writer. Impediments include censorship, political expediency, and squeamishness. The premium on firsthand experience (autopsy) – earning the right to write about war through being there – makes it difficult for those traditionally denied access to the war zone (primarily women) to claim validity for their accounts. Finding words for war is, above all, a complex ethical issue. "Fascism," wrote Walter Benjamin, "expects war to supply the artistic gratification of a sense perception that has been changed by techno- logy,"[6] and there is no reason why this chilling analysis should be confined to the twentieth century. Graphically realistic accounts of war have the disad- vantage that sadists might enjoy them. It is for this reason that the art critic Jonathan Jones argues that the disintegration of the realist image is the only thoughtful solution to representing war.[7] A good example of disintegrated, or fragmented, writing is the list or, to give it its rhetorical title, congeries. Here is an example from Ernst Jünger's First World War novel *Storm of Steel* (*In Stahlgewittern*) (1920):

> On the floor were drifts, sometimes several feet deep, of drawers pulled out of chests, linen, corsets, books, newspapers, nightstands, broken glass, bottles, musical scores, chair legs, shirts, coats, lamps, curtains, shutters, doors off their hinges, lace, photographs, oil paintings, albums, smashed chests, ladies' hats, flowerpots and wallpaper, all tangled together.[8]

Piling up random items of debris, this list evokes the bewilderment of where and how to start disentangling the wreckage: attempting to make sense of the accumulation is the readerly equivalent of picking through the rubble.

But, for some, even attempts to denature the realist image are an insufficient ethical response to the representation of conflict. Famously, in 1949, Theodor Adorno remarked that to write poetry after Auschwitz was barbaric.[9] Revisiting the point in 1965, he "felt no wish to soften the saying."[10] But he used the word *Gedicht* (poem) in his 1949 formulation of the thought (in his essay "Kulturkritik und Gesellschaft"), while in 1965 (in his "Commitment" essay) he substituted the word *Lyrik* (lyric poem).[11] The substitution created a new sense: that it was barbaric to write anything other than *protest* literature after Auschwitz. A more extreme stance is that any literary representation is a form of accommodation and that the arts' supposedly humanizing influence is no bulwark against atrocity. "We know now," wrote George Steiner, whose family escaped Nazi-occupied Paris in 1940, "that a man can read Goethe or Rilke in the evening, that he can play Bach and Schubert, and go to his day's work at Auschwitz in the morning."[12] In the collapse of civilization, "silence *is* an alternative": "when the words in the city are full of savagery and lies, nothing speaks louder than the unwritten poem."[13]

But how can an unwritten poem be registered? Like the two-minute silence held in London on Armistice Day, defined as the space between the chimes of Big Ben and the sounding of the Last Post, writerly tacitness may reside between things: in the lexical gaps, the spaces separating lines, the structural interstices of fragmented writing. Maurice Blanchot suggests that it is linked to "the voiceless cry, which breaks with all utterances, which is addressed to no one and which no one receives, the cry that lapses and decries,"[14] a formulation which accords with Elaine Scarry's finding that physical pain "has no voice ... resists language and destroys it ... reverts to the state anterior to language."[15] The purest word of war would therefore be an unquotable scream of pain, the verbal equivalent of Picasso's *Guernica*.

Such inarticulacy, like silence itself, is an ethical-aesthetic response to the challenges of conveying conflict. But war can also produce a different kind of silence – a psycho-physiological silence – that constitutes another obstacle to its representation. This kind of silence, in which individuals' literal ability to speak is impaired, is a well-documented response to trauma and particularly associated with grief. Faced with the impossibility of concatenating significance, writes Julia Kristeva, the broken-hearted utter sentences that are "interrupted, exhausted, come to a standstill."[16] Paul Marcus and Alan Rosenberg diagnose these symptoms in Holocaust survivors as "alexithymia" – the inability to identify, symbolize, and express feelings.[17] Frequently encountered in war writing is the proposition that war defeats language, as though words themselves have been blasted to smithereens or else suffer from combat fatigue. Such is the view of Frederic Henry in *A Farewell to Arms* (1929):

> I was always embarrassed by the words sacred, glorious, and sacrifice and the expression in vain ... I had seen nothing sacred, and the things that were glorious had no glory and the sacrifices were like the stockyards of Chicago if nothing was done with the meat except to bury it. There were many words that you could not stand to hear and finally only the names of places had dignity ... Abstract words such as glory, honor, courage, or hallow were obscene beside the concrete names of villages.[18]

But this is a verbally rich description of linguistic paucity, featuring the very war-weary words Henry rejects. To recreate the symptoms of alexithymia, war writers make use of rhetorical tropes such as *correctio* (hesitation, amendment, and restatement) and delay. In his "How To Tell A True War Story" (1990) the Vietnam War writer Tim O'Brien deploys *correctio* as a structural principle, while Italo Calvino's "Ricordo di una battaglia" ("Memory of a Battle") (1963) interrupts and postpones the recounting of an encounter with reflections on the nature of recollection itself.[19]

Why must words be found?

Despite the logistical, ethical, psychological, and myriad other reasons why war is difficult to write about, nonetheless it *is* written about. Indeed, the media and modes of its representation are multifarious: an inexhaustive list would include literature, art, music, and dance of every genre; film, television, radio, and the internet; games of every description; and even models, playing cards, pastry cutters, and teddy bears.[20] And the reasons why words must be found for war are as many as the reasons why they are elusive.

In *The Sorrow of War* (1991) by the Vietnamese author Bao Ninh, the writer-protagonist Kien feels it is his "sacred duty" to write about the war.[21] Indeed, the nature of his compulsion is not that war must be written about, *but that it cannot not be written about*:

> Why choose war? Why must he write of the war? ... Is this the author who avoids reading anything about any war, the Vietnam war or any other great wars? The one who is frightened by war stories? Yet who himself cannot stop writing war stories, stories of rifles firing, bombs dropping, enemies and comrades, wet and dry seasons in battle. In fact, the one who can't write about anything else?[22]

When his novel is finished, Kien does not know what to do with it. He only knows that he has "written for the sake of writing"[23] – the great, inarticulable motive at the base of all war literature.

But it is possible to go further than the notion that war must be written about because it must be written about. Seldom stated, though nonetheless espoused, is the thought that writing about war brings about peace. This massive idea emerges – tentatively – through the poignant hesitations of Wilfred Owen's draft Preface to the volume of poems he planned but did not live to see appear:

> I have no hesitation in making public
>   [-?] publishing such
> Yet These   to this generation
>   My ⅄ elegies are not for the consolation
>   th^is in no sense consolatory
>   ^ea bereaved
>   They
>   to this generation.   They may be to the
>   next.   If I thought the letter of this
>   book would last, I woul might have
>   to
>   All a poet can do today is warn.[24]

But poetry – even monitory poetry of the order of Wilfred Owen's – makes nothing happen: conflict shows no signs of letting up. (And, indeed, writing can compellingly make the case for more war.) More realistic is the thought that writing about war somehow controls it: imposing at least verbal order on the chaos makes it seem more comprehensible and therefore feel safer.

To prevent or at least to control war are worthy aims, but attempts to circumscribe it often founder – and fortunately so, if the view is taken that rendering something comprehensible is a step towards rendering it acceptable. But, at the very least, the record can be kept. Often, it is a personal record. Watching a pantomime years after the Vietnam War, Ninh's Kien remembers an incident in which he found a blood-soaked bra belonging to the girlfriend of one of his colleagues, a girl who had apparently been raped by American commandos. The experience is so intense that he wants to "etch" the memories "into his heart,"[25] a sobering response from one who has witnessed firsthand the effects of war on the human frame. To register what has happened – on the page, if not on the body – becomes one of his motives for writing.

But war literature as record keeping is more often expressed as the need to keep the record for others – those who were there and can no longer speak for themselves, and those who were not there and need to be told. Here is the German war correspondent Carolin Emcke on the point:

> I travel to war zones because the experience of violence often leads to the inability to give an account of the injustice endured, to the speechlessness of the victim, to their being forgotten.[26]

The war reporter's task is then to carry the victims "out of the zone of silence."[27] This ethical-aesthetic burden – those who can write must write – is felt particularly acutely by those with survivor guilt. Kien's novel is also composed for and on behalf of his peers:

> He had the burden of his generation, a debt to repay before dying. It would be tragic and unjust in the extreme if he were … to be buried deep in the wet earth, carrying with him the history of his generation.[28]

To give meaning to mass death can be understood in two senses: to make the deaths matter and to explain why they occurred. The latter impulse is made more acute by the discrepancy between the understanding of war of the combatant and that of the civilian on whose behalf he is fighting. That the latter often cheerfully supports the carnage in which the former is suffering and dying is an irony not lost on war writers:

> my sweet old etcetera
> aunt lucy during the recent

> war could and what
> is more did tell you just
> what everybody was fighting
> for[29]

The combatant-civilian gap is at its most acute in "returning veteran" or *Heimkehrer* literature, which records the experience of those who, in Ezra Pound's words:

> [come] home, home to a lie,
> home to many deceits,
> home to old lies and new infamy;
> usury age-old and age-thick
> and liars in public places.[30]

Marked and changed by their experiences, homecoming veterans have been militarized, brutalized, and subjected to unthinkable horrors, yet they often have no obvious means of reintegration into peacetime society. Public ignorance and apathy provoke war writing that is amongst the angriest and most purposeful: at the very least having "the truth told" about combat constitutes a vital opportunity for veterans to reconnect with their former lives.

When combatants express their sense of a duty to act as a spokesperson for others, it is clear that the duty is felt as personally onerous. Discharging it is in some sense liberating – Ninh's "debt to repay before dying." Another major reason for writing about war is that it is cathartic,[31] even curative. Clinical evidence indicates that articulating pain is the necessary precondition of its alleviation[32] – the so-called "talking-cure."[33] Jonathan Shay, a psychiatrist who works with Vietnam veterans suffering from post-traumatic stress disorder, argues that psychological recovery from such trauma is dependent upon the construction of a personal narrative of events that receives sympathetic hearing.[34] Lawrence Tritle concurs with this, citing research that has shown that the re-experiencing of traumatic situations stimulates the production of neurohormones with psychoactive tranquilizing properties.[35] Telling and retelling war can be, then, at some psychic level, therapeutic, as an early literary instance of a veteran hearing recounts of the combat he has participated in suggests: "This song [of Troy] the famous minstrel sang. But the heart of Odysseus was melted and tears wet his cheeks beneath his eyelids."[36] Shay emphasizes that the key element of curative telling is communalization: the traumatized require a community of hearers who are "strong, compassionate, empathetic."[37] Anticipating the lack of such a community, Primo Levi was caused "desolating grief" in Auschwitz by a dream in which he described his experiences to his family but they failed to follow him and spoke of other things as if he were not there.[38]

Finally, the excitement of the fight is a compelling, if distasteful, motive for writing about war. Joanna Bourke, who has insisted upon the element of enjoyment in her intimate history of killing, writes of twentieth-century veterans from the USA, Britain, and Australia: "typically, combatants were able to construct a story around acts of exceptional violence which could render their actions pleasurable."[39] Wrestling with the same unpalatable truth in his analysis of why tragedy gives pleasure, A. D. Nuttall is able to reject the death drive as a motive because of the presence of catharsis.[40] But in war, even if there is an ending, there is no guarantee of a tragic resolution: the pleasure that is taken in pain – if it is taken – is unredeemed.

Or almost unredeemed. Imposing meaning on the chaos of combat through representing it may prove, in Joanna Bourke's words, "a personal bulwark against brutalization"[41] – a harmless enough outlet for aggressive tendencies. Contemplating the pain of others as a means of self-improvement has a respectable history.[42] Words do not bring about peace but, properly used, might make the old lies slightly less credible, occasionally at least.

How can linguistic disclaimers in war writing be explained?

Given that war is widely, and successfully, written about, how can the linguistic disclaimers identified at the opening of this chapter be explained? One suggestion is that they function in the same manner as expressions of the sublime. Kant writes in his "Analytic of the Sublime," contained in his *Critique of the Power of Judgment* (1790):

> What is properly sublime cannot be contained in any sensible form, but concerns only ideas of reason, which, though no presentation adequate to them is possible, are provoked and called to mind precisely by this inadequacy, which does allow of sensible presentation.[43]

To expand this: the sublime brings with itself "the idea of its infinity" and causes the recipient a feeling of "displeasure" at the inability of the imagination to apprehend it.[44] But the failure of the imagination in turn "makes intuitable the superiority of the rational vocation of our cognitive faculty," and this, in its turn, evokes a feeling of "pleasure."[45] In a complex power play between the faculties, the Kantian sublime renders the despair of imaginative failure the precondition of joyful aesthetic judgment.

The adynaton or impossibility trope resonates at various junctures with Kant's "Analytic." When Homer, in the middle of what seems to be a more than adequate narrative of horrific battle, despairs that it would take a god to tell the tale, the reader must pause to revise preconceptions and recalibrate his or her apprehension of the atrocities. The rhetorical trick of communication-by-implication is that absence conjures up presence: a reader informed that a battle is too shocking to be described is likely to envision horrors exceeding anything that straightforward description could invoke. Successful execution of this trick necessitates a curious disempowerment. As a linguistic disclaimer, adynaton makes hyperbolic claims, but they are, para-doxically, large-scale confessions of smallness and ineptitude. Moments of mortification, each deployment of adynaton is an authorial distress flare signaling a linguistic miniature mayday.

But an instant later comes Kant's "vital outpouring"[46] – the point at which the reason apprehends what is beyond the limits of the imagination. In this sense, each occurrence of adynaton is also a cause for celebration, marking the moment when representative possibilities are released and aesthetic judg-ment is given free rein. Hence, the trope figures the beginning, as well as the end, of communication, which makes its presence in successful war represen-tations more comprehensible. Indeed, "success" is twofold, since the ensuing depiction comprises both all that the writer can convey and all that the reader can apprehend.

Words and war

Not finding words for war – or at least claiming not to find them – may therefore be the most potent technique for conveying its magnitude. When words are used, the temptation to repeat outworn ones, to rehearse a version of battle that has more to do with how battles ought to be than how they really are, is difficult to resist. Tolstoy demonstrates this in *War and Peace* (1865–69) through the character of the timorous and ineffectual Berg:

> Not in vain had Berg shown everybody his right arm wounded at Austerlitz, and affected to hold his wholly unnecessary sword in his left hand. He related the episode so persistently and with so important an air that everyone had come to believe in the expediency and merit of his action, and he had received two decorations for Austerlitz.[47]

Berg's recapitulations assume the guise of truth, representation triumphs over reality. In this way, "war" overwrites, and becomes anterior to, war. But difficulties in disentangling war from "war" do not mean that the project of representing conflict should be abandoned. Equally crucial is to find the words for war and to interrogate them at every stage.

NOTES

1. 12.176–7; Homer, *The Iliad*, trans. E. V. Rieu (Harmondsworth: Penguin, 1950), 225.
2. Brian Vickers, *In Defence of Rhetoric* (Oxford University Press, 1988), 491.

3. Martin Gilbert, *Second World War* (London: Phoenix, 1989), 1.
4. William Shakespeare, *Henry V*: Prologue: 11–14.
5. Ibid., 18.
6. Walter Benjamin, *Illuminations*, ed. Hannah Arendt, trans. Harry Zohn (London: Cape, 1970), 244.
7. Jonathan Jones, "The Shame and the Glory," *Guardian* (2 September 2006), 28–33: 32.
8. Ernst Jünger, *Storm of Steel*, trans. Michael Hofmann (London: Penguin, 2003), 94.
9. Theodor Adorno, *Prisms*, ed. Samuel Weber and Shierry Weber (Cambridge, MA: MIT Press, 1981), 34.
10. Adorno, "Commitment," *Aesthetics and Politics*, ed. Ernest Bloch *et al.* (London: NLB, 1977), 177–95: 188.
11. See Klaus Hofmann, "Poetry After Auschwitz: Adorno's Dictum," *German Life and Letters* 58.2 (April 2005), 182–94.
12. George Steiner, *Language and Silence* (Harmondsworth: Penguin, 1969), 15.
13. Ibid., 76.
14. Maurice Blanchot, *The Writing of the Disaster*, trans. Anne Smock (Lincoln: University of Nebraska Press, 1986), 51.
15. Elaine Scarry, *The Body in Pain: The Making and Unmaking of the World* (Oxford University Press, 1985), 3–4.
16. Julia Kristeva, *Black Sun: Depression and Melancholia*, trans. Leon S. Roudiez (New York: Columbia University Press, 1989), 33.
17. Paul Marcus and Alan Rosenberg, "The Religious Life of Holocaust Survivors and its Significance for Psychotherapy," *Bearing Witness to the Holocaust 1939–1989*, ed. Alan L. Berger (Lewiston, Queenston, Lampeter: Edwin Mellen, 1991), 189.
18. Ernest Hemingway, *A Farewell to Arms* (London: Vintage, 1999), 165.
19. Tim O'Brien, *The Things They Carried* (London: Flamingo, 1991); Italo Calvino, *La Strada di San Giovanni* (Milan: Mondadori, 1990).
20. Gifts available from the Imperial War Museum, London: www.iwmshop.org.uk/ (accessed January 2009).
21. Bao Ninh, *The Sorrow of War*, trans. Frank Palmos (London: Minerva, 1994), 51.
22. Ibid., 51.
23. Ibid., 105.
24. Wilfred Owen, *The Complete Poems and Fragments*, ed. Jon Stallworthy, 2 vols. (London: Chatto & Windus, The Hogarth Press, Oxford University Press, 1983), II: 535.
25. Ninh, *The Sorrow of War*, 31.
26. Carolin Emcke, *Echoes of Violence: Letters from a War Reporter* (New Jersey: Princeton University Press, 2007), 199.
27. Ibid., 202.
28. Ninh, *The Sorrow of War*, 112.
29. e.e. cummings, "my sweet old etcetera," *Complete Poems 1904–1962*, ed. George J. Firmage (New York: Liveright, 1991), 275.
30. Ezra Pound, "Hugh Selwyn Mauberley," *Collected Shorter Poems* (London: Faber, 1952), 208.

31. But not "cathartic" in the tragic sense, because it lacks "the complete discharging of the tragic sequence from beginning to end" (A. D. Nuttall, *Why Does Tragedy Give Pleasure?* [Oxford: Clarendon, 1996], 36).
32. See Scarry, *The Body in Pain*, 9; Jean Seaton, *Carnage and the Media: The Making and Breaking of News About Violence* (London: Allen Lane, 2005), 124.
33. The "talking-cure" was widely prescribed, with rest and hypnosis, during the First World War. During the Second World War, techniques such as interviewing or analyzing the "patient" under the influence of hypnotic drugs were used. After the Second World War and during the Vietnam War, the treatments were medication, continued proximity to the battlefield, and constant reassurance of rapid healing (Joanna Bourke, *An Intimate History of Killing: Face-to-Face Killing in Twentieth-Century Warfare* [New York: Basic Books, 1999], 257–8). The talking-cure has its opponents (see Henry Krystal, *Integration and Self-healing. Affect – Trauma – Alexithymia* [Hillsdale, NJ: The Analytic Press, 1988], 253) and should be recognized as a historically and culturally specific activity whose application would distress many veterans.
34. Jonathan Shay, *Achilles in Vietnam: Combat Trauma and the Undoing of Character* (New York and London: Simon & Schuster, Touchstone), 4, 5, 188–92.
35. Lawrence Tritle, *From Melos to My Lai: War and Survival* (London and New York: Routledge, 2000), 69.
36. Homer, *Odyssey*: 8: 521–2.
37. Shay, *Achilles in Vietnam*, 188.
38. Primo Levi, *If This Is A Man / The Truce*, trans. Stuart Woolf (London: Penguin, Abacus, 1979), 66.
39. Bourke, *An Intimate History of Killing*, 42.
40. Nuttall, *Why Does Tragedy Give Pleasure?*, 54, 77, 78, 104.
41. Bourke, *An Intimate History of Killing*, 371.
42. See Seaton, *Carnage and the Media*, 81–101.
43. Kant, *Critique of the Power of Judgment*, trans. Paul Guyer and Eric Matthews (Cambridge University Press, 2000), 129.
44. Ibid., 138.
45. Ibid., 141.
46. Ibid., 128–9.
47. Leo Tolstoy, *War and Peace*, trans. Rosemary Edmonds (London: Penguin, 1957, 1982), 522–3.

FURTHER READING

Michael Bernard-Donals and Richard Glejzer, *Between Witness and Testimony. The Holocaust and the Limits of Representation* (Albany: State University of New York Press, 2001).
Maurice Blanchot, *The Writing of the Disaster*, trans. Anne Smock (Lincoln: University of Nebraska Press, 1986).
Leo Mellor, "Words from the Bombsites: Debris, Modernism and Literary Salvage," *Critical Quarterly* 46.4 (December 2004), 77–90.
Elaine Scarry, *The Body in Pain: The Making and Unmaking of the World* (Oxford University Press, 1985).
George Steiner, *Language and Silence* (Harmondsworth: Penguin, 1969).

3

SARAH COLE

People in war

> Billy was preposterous – six feet and three inches tall, with a chest and shoulders like a box of kitchen matches. He had no helmet, no overcoat, no weapon, and no boots … He didn't look like a soldier at all. He looked like a filthy flamingo.[1]
>
> Kurt Vonnegut, *Slaughterhouse-Five* (1969)

What does it mean to fight in a war? What constitutes a soldier, a civilian, a victim, an aggressor? How do wars change populations and individuals, in an instant and over the course of many years? How does war define a generation or a community? What, in short, does war do to people? Such questions about the profound human consequences of war have always been at the core of war writing, from the *Iliad* (*c.*750 BCE) to *War and Peace* (1865–69) to *Slaughterhouse-Five*. Homer, inaugurating the western epic tradition, imagined superlative men-of-war whose very essence was forged in the crucible of combat. Only war could test and develop what men valued above all else – honor, bravery, masculinity, leadership, and what we might describe as sheer power. Leo Tolstoy, melding his understanding of war into the formal and ethical demands of the emergent novel, figured combatant and civilian life in an ongoing mutual tension, as the long war ebbs and flows over the novel's life-span, simultaneously changing everything and changing nothing for its aristocratic characters. And in Billy Pilgrim, the unlikely protagonist of *Slaughterhouse-Five*, Kurt Vonnegut created an everyman whose absurdity as a warrior ironizes and destabilizes the very category of soldier. In Vonnegut's interplanetary universe, war takes people as they already are – deeply flawed, fully unheroic, brutally savage, at times strangely beautiful – and sweeps them into its destructive vortex. *Slaughterhouse-Five* thus epitomizes what the twentieth century, perhaps for the first time in history, often concluded about war and people: in the face of the former, the latter resemble matchstick figures. They look pathetic, vulnerable, negligible.

To consider people in their relation to war is, almost inevitably, to think in categorical and binary terms – combatant and civilian, men and women, young and old, injured and healthy, prewar and postwar, enemy and friend. And yet, as the trajectory from classical to contemporary war protagonists so clearly shows, to consider people in their relation to war is, equally inevitably, to see those categories disintegrating and losing their force. Billy Pilgrim is hardly man, soldier, American, or member of his generation, and his implausibility as a representative of any of those groups is paralleled and expressed by the nature of the war that produced him. The firebombing of Dresden is the event at the center of *Slaughterhouse-Five*, a staggering wiping away of life that erased any meaningful distinction between civilian and soldier. What Dresden emphatically shows, for this 1969 war novel, is that binaries are irrelevant – even the most central dividing line of death and life is queried in the novel's science-fictional theology. Yet if it was the age of "total war" that eclipsed the protectiveness of civilian life in the most visible and overwhelming ways, the dichotomizing categories that underpin the structure of war have, in fact, always invited skepticism. When it comes to the subject of war's human consequences, its writing almost inevitably follows a deconstructive pattern: war creates distinct types only to miscegenate them; it posits insurmountable differences only to surmount them (at least partially); it organizes the world by animosity only to forge imaginative unities. I propose that, in mapping out some of the central ways that British and American literature has placed people in relation to war, we follow this logic, arranging people tentatively in their seemingly fixed locations, only to see how war smashes apart and rearranges its human participants.

For each of the four categories I shall explore – enemy and friend, civilian and combatant (with subcategories of volunteer and conscript), men and women, injured and healthy – it will be the body that most palpably and irrevocably disrupts the sense of distinctiveness or boundary. Death, as every soldier in every war has noted, is indiscriminate. More specifically, the gruesomely wounded body, so visible and widespread in war, has its own mortality story to tell. In *The Body in Pain: The Making and Unmaking of the World* (1985), Elaine Scarry writes forcefully about the mutability of distinctions that accrue to the injured and dead bodies in war. Even if wounding is the central dividing activity of war, she observes, the dead body itself refutes these divisions:

> [I]f the wounded bodies of a Union and a Confederate soldier were placed side by side during the American Civil War, nothing in those wounds themselves would indicate the different political beliefs of the two sides, as in World War II there would not be anything in the three bodies of a wounded Russian soldier, a Jewish prisoner from a concentration camp, a civilian who had been on a street in Hiroshima, to differentiate the character of the issues on the Allied and Axis sides. But neither would those injuries make visible who had won and who had lost.[2]

Scarry's examples are deliberately challenging – after all, the bodies of Auschwitz prisoners and burned Hiroshima victims are among the most distinctively marked of any casualties of the twentieth century – in order to emphasize that the wounded body is all the more universalizing for its being the victim of very particular regimes and weapons. What the all-important uniform declares, the wounded flesh defies.

As a literary motif, this notion is ubiquitous: over and over, we find in war writing the provocation that the dead and wounded body, perhaps counter-intuitively, pushes back against the organizing oppositions of war. "Then I remembered someone that I'd seen / Dead in a squalid, miserable ditch," recalls the poetic voice of Siegfried Sassoon's poem "A Night Attack" (1916) in a memory sequence inaugurated by the speaker's recent days in heated battle.[3] The poet sympathetically considers the man behind the corpse:

> He was a Prussian with a decent face,
> Young, fresh, and pleasant, so I dare to say.
> No doubt he loathed the war and longed for peace,
> And cursed our souls because we'd killed his friends.[4]

In shifting from the dead body to the imagined narrative of the live man, Sassoon immediately crosses enemy lines. The verb "loathe," for instance, is a key word for his poetry, one of the terms he most often employs for his own expressive animus, and the anger at the death of friends represents a ubiquitous emotional configuration of English writers from the First World War generation. Moreover, from here, the poem launches into an imaginative sequence about the German's earlier experiences, which only ends when the poem returns to his degraded body: "His face was in the mud; one arm flung out / As when he crumpled up; his sturdy legs / Were bent beneath his trunk; heels to the sky."[5] The displayed corpse might seem to put an end to Sassoon's cross-trench musings, yet even at this final moment, the body points back towards narrative; the phrase "as when he crumpled up" reignites the story line, the moment of injuring, as against the dehumanizingly geometric, fixed sight of the body in the landscape.

Moments of unity across enemy lines can be sparked by living connections, too, as with the famous Christmas truce on the Western Front in 1914, which included a British–German soccer match in no-man's-land. The First World War poet Herbert Read has a narrator describe a pleasant moment with a captive German officer, in a sequence evocative of many such moments in twentieth-century war writing: "In broken French," he says, "we discussed / Beethoven, Nietzsche and the International."[6] High culture, socialism, sports, even the simple desire for rest and a shared cigarette: these are among the most frequently avowed principles that align war's human actors across the enemy/friend division. What is distinctive about the encounter with a mutilated enemy corpse, however, is the urge it ignites to give back to the dead man a personal history.

Tim O'Brien begins his searing version of this scenario – in which the sight of a dead Vietnamese body, "The Man I Killed," creates spirals of imaginary narrative – with a detailed, almost aesthetic accounting of the body. Replayed and rewritten, as with many other violent events in *The Things They Carried* (1990), the narrator's reckoning with his own victim functions as a primal scene:

> His jaw was in his throat, his upper lip and teeth were gone, his one eye was shut, his other eye was a star-shaped hole, his eyebrows were thin and arched like a woman's, his nose was undamaged, there was a slight tear at the lobe of one ear, his clean black hair was swept upward into a cowlick at the rear of the skull, his forehead was lightly freckled, his fingernails were clean, the skin at his left cheek was peeled back in three ragged strips, his right cheek was smooth and hairless, there was a butterfly on his chin, his neck was open to the spinal cord and the blood there was thick and shiny and it was this wound that had killed him. He lay face-up in the center of the trail, a slim, dead, almost dainty young man.[7]

Unlike Sassoon and other British First World War writers, O'Brien deliberately avoids any suggestions of shared history, culture, or personal motivation with the dead man, but his meticulous rendering of that body has a similarly enlarging effect. Fantasies of the man's life and interiority flood O'Brien's pages, while the literary figures very consciously used to signpost the body – the star-shaped hole, the butterfly – inflect and organize O'Brien's language throughout the chapter and beyond. There is much of the narrator's own psychic need in these passages; the story of the enemy's body, like his "peeled back" skin or his neck "open to the spinal cord," has an opening effect on the narrator's mental life, which is vividly displayed in these parts of the text. "Even now," he writes, "I haven't finished sorting it out. Sometimes I forgive myself, other times I don't."[8]

These are battlefield moments, scenes that emblematize the experience of combat in terms of a strange, and in some cases deeply troubling, sense of commonality with the enemy. They thus test the first and most overarching distinction of war – us and them. In a civil war, however, those splits are already agonizingly visible. National unity may be a pure fiction, but when it is violently disrupted, as in civil war, it becomes an abiding ideal towards which the imagination constantly reaches. For some writers of the American Civil War, it was the dead and injured bodies of soldiers that provided that very material linkage, as in Herman Melville's commemorative poem, "Shiloh" (1862). In this "requiem" for the dead of a terrible battle near the Shiloh church in Tennessee, Melville movingly indicates the tractability of enemy/friend categories, in grisly death but also in life. With the image of swallows skimming over the corpses providing an opening and closing frame, the short poem impacts, at its center, the conjoined and overlapped bodies of northern and southern dead. It is a poem of configural prepositions – "Over," "Over," "Through," and "Around" inaugurating four lines in its first half – but all of this relationality halts at the church, which literally and figuratively facilitates convergences:

> The church so lone, the log-built one,
> That echoed to many a parting groan
> And natural prayer
> Of dying foemen mingled there –
> Foemen at morn, but friends at eve –
> Fame or country least their care:
> (What like a bullet can undeceive!)
> But now they lie low.[9]

The mingling of "dying foemen" forms the crux of the poem, that which turns enemies back to friends, and this return, the poet indicates, represents a resuscitation of the alignments that should have been in place all along. "What like a bullet can undeceive!" – the line, no parenthetical to the poem's message, makes succinct what many war texts suggest: for all war's language of necessity, its divisions are profoundly, indecently untenable.

In "Shiloh," the poet's voice is that of an observer; not a combatant, but a civilian who sees, imagines, and records. And this is a pivotal perspective in war writing, the outside viewer who in one form or another comes upon the scene of war, and whose distance from the brute realities and intense loyalties of combat might provide him/her with a perspective that can cut through and across war's dichotomies. That such a position necessarily lacks the authority granted soldiers by war's combat violence does not diminish its significance. When Virginia Woolf opens *Three Guineas* (1938) with a description of herself viewing gruesome photographs of destroyed civilians and their homes during the Spanish Civil War, she inevitably calls up the disjunction between her own comfortable domestic position and the ripped-apart world of the people in the photographs, victims of fascist bombs.[10] Notably, she does not reproduce these photographs in her text (an omission whose deliberateness is accentuated by the fact that she did include other photos in the original edition of *Three Guineas*). The effect of Woolf's description is two-fold: she wants to bring her reader into a position akin to a viewer of the photograph, to have us, in essence, read through her prose to a scene of horrible violence. But she also wants to call attention to the mechanics by which that happens – first photography, then the transmission technology that makes the photograph available to a viewer in England, finally her own writing – and hence to highlight a reader's necessary distance from the war and its suffering. It is only with that combination of immediacy and distance, Woolf believes, that we can begin to change our whole attitude towards militarism, war, violence, and patriarchal authority – those conditions which, in her view, have always been the enemy of humankind.

Or, to take a very different kind of example of a narrative that considers the external vantage point to war as a vital one, in *The Return of the Soldier* (1918), Rebecca West has her female narrator (rather than the novella's actual soldier) provide the only window into the battle zone of France. The novel was written and set while the First World War was underway and it bears the markers, via its home-front narrator (Jenny) and its overall atmosphere, of the intense strain entailed by experiencing war vicariously and from afar. Comfortably ensconced in a well-manicured estate, Jenny could not be further from the trenches. Yet her mediated relationship to that landscape, intense and visionary, is richly construed:

> By night I saw Chris running across the brown rottenness of No Man's Land, starting back here because he trod upon a hand, not even looking there because of the awfulness of an unburied head, and not till my dream was packed full of horror did I see him pitch forward on his knees as he reached safety – if it was that. For on the war-films I have seen men slip down as softly from the trench parapet, and none but the grimmer philosophers would say that they had reached safety by their fall. And when I escaped into wakefulness it was only to lie stiff and think of stories I had heard in the boyish voice, that rings indomitable yet has most of its gay notes flattened, of the modern subaltern.
> "We were all of us in a barn one night, and a shell came along. My pal sang out, '*Help me, old man, I've got no legs!*' and I had to answer, '*I can't, old man, I've got no hands!*'"[11]

As in the passage from O'Brien's *The Things They Carried*, much here can be traced to the narrator's psychic needs and desires. To identify with the beloved (her cousin Chris) by participating imaginatively in his war-induced trauma, to traverse the confines of middle-class femininity by entering into the spaces and dialogue of working-class soldiers, to rescript a variety of visual and verbal forms associated with combat into her own language: all of these threshold-crossing desires point back to one primary division whose quiet presence shapes all aspects of the novel. That division is, of course, there and here: the western front of France (invisible, its grim horrors deliberately repressed) versus the home front of peaceful England (jarringly, excessively aesthetic). In these dissimilar sequences, then, Woolf and West each gesture towards a dynamic interplay of war and home, where the proximity and distance with respect to war's most harrowing scenes of violence work in part to reify the discreteness of each sphere, but equally to create opportunities for significant forms of imaginative transgression.

As these and countless other works suggest, a primary distinction that strenuously and inevitably organizes the terrain of "people in war" is that of soldiers versus civilians. And yet, this core distinction is one which the twentieth century has done much to challenge, in some ways even to supersede, for two primary reasons: first, because conscription has made the "citizen soldier," a temporary and often non-voluntary combatant, into the world's primary icon of war (as distinct from the regular army officer, one for whom war is a career choice); and second, because the attack on civilians in modern war has become so vast. I began this chapter with Vonnegut's invocation of the Allied bombing of Dresden in the Second World War, which functions in the novel as a representative event for the war's gigantic swath of civilian catastrophes. Today – with memory of the extermination camps, the explosion of atomic weapons, and the carpet bombing of many parts of the world in mind; with the ever-escalating facts of war-caused statelessness and refugeeism as defining features of the twentieth and twenty-first centuries; with children captured and forced into military service in war-ridden countries – it is difficult to imagine ourselves as fully excluded from the terrain of total war. But even well before the events of the mid-twentieth century made a mockery of the notion of a civilian safety zone, the division between combatant and civilian had repeatedly been breached.

Conscription, after all, creates a field of combatants who belong by desire and identification to the civilian world. The vast conscripted armies of modern warfare are replete with men who do not view themselves as belonging, in fundamental ways, to the codes and realities of the military. Indeed, they create their own worlds around that disjunction. In the journalist Michael Herr's genre-bending memoir *Dispatches* (1977), the Vietnam "grunts" he chronicles – nearly all draftees, of course – create their own lexicon through slogans emblazoned on helmets and flak jackets, many of which reach back to the urban neighborhoods where they grew up and where they expect to return. In *Catch-22* (1961), Joseph Heller makes the crisscrossing between war and civilian life a condition of being, as his panoply of half-mad pilots carry on multiple lives in various continents. Some of his most marvelous comic inventions are generated from this structure, such as the ever-self-transforming Milo Minderbinder, who takes on identity after identity as he is absorbed into the world that surrounds and feeds off of the war's organization. The one thing Milo is not, in any conventional sense, is a combatant. (After all, he is responsible for bombing his own forces.) For the soldier, the invariable point about the line that divides him from the civilian world is that this seemingly stark division is both real and imagined, absolute and porous. In *Catch-22* these contrasts fuel Heller's madcap humor, but in most cases they are the subject of confusion and anxiety. As Private John Ball, David Jones's First World War everyman has it: "You feel exposed and apprehensive in this new world."[12]

War creates such liminalities in abundance. Whole industries grow up in and around areas of combat, including prostitution and black markets, alongside official forms of commerce and management. And since the early twentieth century, journalism has become a primary companion to war, its *personae* of war correspondents and photojournalists adding significantly to the roster of people formed and in some cases killed by war. But it is in the work of healing that perhaps the most pronounced and powerful statements of categorical fluidity have developed. Indeed, of all the many forms of war work, none is more resonant as a site for the complex and self-conscious bridging of differences than nursing. In America, Walt Whitman, who volunteered as a nurse during the Civil War, helped to inaugurate the tradition of nursing literature for the modern age. An attitude of the deepest reverence runs throughout Whitman's *Drum-Taps* sequence, the group of war-related poems added to the 1867 edition of *Leaves of Grass*. Over and over, in these lyrics, the poet's voice breaks through in lament, offering gestures of admiration, sympathy, identification, desire, mourning, and love to anonymous men in and around the battle areas. "The Wound-Dresser," which trains its eyes unflinchingly on a ward of wounded men, is perhaps the most personally wrenching of the sequence. It is a poem, once again, of a dizzying proximity to injury that calls up a reminder of necessary distance, yet these gaps are partially traversed by the gentle touch of the speaker's hand. Above all, what "The Wound-Dresser" offers is a statement of extraordinary empathy, writ through the prism of the speaker's own wholeness and health, in relation to his grievously suffering patients:

> From the stump of the arm, the amputated hand,
> I undo the clotted lint, remove the slough, wash off the matter and blood,
> Back on his pillow the soldier bends with curv'd neck and side-falling head
> His eyes are closed, his face is pale, he dares not look on the bloody stump,
> And has not yet look'd on it ...
> * * *
> Thus in silence in dreams projections,
> Returning, resuming, I thread my way through the hospitals,
> The hurt and wounded I pacify with soothing hand,
> I sit by the restless all the dark night, some are so young,
> Some suffer so much, I recall the experience sweet and sad.[13]

What gives the poem its unique quality is its intertwining of the speaker's compassion with his visceral portrayal of his patients, whose traumatic responses to their wounds are suggested through their physical gestures and involuntary movements, and through their silence. Yet, as always with Whitman, the "I" voice sounds loudly, in this case as a statement of medical competence and stability, and also as an articulation of shared reaction to war's assault, the many references to the speaker's own legacy of anguish shifting the narrative from the patients, who, after all, seem lost in their pain, back to the poet, whose voice prevails.

This configuration – a combination of writerly sympathy, stress on the damaged soldier's body, keen awareness of difference, ambivalent focus on the nurse's subjectivity, and consciousness that this voice has something crucial to say about war – anchors a great number of nurses' war writings. To this we must add, of course, the important question of gender, with nursing memoirs in the twentieth century overwhelmingly authored by women (military nursing having previously been largely a male occupation). Whitman's heavily homoerotic war poetry had uneasily raised the question of sexual desire for the male combatant. With women nurses, the arena of healing becomes very directly and almost universally sexualized. Ernest Hemingway's *A Farewell to Arms* (1929) offers a clear case in point, with the protagonist Henry's distinctly sexual relationship with his nurse Catherine charting an eventual (and illegal) path out of combat for the war-wearied pair. Or one might point again to *Catch-22*, where the sexual high jinks between male combatants and women nurses reach comic-epic proportions (prostitutes, here called "whores," also figure prominently in Heller's war universe). This legacy of sexualized, often misogynistic, portrayals of female nurses reaches deep into contemporary culture, as expressed in the influential Robert Altman film *M*A*S*H* (1970), where the sexual humiliation of the head nurse "Hot Lips" effectively organizes the film's episodic plot. In all of these cases, a central premise is that (hetero)sexual activity is good for recovery. A sign of normalcy and a return to healthy masculinity (with all that implies individually and culturally), to desire the nurse and to have sexual relations with her is, for these texts, to exit the war domain and reenter a productively civilian one.

We find in many women nurses' writings, by contrast, an extremely sensitive, compelling, and at times disruptive account of the gender dynamics created in and by the nursing environment. These works, which engage pointedly with their own writerly status in relation to both war and readers, recall the complex dynamics of desire, unity, and difference developed in Whitman's "The Wound-Dresser." Moreover, nurses often relay their own experiences of crossing the enemy/friend divide. In her First World War memoir, *Testament of Youth* (1933), Vera Brittain depicts her tending of injured German prisoners – again stressing the touch of hands – in terms of common kindness:

> Another badly wounded boy – a Prussian lieutenant who was being transferred to England – held out an emaciated hand to me as he lay on the stretcher waiting to go, and murmured: "I tank you, Sister." After barely a second's hesitation I took the pale fingers in mine, thinking how ridiculous it was that I should be holding this man's hand in friendship when perhaps, only a week or two earlier, Edward [her brother] up at Ypres had been doing his best to kill him. The world was mad and we were all victims; that was the only way to look at it. These shattered, dying boys and I were paying alike for a situation that none of us had desired or done anything to bring about.[14]

Expressions like this one, found throughout the writings of nurses and other women serving in war-related capacities, take direct aim at the logic and meaning underlying the ordering dichotomies of war.

Perhaps the most remarkable text written by a nurse from the First World War, whose imaginative formal responses to the experience of frontline nursing are illuminating, original, and moving, is Mary Borden's *The Forbidden Zone* (1929). As its title announces, *The Forbidden Zone* is interested in what falls between the clear lines of demarcation. Borden's mutable zones include not only the terrains of combatant and civilian, men and women, healers and warmongers, but also of mixed genres: the text, a collection of stories and sketches, represents a pastiche of styles and voices, which reflect different aspects of Borden's years as a nurse in a French unit. For all its internal heterogeneity, at the base of her text is always the human body, often broken into pieces in a quite literal sense, and the human voice, calling out in the frailest of tones. In focusing on war's attack on body and voice, what these sketches ultimately undertake is to derail the fundamental structures that organize "people in war." To see men rearranged into units of bodily dismemberment and mutilation, to feel their weakening will and quiet gratitude for minor gestures of kindness, to recognize the nurse's own place as both a healer and a contributor to war (caring for wounded men so that they can return to combat and be wounded once again, or killed), to feel a strange exaltation along with a numbing of her whole emotional being: all of this burdens the most fundamental category, that of a person's humanity. Over and over, she attempts to break out of a frame of mind that normalizes war's assaults, to stand back from the logic of war and see anew what it does to our humanity. Perhaps most pointedly, in a chapter entitled "The City in the Desert," Borden posits a visitor from another world, who comes upon a field hospital and attempts to make sense of its awful wreckage and counterintuitive physical objects:

> You say that these bundles are the citizens of the town? What do you mean? Those heavy brown packages that are carried back and forth, up and down, from shed to shed, those inert lumps cannot be men ... What do you mean by telling me they are men?
>
> Why, if they are men, don't they walk? Why don't they talk? Why don't they protest? They lie perfectly still. They make no sound. They are covered up. You do not expect me to believe that inside that roll there is a man, and in that one, and in that one?
>
> Ah, dear God, it's true! ...
>
> But how queer they are! How strangely they lie there. They are not the usual shape. They only remind one of men. Some, to be sure, are wearing coats, and some have on iron hats, but all of them seem to be broken and tied together with white rags. And how dirty they are! The mud is crusted on them. Their boots are lumps of mud. Their faces are grey and wet as if modelled of pale mud. But what are those red, rusty stains on their dirty white rags? They have gone rusty and are lying out there in the mud, in the backwash. Ah, what a pity. Here is one without an arm, and another and another, and there, dear God, is one without a face! Oh! Oh![15]

At the center of this bewildered passage is the problem of "men," of what it means to be a man under these apparently insane conditions. Borden's narrator is referring, in part, to ordinary norms of masculinity: would "men," conventionally imagined, submit to such erasure – "why," we may indeed ask, "don't they protest?" But she is also thinking about common humanity: in these states of mutilation and degradation, how can we assert that our very personhood remains intact? When physical wholeness and the ability to speak are both reduced to shards, and when the organization of the world has shifted to enable and perpetuate such reduction, Borden intimates, there are no full "people" anymore.

In Borden's example, then, the dichotomy that most powerfully challenges the belief structure of war is that of injury versus health. Confronted by a man without limbs, "and another and another," having to face a person who himself has no face, is almost too much for the narrator, whose language shrinks back to a cry, "Oh! Oh!" That the shattered body should have the effect of destabilizing any and all structures of division should not, however, surprise us. For we have noted this pattern repeatedly. The injured or dead body, which magnetically draws forth sympathy, has functioned to expand and to link. From its graphic dehumanization, it has made the category of human seem all the more extensive, and, in this sense, it might be conceived as a force for bridging differences in larger ways as well. Let us end with one such vision, one of history's great statements of healing after war – or rather, of war itself as, paradoxically, the force for healing, even as it divides and destroys. Abraham Lincoln majestically concludes his Second Inaugural Address (1865) by sweeping the violently divided halves of the nation back into the "we" of the union, and by envisioning healing as an operation that metaphorically sutures its wounds. As the war continues in its last stages, Lincoln reaches towards its end, imagining care as the final gesture that will bring together all survivors, whether from north or south, men or women, combatants or civilians: "let us strive on to finish the work we are in," the address famously enjoins, "to bind up the nation's wounds, to care for him who should have borne the battle and for his widow and his orphan."[16] Only the dead, alas, cannot be brought into the fold.

NOTES

1. Kurt Vonnegut, *Slaughterhouse-Five* (New York: Dial, 2005), 41, 42.
2. Elaine Scarry, *The Body in Pain: The Making and Unmaking of the World* (Oxford University Press, 1985), 115–16.
3. Siegfried Sassoon, *The War Poems* (London: Faber, 1983), 42.
4. Ibid., 43.
5. Ibid., 43.
6. Herbert Read, *Collected Poems* (New York: Horizon, 1966), 36.
7. Tim O'Brien, *The Things They Carried* (New York: Houghton Mifflin, 1990), 139.
8. Ibid., 149.
9. Herman Melville, *Battle-Pieces and Aspects of the War* (Gainesville, TN: Scholars' Facsimiles and Reprints, 1960), 63.
10. See Virginia Woolf, *Three Guineas* (San Diego, CA: Harvest, 1966), 10–11.
11. Rebecca West, *The Return of the Soldier* (New York: Penguin, 1998), 5. Italics original.
12. David Jones, *In Parenthesis* (New York: New Review Books, 2003), 9.
13. Walt Whitman, *Complete Poetry and Selected Prose* (New York: Library of America, 1982), 444–5.
14. Vera Brittain, *Testament of Youth: An Autobiographical Study of the Years 1900–1925* (New York: Penguin, 1989), 376.
15. Mary Borden, *The Forbidden Zone* (New York: Doubleday, 1930), 120–1.
16. Abraham Lincoln, "Second Inaugural Address," *Norton Anthology of American Literature*, 2nd edn., 2 vols. (New York: Norton, 1985), I: 1466.

FURTHER READING

James Dawes, *The Language of War: Literature and Culture in the U.S. from the Civil War through World War II* (Boston, MA: Harvard University Press, 2002).

Drew Gilpin Faust, *This Republic of Suffering: Death and the American Civil War* (New York: Knopf, 2008).

Elaine Scarry, *The Body in Pain: The Making and Unmaking of the World* (Oxford University Press, 1985).

James Tatum, *The Mourner's Song: War and Remembrance from The Iliad to Vietnam* (University of Chicago Press, 2003).

4

ADAM PIETTE

War zones

Approaching the war zone

War zones destructure any narrative that attempts to describe them with powers of menace capable of warping civilian space-time: the war story's wartime is spatialized into different zones of mind-threatening danger; its narrative coordinates are temporalized into overlapping waves of presents and pasts and futures, lives and afterlives and war-machinic phases intermixed. The approach to the war is a journey into this war-scrambled spatiotemporal zone, and has classic status in any war story. Romance and folk tale establish the generic scene. The hero of the fourteenth-century poem *Gawain and the Green Knight* enters a wild, rugged landscape at the end of his movement through dangerous territory to meet the creature of unreason, the Green Knight. The battle zone is a place of sacrifice, a testing of honor and virtue, a space of punishment. But it is at its core a zone which picks up and decreates the features of Gawain's old world – the green chapel, the courtliness of the enemy, the parade of erotic as well as military honor – by feeding on forces outside Gawain's control, his fear of his own darkest fears, his guilt, his alienation from culture. All this is concentrated into the terrible whirring, rushing, ringing noise Gawain hears as he makes his way up through the "corsedest kyrk."[1]

Browning, in "Childe Roland to the Dark Tower Came" (1855), working with similar folk material, imagines the journey to warfare as an inward spiritual exploration of nature as a series of devastated landscapes, staging posts to catastrophe. All features of the ordinary world are infused with uncanny menace in the combatant's mind as he travels to the war zone, dark memories fusing with apprehensions and confused sensations. Death as the Dark Tower casts its shadow over all things, the unmasked world revealing itself as always already destroyed. The combatant cannot be said merely to be projecting suicidal, pathological symptoms onto the landscape, since it is the landscape's central defining feature, the Dark Tower, which is the core decreating agent. The Dark Tower is the terminus, the killing end to

38

all quests, heart of the "ominous tract" of the war zone.[2] The zone is intense with a specific form of the uncanny, the composite recognition of all things as evil omens marking one out for imminent death. Fording a simple stream becomes a nightmare of fear and paranoia for Childe Roland, the water a hellish "black eddy bespate with flakes and spumes," the willows overhanging it "a suicidal throng," the cow-trampled bank summoning savage warriors past: "Who were the strugglers, what war did they wage, / Whose savage trample could thus pad the dank / Soil to a plash?"[3] The journey to the zone maddens the mind, unhinged by lethal apprehensions and sensations.

Nature is staged as battleground and burial ground, theater of war for the spectating giants of warlike death ("the hills, like giants at a hunting, lay, / Chin upon hand, to see the game at play").[4] And the same uncanny noise that frightened Gawain signals the war zone to Roland: "noise was everywhere! It tolled / Increasing like a bell. Names in my ears / Of all the lost adventurers my peers."[5] The war zone is an echo chamber for the warrior's massed fears, fears that toll the names of all previous warriors, internalized monitory ancestor spirits destroyed by war, brute witnesses (like the hill giants) of lethal breakdown at the terminus. The moment of death, in these circumstances, is both an instant of sudden incomprehensible violence and the image-making of a photographer's flash: "one more picture! in a sheet of flame." War technology freezes the image of the killed for the delectation of the survivors "ranged along the hill-sides," trivializing the death to a cliché image.[6]

Entering the zone

The First World War is, for modern Western culture, the active realization of the folk nightmare of the war-zone quest and its terminal space-time. Wyndham Lewis's account of his first approach to the front line in *Blasting and Bombardiering* (1937) finds all the folk features realized for him, right down to the uncanniest detail. "At this point civilization ended":[7] the journey through the lines discovers the clear point of entry into the war zone where nature is utterly transformed by war – the "shell-pitted nothingness" of Browning's wasteland, the "arid and blistering vacuum," the "lunar landscapes" inhabited by the war dead ("grinning skeletons in field-gray"). As in "Childe Roland," nature is ghosted by its blasted uncanny counterpart, "those festoons of mud-caked wire, those miniature ranges of saffron earth, and trees like gibbets," the world reduced by war technology to a mass graveyard. All is staged as though for gigantic spectators, figures for the dying soldiers of all wars: "these were the properties only of those titanic casts of dying and shell-shocked actors, who charged this stage with a romantic electricity."[8] The uncanniness of the combat zone is defined precisely here as the charging of the atmosphere with the collective trauma generated by all those lethal charges across the landscape. Trauma has theatricalized the zone into a spectacle of deaths repeatedly imagined, space a conductor of lethal energies across circuits connecting all wartimes.

But this is just preliminary territory: Lewis and his companion must cross the old front line, and the German trenches "lined with fresh corpses," with no time for trauma ("I hated all those bodies, but put that impression away, to be pondered at a later time").[9] They must approach the Dark Tower of the new front line. What is astounding to Lewis is that even during the final approach, though heralded by the infernal noise of the artillery, the "angry hammering"[10] of some Green Knight, there is still not a soul to be seen. The trenches have buried their combatants deep in the earth, as though to prepare them for their graves, leaving the zone as solitary as the "grey plain all around":

> Now we were in the heart of this sinister little desert. Despite the angry hammering from the world of batteries we had left, and that from the world of batteries whose frontiers lay not so far ahead, but still not near enough to sound very loud – in spite of that agitated framework to our "mystery land," nothing could have been more solitary.[11]

In the interzone between both sets of guns, designed to clear the land of human presence, it is as though they have succeeded in burying the dying and shell-shocked beneath "this parched, hollow, breathless desert." The war zone is "terrible in its emptiness"[12] precisely because at this point the observing subject is being singled out, as atomized target, the war's sole intended victim.

The zone is unimaginable in civilian space and time, for this is "a museum of sensations, not a collection of objects." In other words, civilians cannot see what the soldiers see, free as they are from the soldiers' fear. To reconstruct the landscape for a civilian "millionaire sightseer" would be to construct the museum without the core features of the war zone, Death and the dead: "For your reconstruction you would have to admit Death as well, and he would never put in an appearance, upon those terms. You would have to line the trenches with bodies guaranteed freshly killed that morning. No hospital would provide it." To obtain the desert that is the war zone you would also need the incredible massed ordnance to create the destroyed landscape, and that is to "postulate madmen." And it is this that gives Lewis the clue to all war zones: "It was the hollow centre of a madman's dream we had got into."[13] The hollow centre, the empty site of destroyed nature inhabited by the hammering of a madman's technology and the uncanny electricity of the war dead, is a fool's inferno. At the hollow core of the war zone is this triple recognition: this is Death's country; it is empty of civilization and culture – only the names and ghosts of the dead and those about to die exist amid blasted parodies of all ordinary objects; and it is here that time and space meet and tangle into awful shapes as if at some mad destructive terminus. The "cratered nothingness" of the interzone is a kind of hillside "terminating eventually in another ridge."[14] Lewis and his companion meet two soldiers crouching behind a wall at the summit of the incline "terminating in this fragment of wall." They can only hear their own feet on the move, "echoing faintly from end to end of this mysterious place of death."[15] Everything echoes within this closed-in zone of ends and terminations, a hollowness that marks each step as a gamble with Death under the shadow of the Dark Tower. Death in this place is a gigantic observer with a flashgun, capturing its targets in its own wartime, forcing combatants inwards to inhabit as desolate a mental war zone: "We met an infantry party coming up, about ten men, with earthen faces and heads bowed, their eyes turned inward as it seemed, to shut out this too-familiar scene. As a shell came bursting down beside them, they did not notice it. There was no sidestepping death if this was where you *lived.*"[16]

The Dantescan inwardness of the combatants is matched by a further warping of all war story. All war stories, if based on the real death of combatants, must suffer the painful difference constituted by the post-mortem status of elegiac writing. It is this post-mortem timing which must alter the representation of the war zone according to other forms of echo, the echo of conventions, necessarily restabilizing the warped sensations of the zone.

The war zone as elegiac space

On June 9, 1944, Keith Douglas was killed near St. Pierre in Normandy after patrolling ahead of his regiment to locate enemy tanks. Desmond Graham's biography of Douglas ends with this brief paragraph describing the strange way he died:

> Douglas had climbed from his tank to make his report, when the mortar fire started. As he ran along the ditch one of the shells exploded in a tree above him. He must have been hit by a tiny fragment, for although no mark was found on his body, he was instantly killed.[17]

The last words of Graham's biography, strange tale of a poet's body miraculously preserved – the paragraph is quietly elegiac. The prose celebrates its hero *sotto voce*, with the odd hagiographical intervention from the post-mortem report participating within the very sentence describing the death.

In the manner of his dying, Douglas was confirmed as the Second World War's Adonis, its darling child and voice, body preserved in its perfection to enable posterity to mourn the passing of the miraculous voice of the war's own poet. Douglas's death makes the war zone a strange, quiet graveyard, his untouched body a sign of the preserved privacy and sanctity of his gift. The footnote to those last words in Graham's biography reads: "Skinner and [John Bethell-Fox] made a temporary grave for him on the hillside; Keith Douglas's body now lies in the War Cemetery, Tilly-sur-Seulles, plot 1, row B, grave no. 2."[18] These lapidary words perform the ceremony that transforms the remains of the poet's body into a future site of pilgrimage. Matching the mystery of the war zone and its lethal tree (the makeshift grave on the hillside) to the war grave memorial creates twin sites preserving the double memory of the poet's body for those of us ranged along other hillsides.

The war zone as elegiac space is a construct of postwar record narratives. Graham's biography is a war elegy based on a fragmentary narrative: Douglas's fellow officer John Bethell-Fox's *Green Beaches* (1944), which he wrote in hospital after being wounded in Normandy.[19] The hospital text is an aftermath narrative of Douglas's death and Graham supplements Bethell-Fox's story of the death under the fatal tree with details from the post-mortem report. War itself, however, in its own time, has no time for elegy. The war zone is destructive of elegy, warping the time needed to mourn, forcing the mourner to "put that impression away, to be pondered at a later time."

There exists a narrative of Douglas's death written the same day, a text written in something approaching real wartime rather than as a postwar record. Rev. Leslie Skinner, Chaplain to the 8th (Independent) Armored Brigade (Douglas's regiment), published his war diary after the war, and this is the entry for June 9, D-Day+3:

> News of death Captain K. Douglas on forward slopes Pt. 102. CO refused permission for me to go forward recover body – enemy dug in with tank support. Two drivers of A. Echelon taking up replenishments wounded. Helped bring them in – then evacuated to ADS. Back 20.00. News death Lt. Peter Pepler on same slopes as Douglas. Clearing area forward of Pt. 102 effective but costly. Tanks forward 1 mile on downward slopes to allow infantry and anti-tank to dig in and cover approaches to St. Pierre and Tilly sur Seulles – ditto on left towards Fontenay and Cruelly. By midnight our tanks pulling back, refuel etc., leaving one squadron in open leaguer to hold the hill.
>
> Remaining tanks joined A. Echelon at Brecy above and south of Cruelly near St. Gabriel. All safely back in by 02.00 hours. Stayed up to see tanks in and check casualties etc. Bed by 03.00 after sharp words with CO about not being allowed forward to recover bodies of Douglas and Pepler.[20]

In the war zone, the body of the poet is an insignificant encumbrance, a simple casualty lost at the back of the CO's mind, lost within Rev. Skinner's own narrative, despite his pastoral concern for the fate of the dead. Douglas's death is just one item in a bewildering narrative of military movements and events, a word ("body") lost in the military jargon and telegraphic urgencies of wartime history. For Skinner is recording history in the making, D-Day+3, the regiment's history, the military story of the struggle for the hillsides of France. His sharp words to his CO have true pastoral feeling, but his diary entry shares his commanding officer's urgent concern with the military vision of the day. We need only compare the elegiac pathos of the postwar record – "although no mark was found on his body" – with Skinner's bare account – "CO refused permission for me to go forward recover body ... not being allowed forward to recover bodies of Douglas and Pepler" – to hear the gulf between wartime expediencies and war record plangencies.

Echoes in the war zone

Both hagiography and wartime diary interpose the ghosts of other voices to articulate Douglas's death: Graham resorts to the conventions of elegy; Rev. Skinner to the language of the military machine. In most accounts of war zones, a similar ghostly echoing occurs, a tolling noise of names of all the "lost adventurers." The echoic effect rang in Douglas's ears before he died, as shown in the *obiter dicta* of "Desert Flowers" (1943): "Rosenberg I only repeat what you were saying."[21] The burden of the First World War's shaping of the practice of Second World War writing is that war writing is always implicitly a matter of painful recall, of repetition of other wars dramatized as a guilty working through, repression of, and struggle with the terrible deaths of other past combatants. The repetition mimics the tolling echoes of the war zone.

Douglas's three "Landscape with Figures" poems (1943) concern this uncomfortable derivativeness. In the first, the poet flies over the battlefield hungry for the dead, adopting the subject position of the giant observers conjured by the First World War poets, specifically Wilfred Owen in "The Show" (1918): "My soul looked down from a vague height, with Death." Owen's airman observer, with his Death's point-of-view, looks down on a lunar landscape, the soldiers crawling to their deaths like caterpillars.[22] But Douglas finds only destroyed machines, "monuments and metal posies."[23] "Landscape with Figures II" meditates on the second war's theatricality, the dead mere "mimes" "crawling on the boards of the stage like walls," Douglas again viewing them from demonic heights. Adopting the view of the machinic observers of another war zone, Douglas is in guilty torment over his incapacity to feel. "I am the figure writing on the backcloth"[24] is revealed as one of the damned in "Landscape with Figures III": "I am the figure burning in hell."[25] What damns him is this sick inhabiting of the subject position of First World War reportage and war-zone witness.

War-zone writing is at once a mad slandering of the dead, an obscenely voyeuristic act of observation, a pruriently self-luxurious writhing in one's own guilt, and a cool, technically accomplished charting of these derivative attitudes. What is generated by this ghosting of the war zone by other wars is a demonic hunger for gory detail in the war reporter, an indifference to the meaning of the many deaths. The energy expended struggling to emulate the war poets of the First World War, Douglas's poems argue, is so debilitating that the mind is corrupted from engagement with the landscapes and figures of the real desert war, except as rhetorical figures, as contexts merely mechanically occasional to the production of derivative texts.

The echoic nature of war writing unpicks a too facile contrast between First and Second World War writing, for representations of all war zones must necessarily derive from other zones. Isaac Rosenberg, writing from the trenches, felt keenly the second-hand nature of his representations, not in the sense of commonplace cliché, but as a repeat of the war work of Walt Whitman: "[The war] should be approached in a colder way, more abstract, with less of the million feelings everybody feels; or all should be concentrated in one distinguished emotion. Walt Whitman in 'Beat, drums, beat,' [sic] has the noblest thing on war."[26] The approach to the war zone is governed, in other words, by other words: Whitman's voices from the American Civil War. "The Homer for the war has yet to be found," argued Rosenberg, unless his name echoes Whitman's: "Whitman got very near the mark 50 years ago with 'Drum Taps'."[27] Rosenberg's war zone is full of the noise of Whitman's drumming: "'Drum Taps' stands unique as War Poetry in my mind. I have written a few war poems but when I think of 'Drum Taps' mine are absurd."[28]

Moreover, Whitman's own work is subject to the same form of echolalia, his war zone haunted by the chronotopes of other wars. In the 1865 "The Centenarian's Story," the battlefields of the civil war are inhabited by the ghosts of the dead ("the phantoms return"), the dead of another war, the Revolutionary War, and his war writing is troped as a story repeating the war songs of that time: "I must copy the story and send it eastward and westward," sings the voice of the war dead, Terminus.[29] It is Terminus who rules the zone of war writing, writing which is always a traumatic return to the real zone of suffering and death, writing which is always recollected, belated, painfully derivative of the collective experiences of the war dead, the dead of the "other" war that has happened. Terminus is the god of the war zone's Dark Tower, the terminating observer of each soldier's end.

Terminus

The First World War poets wrote their poems under the sign of Terminus, the war zone recollected as a zone of all the war dead. Rosenberg's "Dead Man's Dump" (1917) recalls the dead of the battle as timelessly repeating their last strides towards the terminus:

> Timelessly now, some minutes past,
> These dead strode time with vigorous life,
> Till the shrapnel called "an end!"[30]

The dying soldier lies among these dead: "They left this dead with the older dead."[31] Terminus governs the belated, derivative space of the war zone, where the dying make echoic noise, like the half-conscious composing mind of the poet, haunted by the presences of "the older dead."

The terminal noise of death's effects at the war zone has not remained a soldier's dark privilege, however. The distinction between military and civilian zones which the front lines of the First World War preserved has fallen away as war technology has trained its terrible eye on civilian populations. The genocidal wars of the twentieth century, the blitzes and area bombing campaigns of the Second World War, the Holocaust, the deliberate terrorist shelling of civilians in war zone cities, the Cold-War targeting of entire populations by nuclear weapons systems have expanded the potential war zone to include the whole world and all its civilians. Wendell Stevenson, in a piece of war reportage from Lebanon in *Granta's War Zones* issue, passed on the story of the Shaito family, Beirut Shi'as trying to escape from the city under Israeli bombardment. Crammed into a minivan, they drive through the hills of southern Lebanon, only to suffer a rocket attack. When the second missile hits the hired minivan, "there was a silence of shock and burst eardrums. Everyone was covered in blood. Still they were quiet; no one screamed. Ali and Abbas had their clothes torn to shreds, their faces blasted with sooty debris. 'When we were hit,' Ali said, 'there was no sound, only blood splashing.'"[32] In the wars on civilians, it is the war zone which tracks the family down, ambushes it from peaceable hills and skies. The shock of the attack, though announced by the ear-splitting missile strike, generates its own quiet wartime, a stillness of horror that this car, these bodies, this little civilian space and time, have become war zone, the zone of no sound, only blood splashing.

NOTES

1. J.R.R. Tolkien and E.V. Gordon (eds.), *Sir Gawain and the Green Knight* (Oxford: Clarendon, 1925), 60.

2. Robert Browning, "Childe Roland to the Dark Tower Came," *Poetical Works*, 17 vols. (London: Smith, Elder, 1888–94), V: 195.
3. Ibid., 200–1.
4. Ibid., 204.
5. Ibid., 205.
6. Ibid., 205.
7. Wyndham Lewis, "A Day of Attack," *A Soldier of Humour and Selected Writings*, ed. Raymond Rosenthal (New York: Signet Classics, 1966), 221.
8. Ibid., 221.
9. Ibid., 222.
10. Ibid., 222.
11. Ibid., 222.
12. Ibid., 221.
13. Ibid., 223.
14. Ibid., 221.
15. Ibid., 223.
16. Ibid., 224–5.
17. Desmond Graham, *Keith Douglas, 1920–1944: A Biography* (Oxford University Press, 1974), 256.
18. Ibid., 283.
19. Ibid., 293.
20. Leslie Skinner, *The Man Who Worked on Sundays* (privately published, 1991), 17.
21. Keith Douglas, "Desert Flowers," *The Complete Poems*, ed. Desmond Graham (Oxford University Press, 1978), 102.
22. Wilfred Owen, "The Show," *The Complete Poems and Fragments*, ed. Jon Stallworthy, 2 vols. (London: Chatto & Windus, The Hogarth Press, Oxford University Press, 1984), I: 155.
23. Douglas, *The Complete Poems*, 103.
24. Ibid., 103.
25. Ibid., 104.
26. Letter to Mrs. Cohen of June/July 1916, *The Collected Works of Isaac Rosenberg: Poetry, Prose, Letters, Paintings and Drawings*, ed. Ian Parsons (London: Chatto & Windus, 1979), 237.
27. Letter to Marsh of December 1916, Rosenberg, *The Collected Works*, 250.
28. Letter to Joseph Leftwich of 8 December 1917, Rosenberg, *The Collected Works*, 266.
29. Walt Whitman, *Complete Poetry and Selected Prose* (New York: Library of America, 1982), 434.
30. "Dead Man's Dump," Rosenberg, *The Collected Works*, 110.
31. Ibid., 110.
32. Wendell Stevenson, "Victory in Lebanon," *Granta* 96 (Winter 2006), 43–58: 48.

FURTHER READING

Harold Bloom, "The Internalization of the Quest-Romance," *Romanticism and Consciousness: Essays in Criticism*, ed. Harold Bloom (New York: Norton, 1970), 3–24.
Lynne Hanley, *Writing War: Fiction, Gender, and Memory* (Amherst: University of Massachusetts Press, 1991).

5

KATE McLOUGHLIN

War in print journalism

Until the nineteenth century, British and American newspapers obtained accounts of battles from participants or chance observers. One of the earliest instances of a war report in the American press, "French and Indians Murder Settlers on Virginia Frontier," appeared in the *Pennsylvania Gazette* (proprietor: Benjamin Franklin) on July 5, 1753:

> New York, July 2 …
>
> By a Gentleman who came Passenger in Captain Kiersted, who arrived here last Friday, in 9 Days from Topsail Inlet, in North-Carolina, we learn that the Day before he sailed from thence, they had Advice there, that an Express was arrived at Charles-Town, in South-Carolina, from Virginia, with an Account, that a large Body of French and Indians, amounting to between 7 and 800, were arrived on their back Settlements, and had murdered all the Inhabitants of an out Village in the Province of Virginia, except a Girl of about 10 Years old, who fled into the Wood, and by that Means escaped the Cruelty of these Merciless Savages.[1]

The hallmarks of print war journalism are present even in this simple synopsis. A dateline ("New York, July 2") is provided to set the place and time from which the news derives; partisanship is not eschewed ("murdered," "cruelty," "merciless savages"); and the survival of a little girl provides a human interest element. Above all, care is taken to establish as precisely as possible the source and age of the data. The "news," when it reaches the reader, is some two weeks old, but what is significant is the effort made to render the links in the chain of information exchange as strong as possible. Though what is published is at least third-hand hearsay, the underlying principle is that the credibility of an account is in direct proportion to the news-gatherer's proximity to events.

The media of written war reporting are newspapers, magazines, and, now, the virtual texts available on the internet. Each medium has its own poesis or approach to writing: variables such as deadline dates, frequency of publication, editorial policy and etiquette, amount of space devoted to the story, and the availability of illustration result in pieces ranging from the urgently laconic to the leisurely reflective, from the briefly factual to the complexly opinionated, from the quirkily personal to the broadly synoptic. (Television and radio war journalism have their own set of variables.) But despite these variations, modern war correspondence, from its beginnings, has had a primary objective – to achieve believability through an *ethos* (the Aristotelian term for persuasive appeal located in character) based on *autopsy* or firsthand experience. It is this objective that underlies the practice that was in its infancy in 1808 when the London *Times* sent Henry Crabb Robinson to Spain to report on the British forces fighting the Peninsular War.[2] The first conflict to which American newspapers sent correspondents on a significant scale was the Mexican War (1846–48): indeed, newspaper proprietors such as George Wilkins Kendall, founder of the New Orleans *Picayune*, actually agitated for the conflict in the first place. John Hohenberg observes that "it was the fashion for correspondents to prove their daring by fighting rather than sit on the side-lines as non-combatants" and, proving his proximity to the action, Kendall, one of forty correspondents in Mexico, captured a Mexican Cavalry flag, was mentioned twice in dispatches, and was wounded in the knee.[3]

The inchoate war correspondent was therefore already performing on behalf of readers what Géraldine Muhlmann has characterized as the "witness-ambassador" role.[4] The nature of this role is further illuminated by the dispatches sent to Horace Greeley's *New York Tribune* by another proto-war reporter, Sarah Margaret Fuller Ossoli (Margaret Fuller), who was based in Rome during the revolutionary years of 1848–49. Each dispatch was personally posted by Fuller and took around a month to reach America, appearing in the newspaper with a dateline and the opening "Messrs. Greeley and McElrath:."[5] The letter-like characteristics of these early dispatches reveal the epistolary element of war correspondence. Though newspaper articles about war lack the true dialogic nature implied by the etymology of "correspondence," their epistolary qualities suggest the necessary mutual confidence of the reader–war reporter relationship. The importance of maintaining this confidence is evident in an anecdote told by Emmet Crozier, who, in 1918, was working on the *New York Globe* and nursing a desire to go to France as a war correspondent. A colleague brought Crozier "odd fragments" about the war, "second hand" material some of which Crozier suspected was contrived, but which represented his "only chance, albeit vicarious, to be a war correspondent." After the war, Crozier discovered that *all* the material was fabricated and felt that "a shabby trick" had been played "on *Globe* readers and on the integrity of journalism."[6] What had been attenuated, to the loss of both sides, was the autopsy-based ethos.

The reader–war reporter relationship, then, is founded on a credibility/ closeness ratio. Next to proximity in importance is priority. George Washburn Smalley, founder of the first overseas news bureau (for the New York *Herald Tribune*), believed that:

> In modern war correspondence, the race is emphatically to the swift, the battle to the strong. The best organizer of the means for expediting his intelligence, he it is who is the most successful man – not just your deliberate manufacturer of telling phrases, your piler-up of coruscating adjectives.[7]

News of war, in other words, must be *fast* as well as accurate. Legendary "scoops" include Marguerite Duras reaching Dachau for the *Herald Tribune* before the American troops arrived; Doon Campbell getting first to the Normandy beaches for Reuters; Max Hastings of the London *Evening Standard* walking first into Port Stanley in 1982; Bob McKeown making the first live broadcast (for CBS) from Kuwait City in 1991; Tim Marshall (Sky News) welcoming British forces into Pristina in 1999; and, in the War in Afghanistan, John Simpson "liberating" Kabul for the BBC.[8] Such "firsts" themselves become the "peg" or "frame"[9] for the news material, often with the (undesirable) result of transforming the reporter into the story. As may be inferred from these instances, accessing the war zone requires considerable resourcefulness and resilience on the part of the war correspondent, who must operate as what the French sociologist Michel de Certeau has termed a "tactician." For de Certeau, tactics are cunning and subtle "ways of operating" that constitute a means for the individual to thrive within dominant power structures (in the context of war, the military authorities). Using clever tricks, the knowledge of how to get away with things, "hunter's cunning," maneuvers, polymorphic simulations, and joyful discoveries, the successful war recorder insinuates himself or herself into the arena of war.[10]

Success has been more elusive for women war correspondents, traditionally denied access to this arena. In *Journalism for Women: A Practical Guide* (1898), Arnold Bennett advised female journalists to confine themselves to the "woman's sphere" – "fashion, cookery and domestic economics, furniture, the toilet, and (less exclusively) weddings and what is called society news."[11] In the context of conflict, this mentality limits women to what may be called *parapolemics* – those spatial and temporal margins of war that include such phenomena as visits to hospitals and orphanages, the home front, interviews of the waiting and the bereaved, and the domestic war effort. These were the subjects to which Cora Crane was expected to devote herself when she accompanied her partner, Stephen Crane, to report on the Greco-Turkish war in 1897. Under the name Imogene Carter, she wrote in the *New York Journal* on May 14, 1897:

> In Athens one can get an idea of war which satisfied, it is true, the correspondents of many London newspapers, but surely this is not the whole of war. War here is tears and flowers and blood and oratory. Surely there must be other things. I am going to try and find out at the front.[12]

Emphatically rejecting parapolemical "tears and flowers and blood and oratory," Cora Crane did reach the war zone, where the soldiers were "amazed at the presence of a woman during the fighting."[13] The idea that the presence of women in battle is anomalous was slow to die. Twenty years after Cora Crane's experiences in Greece, the US Army still refused to accredit women journalists to cover American action on the western front during the First World War.[14] Notwithstanding, Mary Roberts Rinehart entered no-man's-land before the first official visit organized for correspondents and Rheta Childe Dorr (*New York Mail*), Bessie Beatty (*San Francisco Bulletin*), and Louise Bryant (Bell Syndicate) covered the war between Germany and Russia.[15] Edith Wharton also visited the trenches, sending dispatches to *Scribner's* magazine (collected as *Fighting France: From Dunkerque to Belfort* [1915]).

In her pointedly titled memoirs, *No Woman's World* (1946), Iris Carpenter, correspondent for the North Atlantic Newspaper Alliance, gives a clear idea of the restrictions still faced by female reporters during the Second World War. In France, women correspondents were confined to field hospitals that were, paradoxically, nearer to the enemy lines than the press camps occupied by the male journalists and therefore more dangerous.[16] Their copy had to be sent through the ordinary field-message service, arriving four to seven days after it was written and making no sense anyway as it was censored away from the field.[17] Nonetheless, despite these limitations, American and British women did attain the war zone – and often attained it first. Since Vietnam, the US Defense Department has allowed women to cover combat on an equal footing with men,[18] thus granting them the opportunity to establish the credentials that come with autopsy.

Indispensable as proximity is to the war reporter's credibility, it nonetheless poses a nagging question. Is it possible to become *too* close? One version of autopsy has itself become the subject of intense reporting (or meta-reporting) and a heavily politicized issue. The Iraq War beginning in 2003 inaugurated the term, if not the concept of, "embedded" journalism,[19] with the US Armed Forces announcing on 3 March 2003:

> About 800 members of the press – including 20 percent from non-US media – will be assigned slots in specific ground units, aviation units, ships and

headquarters throughout the combat zone. They will remain "embedded" with those units as long as they wish and are supposed to have what these Pentagon ground rules described as "minimally restrictive" access to US forces through-out their day.[20]

Eventually, out of the 1,000 journalists covering the war, around 660 were embedded with the American forces and 150 with the British.[21] For some commentators, the result was that "the coverage of certain aspects of the war was more detailed, because of the privileged access that these journalists were granted."[22] Disputing this view were those who believed that embedding resulted in an inability to see the forest for the trees and an irresistible bias towards those being reported on. But *not* being embedded had other con-sequences. Emily Nelson and Matthew Rose report:

> The Pentagon, in several meetings with editors, warned of the safety risks in covering a war. "The battlefield's a dangerous place, and it's going to be a dangerous place even embedded with our forces. It will be an even more dangerous place, though, for reporters that are out there not in an embedded status," said deputy Pentagon spokesman Bryan Whitman at a late February briefing.[23]

There are hints here that non-embeds might actually be targeted by *coalition* forces. Many saw embedding as a means for the military to control the media, hence its institution and encouragement by the Pentagon.

In a phenomenon similar to embedding, war reporters assimilate them-selves with actual combatants. The glamorous American war correspondent Richard Harding Davis reported on Theodore Roosevelt's Rough Riders during the Spanish-American War (1898). In his memoirs, Roosevelt recalled:

> It was Richard Harding Davis who gave us our first opportunity to shoot back with effect. He was behaving precisely like my officers, being on the extreme front of the line, and taking every opportunity to study with his glasses the ground where we thought the Spaniards were ... "There they are, Colonel; look over there; I can see their hats near that glade."[24]

Though Davis is in the role of observer here, he is observing on behalf of Roosevelt's forces (rather than observing *them*) and facilitating their opera-tions. Correspondent is indistinguishable from combatant: indeed, Davis was made a member of the regiment and given the same medal as the men. Davis's machismo was reprised, and somewhat satirized, in Ernest Hemingway's performance of the role of war correspondent during the Spanish Civil War and Second World War. Nominally covering the latter conflict for *Collier's* magazine, Hemingway attached himself to the 4th Infantry Division and also led some irregulars in defending Rambouillet and a command post in the

Hürtgenwald in 1944. In his dispatches, he identified himself with the
American troops, as in this account of D-Day:

> If you want to know how it was in an LCV(P) on D-Day when we took Fox
> Green beach and Easy Red beach on the sixth of June, 1944, then this is as near
> as I can come to it.[25]

Hemingway did not, in fact, land on a beach on June 6, 1944 – "we" refers to
the American forces – but his adoption of the combatant persona, in field and
in text, was complete. As the Geneva Convention then in force prohibited
correspondents from bearing arms, his activities led to his being interrogated
by the Inspector General of the Third Army. Today, the Geneva Conventions
of 1949, amended by the 1977 Protocols, explicitly recognize journalists to be
civilians and hence due all civilian (as opposed to military) protections.
Consequently, correspondents must distinguish themselves from combatants
by not wearing uniforms or openly carrying firearms.[26] Nonetheless, in the
quest for credibility, the urge to assimilation is still prevalent and the
Hemingwayesque quasi-combatant is still recognizable in some of today's
war reporters.

If proximity to the point of assimilation is legally problematic, it also has
awkward ethico-aesthetic consequences. Mick Hume has written of the dangers of the "journalism of attachment" – reportage that presents human
emotions and suffering as an argument that "something must be done."
Instead of exposing the political and social roots of wars, this kind of reporting depicts conflicts as unnuanced and "exclusively moral struggles between
right and wrong." The primary aim of the journalism of attachment, according to Hume, is "to give a sense of purpose and self-importance to journalists," who use their status as "saintly crusaders abroad" as "a twisted sort of
therapy." For Hume, this brand of war correspondence is a "menace," a
misuse of journalistic power to influence the course of events reported on.[27]

Hume's argument raises questions about the degree of participation that is
possible and fitting on the part of the war correspondent. What (if any) should
be the extent and nature of the intervention he or she makes in the conflict
being reported? And what concrete results might war journalism be expected
to achieve? At one end of the spectrum of participatory possibilities is the
passive observer, but even here, argue Stuart Allan and Barbie Zelizer, the
mere presence of the recording journalist shapes the perception of war:

> Being there suggests that the violence, devastation, suffering, and death that
> inevitably constitute war's underside will somehow be rendered different – more
> amenable to response and perhaps less likely to occur – just because journalists
> are somewhere nearby.[28]

Next to simple presence on the scale of influence is helpful intervention: Iris Carpenter retrieving body parts from London bombsites, for instance, or the American correspondent Martha Gellhorn pouring coffee into bandaged mouths on a D-Day hospital ship.[29] This is a brand of participation that might be said to ease the course of conflict. More spectacular (though no more important) is journalistic activity that effects change in the political sphere. Belief in this possibility was the motivation behind Martha Gellhorn's early reportorial forays:

> When I was young I believed in the perfectibility of man, and in progress, and thought of journalism as a guiding light. If people were told the truth, if dishonor and injustice were clearly shown to them, they would at once demand the saving action, punishment of wrong-doers, and care for the innocent ... A journalist's job was to bring news, to be eyes for their conscience. I think I must have imagined public opinion as a solid force, something like a tornado, always ready to blow on the side of the angels.[30]

Some war reports have indeed led to significant change: the unflinching realism of William Howard Russell's battlefield dispatches from the Crimean War to the London *Times* (among the earliest modern war correspondence), for instance, played a major part in Florence Nightingale's revolution in military nursing, the construction of the Grand Crimean Central Railway, and the fall of Lord Aberdeen's government in 1855. Pro-interventionist US journalists covering the First World War before 1917 and the Second World War before 1941 also aimed to achieve a political objective – to mobilize the support of a suspicious American public (if not an isolationist government) for US entry into the wars. A preferred tactic was to depict potential allies as embodying American values and therefore deserving of American defense. In this vein, Ernie Pyle, roving correspondent for the Scripps Howard newspaper chain, described for his readers the behavior of Londoners during the 1940 Blitz:

> At home you have all read about London's amazing ability to take it, and about the almost amazing calm of Englishmen in the face of Hitler's bombs ... I just want to confirm that what you have read in this connection is true.

Pre-Pearl Harbor, Pyle's objective in depicting Londoners' phlegm in the face of attack and privation was to persuade his American readers that the British both needed and merited their support.

In more simplistic and uninformed versions, Pyle's techniques might now be dismissed as "the journalism of attachment" and consequently, in Hume's words, "a menace." In this configuration, the war correspondent has become meddler, even lethal hindrance, in the course of conflict – the other extreme on the participatory spectrum from the passive, neutral observer. What Hume attacks is the kind of journalism that presents a pile of bodies as an argument for support for one particular side in a war: such an image "cannot inform," he argues, but only "touch raw emotion."[31] But, while the call for more nuanced accounts of the complex causes of wars is laudable, the possibility of a "non-attached" journalism requires careful scrutiny. During and after the First World War, the burgeoning public relations industry spawned a distrust of official facts, chiming with contemporary modernist skepticism and the collapse of the belief that transcendent truth existed and could be accessed. A resolution passed by the American Society of Newspaper Editors in 1933 stated that "editors should devote a larger amount of attention and space to explanatory and interpretative news."[32] By the 1930s, the word "objectivity" was in common parlance,[33] but did not mean – if it had ever meant – unadorned truth neutrally mediated. Instead, in the socialist realism-influenced New Reportage of the 1930s, objectivity comprised the practice of eyewitnessing, an ongoing reluctance to accept official versions of the facts, generic hybridity ("faction"), and techniques such as verbatim reporting, the presentation of statistics, the citation of sources, the incorporation of original documents, and the use of corroborative evidence. In later twentieth-century war journalism, similar attempts to achieve, if not objective accounts, at least objective-sounding accounts, have been characterized by Gaye Tuchman as a "strategic ritual" performed by journalists as a defensive measure against forms of attack from criticism to libel suits.[34] A war journalism seemingly of non-attachment has its own potential, therefore, for contrivance and artificiality.

Artificiality is an ongoing concern with regard to the reporting of conflict and the pitfalls have been variously identified. Censorship, always in place to some degree, obviously separates account from reality. The source of censorship may be military or political, or it may be self-imposed by news organizations or individual journalists taking account of what is acceptable (the degree of graphic description, for instance) to readers. In such cases, the journalist acts as "gate-keeper,"[35] mediating between event and audience. Distortion is also produced by the phenomenon of what Daniel Boorstin has termed the "pseudo-event" – a planned "synthetic novelty" such as an interview or press conference.[36] For long stretches, wartime can be eventless, even boring, and so the pseudo-event is a prevalent phenomenon in its coverage, the "peg" on which to hang a news story. Indeed, Jean Baudrillard's theory is that the events of (post)modern warfare are simulacra stage-managed for the media. In *The Gulf War Did Not Take Place* (1994), he writes:

> The Iraqis blow up civilian buildings in order to give the impression of a dirty war. The Americans disguise satellite information to give the impression of a clean war. Everything is *trompe l'oeil!*[37]

This is not to say that the Gulf War, and the death and injury it entailed, did not happen (though that is often how Baudrillard's claims are interpreted),[38] but that the "Gulf War" was a contrived series of pseudo-events and sound- and action-bites. War, in other words, is only reported war.

The early twenty-first century has seen the impact of rapidly developing communications and information technology on war reporting. The war correspondent is now not only the professional journalist, but also the passerby with a mobile phone; newspapers and magazines are joined as written media of dissemination by the virtual texts of internet chat rooms, bulletin boards, discussion threads, and blogs.[39] The multipartite nature of the data might make comprehension difficult, but it is also arguable that, the more people on the job, the more likely it is that reality (as opposed to hyperreality) will shine through. Indeed, the messier, more random, less coherent war reportage that the technology makes flourish has the advantage of more nearly resembling its subject matter. Scattered across cyberspace, the scraps of information may or may not make sense. But they have in common with the *Pennsylvania Gazette* of 1753 a commitment to shared information and a recognition of the importance of being there.

NOTES

1. David Copeland (gen. ed.), *The Greenwood Library of American War Reporting*, 8 vols. (Westport, CT: Greenwood, 2005), I: 28.
2. Robert B. Downs and Jane B. Downs (eds.), *Journalists of the United States* (Jefferson, NC and London: McFarland, 1991), 14.
3. John Hohenberg, *Foreign Correspondence: The Great Reporters and Their Times* (New York and London: Columbia University Press, 1967), 39, 25, 39, 42.
4. Géraldine Muhlmann, *A Political History of Journalism*, trans. Jean Birrell (Cambridge: Polity, 2008), 6.
5. See, for example, the reproduction of the dispatch of June 10, 1849 in Margaret Fuller, *"These Sad but Glorious Days": Dispatches from Europe, 1846–50*, ed. Larry J. Reynolds and Susan Belasco Smith (New Haven, CT and London: Yale University Press, 1991), xiv.
6. Emmet Crozier, *American Reporters on the Western Front, 1914–1918* (Oxford University Press, 1959), vii, viii.
7. George Washburn Smalley, *Anglo-American Memories* (London: Duckworth, 1911), 245–6, quoted in Hohenberg, *Foreign Correspondence*, 79.
8. Oliver Burkeman, "Simpson of Kabul," *Guardian* (Manchester) (November 14, 2001), G2: 2–3.
9. Pippa Norris, "Introduction: Women, Media, and Politics," *Women, Media, and Politics*, ed. Pippa Norris (Oxford University Press, 1997), 1–18: 2.
10. Michel de Certeau, *The Practice of Everyday Life*, trans. Steven Rendall (Berkeley, Los Angeles and London: University of California Press, 1984), xix, xiv, xix.
11. Arnold Bennett, *Journalism for Women: A Practical Guide* (London and New York: John Lane, The Bodley Head, 1898), 88.

12. Imogene Carter, "War Seen through a Woman's Eyes," *The University of Virginia Edition of the Works of Stephen Crane*, ed. Fredson Bowers, 9 vols. (Charlottesville: University Press of Virginia, 1971), IX: 267–8.
13. Carter, "Imogene Carter's Pen Picture of the Fighting at Velestino," Bowers, *Works of Stephen Crane*, 272.
14. Julia Edwards, *Women of the World. The Great Foreign Correspondents* (Boston, MA: Houghton Mifflin, 1988), 5.
15. Ibid., 27, 32.
16. Iris Carpenter, *No Woman's World* (Boston, MA: Houghton Mifflin, 1946), 47.
17. Ibid., 47–8.
18. Edwards, *Women of the World*, 6.
19. Agnes Smedley, for instance, was embedded with the Chinese Eighth Route Army during the Chinese Civil War of the 1930s: see her *China's Red Army Marches* (1934), *China Fights Back* (1938), and *China Correspondent* (1984).
20. Glenn W. Leaper, Anthony Löwstedt, and Husam Madhoun, *Caught in the Crossfire: The Iraq War and the Media* (Vienna: The International Press Institute, 2003), 3.
21. Emily Nelson and Matthew Rose, "Media Reassess Risks to Reporters in Iraq," *Wall Street Journal* (April 9, 2003), B1, B10: B1.
22. Leaper, Löwstedt, and Madhoun, *Caught in the Crossfire*, 76.
23. Nelson and Rose, "Media Reassess Risks," B10.
24. Theodore Roosevelt, *The Rough Riders* (London: Kegan Paul, Trench, Trübner & Co., 1899), 90–1.
25. Ernest Hemingway, "Voyage to Victory," *Collier's* (July 22, 1944), 11–13, 56–7: 57.
26. http://spj.org/gc-history.asp? (accessed January 2009).
27. Mick Hume, *Whose War Is It Anyway? The Dangers of the Journalism of Attachment* (London: InformInc, 1997), 4, 20, 18, 6.
28. Stuart Allan and Barbie Zelizer, "Rules of Engagement: Journalism and War," *Reporting War. Journalism in Wartime*, ed. Stuart Allan and Barbie Zelizer (London and New York: Routledge, 2004), 3–21: 5.
29. Carpenter, *No Woman's World*, ix; Martha Gellhorn, "The Wounded Come Home," *Collier's* (August 5, 1944), 14–15, 73–5: 15.
30. Gellhorn, *The Face of War* (New York: Simon & Schuster, 1959), 1.
31. Hume, *Whose War Is It Anyway?*, 13.
32. Michael Schudson, *Discovering the News: A Social History of American Newspapers* (New York: Basic Books, 1978), 148.
33. Ibid., 156.
34. Gaye Tuchman, "Objectivity as Strategic Ritual: An Examination of Newsmen's Notions of Objectivity," *American Journal of Sociology* 77.4 (1972), 660–79: 663, 676.
35. Stuart Hall, "A World At One With Itself," *The Manufacture of News. Social Problems, Deviance and the Mass Media*, ed. Stanley Cohen and Jock Young (London: Constable, 1973), 85–94: 87.
36. Daniel Boorstin, *The Image* (London: Weidenfeld & Nicolson, 1961), 9.
37. Jean Baudrillard, *The Gulf War Did Not Take Place*, trans. Paul Patton (London: Power Publications, 1994), 62.
38. See further Richard Keeble, "Information Warfare in an Age of Hyper-Militarism," Allan and Zelizer, *Reporting War*, 43–58.

39. Stuart Allan, "The Culture of Distance: Online Reporting of the Iraq War," Allan and Zelizer, *Reporting War*, 347–65: 349.

FURTHER READING

Phyllis Frus, *The Politics and Poetics of Journalistic Narrative. The Timely and the Timeless* (Cambridge University Press, 1994).

Fred Inglis, *People's Witness. The Journalist in Modern Politics* (New Haven, CT and London: Yale University Press, 2002).

Phillip Knightley, *The First Casualty. The War Correspondent as Hero and Myth-Maker from The Crimea to Kosovo*, rev. edn. (London: Prion, 2000).

Jean Seaton, *Carnage and the Media. The Making and Breaking of News about Violence* (London: Allen Lane, 2005).

PART TWO

Influences

6

DAVID JASPER

The Bible

The presence in the Western world of a Christian tradition as a continuous background, albeit a vaguely defined one without a univocal meaning, is not an element for leveling out conflicts; on the contrary, it is (or has become) a constitutive factor in promoting them, and can exacerbate them.[1]

Almost from its beginning the Bible deals in conflict and is soaked in blood. The enmity foretold between Eve and the serpent (Genesis 3:15)[2] is translated by John Milton to the cosmic battle between the "Son of God Most High," the fruit of Mary's womb, and the Serpent who can expect only "mortal pain."[3] Though traces remain in the Hebrew Bible of mythological stories of primeval warfare between the gods and the cosmic battle between good and evil, these are generally subsumed under the conditions of the Holy War in which Yahweh, the Lord of Hosts, fights for and at the head of his people against their enemies. Such imagery is later translated to the war of the Christian Church against the world, the flesh, and the devil[4] under the banner of Christ. Blake, in "The Everlasting Gospel" (1818), has Jesus seize the "Spiritual Prey" and thus "he bound Old Satan in his Chain."[5]

The great song of Moses in Exodus 15:1-21 (with the briefer song of Miriam to accompany dances of victory) follows the defeat of Pharaoh's army in the Red Sea and, with its parallels in the Psalms, celebrates the triumph of God as warrior-king. Possibly one of the oldest poems in the Bible (dated as early as the eleventh or twelfth century BCE), Moses' song finds its way into English poetry in George Wither's "Now Shall the Praises of the Lord be Sung" (1623) and in the imperial hymn of Rudyard Kipling, "God of our fathers, known of old, / Lord of our far-flung battle-line" (1897), each verse ending with some variant of:

> Lord God of Hosts, be with us yet,
> Lest we forget – lest we forget![6]

In John Bunyan's spiritual allegory *The Holy War* (1682), King Shaddai, whose son Emmanuel is finally sent to command the army which will recover the city of Mansoul, has his origins in the creator God who leads the army of Israel to victory. The "wrath divine" returns to Samson in his final destruction of the Temple of Dagon (whose god dared to deliver the champion of Israel to the Philistines [Judges 16:23]) and later to David himself, whose final words before the defeat of Goliath are the defiant, "for the battle is the Lord's and he will give you into our hand" (I Samuel 17:47) (this victory is given epic treatment in Michael Drayton's poem *David and Goliath* [1630]). Samson and David exemplify the weakened hero strengthened for victory by God, interpreted in the tradition of Christian typology as the prefiguration of Christ.[7]

In the New Testament, the imagery of the Lord of Hosts is introduced in the appearance to the shepherds of the "multitude of the heavenly host" (Luke 2:13) (in Greek, the military term "στρατιᾶς ὀυρανίου"),[8] with Christ revealed as Savior, Messiah, and Lord, continuing Yahweh's purposes of defeating his enemies and finally bringing peace to his people ("on earth peace among those whom he favors" [Luke 2:14]).[9] The infant Christ is graphically described by Robert Southwell as a reminder of the young David:

> With tears he fights and wins the field;
> His naked breast stands for a shield;
> His battering shot are babish cries,
> His arrows looks of weeping eyes,
> His martial ensigns cold and need
> And feeble flesh his warrior's steed.[10]

But the definitive image of the *miles Christi*, the soldier of Christ whose final military victory is on the Day of the Lord, is found in St. Paul's Epistle to the Ephesians (6:10–17), which begins with the injunction, "be strong in the Lord and in the strength of his power" and continues with the description of the "armor of God" in the fight against "the powers of this present darkness, against the spiritual forces of evil in the heavenly places" (6:12).[11] If the most familiar rehearsal of this image is in the poem which forms the Preface to Blake's *Milton* (1804–10) and its description of the Mental Fight to build Jerusalem "in England's green and pleasant Land,"[12] the literary tradition of the *miles Christi* has its origins in two strands of patristic writing. The first is the *Psychomachia* (c.482 CE) of Prudentius, a quasi-epic allegory of the struggle in the Christian between virtue and vice drawing on Ephesians 6. The second is the tradition in preaching, notably that of St. John Chrysostom, of recounting the Passion as a literal battle between Christ and Satan.

The language of this "battle" is found in the seventh-century *Dream of the Rood* and increasingly in the courtly tradition which sees Christ (and therefore also his Christian soldiers) as a knight,[13] but finds its greatest expression in the medieval poets of the Franciscan tradition. St. Francis is said to have called his followers *"fratres mei milites tabulae rotundae"* ("my brothers, knights of the round table") and the imagery is commonplace in English

Franciscan lyrics, with Christian knights armed after the Pauline description. As late as the early sixteenth century, in the mysterious *Corpus Christi* carol, Christ is described as the ever-bleeding knight, his wounds flowing for our redemption:

> And in that bed ther lythe a knight
> His woundes bleding day and night.[14]

By the mid-twentieth century, the image of the warrior Christ and the "verray, parfit gentil"[15] Christian knight, rendered honorable in the holy warfare of the Crusades, had become the surreal "horrifying face" with "putrid flesh, discoloured, flayed" of David Gascoyne's poem "Ecce Homo" (1943), drawing upon the Isaian description of the Suffering Servant (Isaiah 53:4–9), and linking the "Christ of Revolution and Poetry" through close references to the Passion narratives to the horrors of modern violence and warfare. The malefactors crucified with Jesus become "A labourer and a factory hand, / Or one is maybe a lynched Jew," and the crucified one weeps not just for Jerusalem (Luke 19:41–4) but for all the great cities of the world.[16] The nightmare of the world wars turned the crucified Christ from a courtly warrior into a gentle victim of the cruelty of the generals – in Wilfred Owen's poems of the First World War, these become our jingoistic version of the New Testament scribes and uncaring priests at the foot of the cross:

> The scribes on all the people shove
> And brawl allegiance to the state,
> But they who love the greater love
> Lay down their life; they do not hate.[17]

If the Pauline imagery of the *miles Christi* flourished in the age of chivalry, it persisted but underwent changes under the influences of Renaissance Christian humanism. Erasmus's *Enchiridion Militis Christiani* (*Handbook for the Christian Soldier*) (1503; translated into English in 1518) stressed the two primary weapons of Christian warfare – prayer and knowledge. Milton's *Areopagitica* (1644) is clearly descended from Erasmus in a Protestant crusade to reform church and society. A century earlier than Milton, Edmund Spenser in his *Faerie Queene* (1590–96) led his chivalric knights on allegorical quests of virtue, armed, as Spenser informed Raleigh, with "the armour of a Christian man specified by St. Paul,"[18] but also with the civic duties of a St. George of England. Thus, as the Red Cross Knight pursues holiness, his progress sketches the history of the English Church (Elizabeth) in its conflict with Rome (Mary). Drawing upon the same courtly tradition, Shakespeare's Hostess in *Henry V* (c.1599) describes Falstaff on his deathbed as the Arthurian knight, but also as Lazarus the poor man (presumably ironically suggesting his newly elevated companion, Hal, now Henry, to be Dives) in Abraham's (Arthur's) bosom.[19]

Underlying the triumphant tone of *Henry V* and Henry as "the mirror of all Christian kings"[20] is the theme of the instability that is caused by struggling for the temporal kingdom rather than for the salvation of the soul – a kingdom lost (Epilogue: 6–14) in the political wranglings under Henry's son, Henry VI. All the darker in this context is the moment of King Henry's anger at the French slaughter of the baggage boys after the battle:

> we will come to them,
> And make them skirr away, as swift as stones
> Enforcéd from the old Assyrian slings:
> Besides, we'll cut the throats of those we have,
> And not a man of them that we shall take
> Shall taste our mercy.[21]

Aside from the rather obscure reference to the Assyrians,[22] we are here clearly within the ethos of the Holy War, of which the last act or culmination was not victory, but the *herem* – the anathema or curse which is the total destruction of the defeated people (*herem*, unlike Henry's anger, has a biblical defense which is theological – the necessary destruction of all that denies Yahweh). Thus, after the defeat of Jericho, the Israelite army "devoted to destruction by the edge of the sword all in the city, both men and women, young and old, oxen, sheep, and donkeys" (Joshua 6:21).[23]

Apart from Milton, the other major Puritan expression of the *miles Christi* tradition in literature is John Bunyan, above all in *The Pilgrim's Progress* (1678, 1684), in which Christian is armed with Piety, Prudence, Charity, and "all manner of Furniture, which their Lord had provided for Pilgrims, as Sword, Shield, Helmet and Brest Plate"[24] – weapons with which he quickly defeats Apollyon. In *The Holy War* this Pauline armor is reversed in the description of Diabolus, who wears a breastplate of "an hard heart" and wields the sword of "a Tongue that is set on fire of Hell" with the shield of unbelief.[25] The theme of the soldier of Christ more or less dies out in eighteenth-century literature, to reappear in imperialist hymns (behind which also lie the Songs of Moses and Miriam in Exodus 15) such as Bishop Heber's "The Son of God Goes Forth to War" (1827) (taken up by Kipling in his story "The Man Who Would be King" [1888] in a moral challenge to British imperialism) and J. S. Arkwright's "O Valiant Hearts" (1919), sung as a memorial to the fallen soldiers of the First World War:

> Proudly you gathered, rank on rank, to war,
> As who had heard God's message from afar;
> All you had hoped for, all you had, you gave
> To save mankind – yourself you scorned to save.[26]

The American version of such popular hymns is Julia Ward Howe's "The Battle Hymn of the Republic," published during the Civil War in 1862, and drawing deeply on Isaiah, Matthew 21:33–43 (the Parable of the Wicked Tenants), and, above all, Revelation 14:18–20, with its apocalyptic imagery of the pressing-out of the final vintage in "the great wine press of the wrath of God." She described its message as "the sacredness of human liberty,"[27] and through the Battle Hymn such imagery has persisted in American literature in novels such as John Steinbeck's *The Grapes of Wrath* (1939), John Updike's *In the Beauty of the Lilies* (1996), and perhaps even Flannery O'Connor's *The Violent Bear it Away* (1960), with its prefatory quotation from Matthew 11:12: "From the days of John the Baptist until now, the Kingdom of Heaven suffereth violence, and the violent bear it away."

Ancient apocalyptic literature was concerned with revealing the future, and above all the end of the present world on "the great and terrible day of the Lord" (Malachi 4:5), when God will finally judge all things, destroying his enemies and establishing his Kingdom for ever.[28] The earliest of the great Jewish apocalypses, the Book of Daniel, was probably written to comfort the Jews during the persecution of Antiochus Epiphanes (175–164 BCE), assuring them of the ultimate intervention and triumph of God. The political theme persists into Christian apocalypses, of which the most important are Revelation and the non-canonical "Apocalypse of Peter."[29] In the Little Apocalypse in Mark 13, drawing clearly on Daniel, reference is probably made to the destruction of the Temple in Jerusalem by the Romans in 70 CE after the Jewish revolt, Jesus' words predicting the time of conflict and confusion which will precede the second coming of the Son of Man, when "he will send out the angels, and gather his elect from the four winds from the ends of the earth to the ends of heaven" (Mark 13:27). Linked to this event of the Second Coming is the theme of the War in Heaven (Revelation 12:7–9) in which "Michael and his angels fought against the dragon" – a final return to and resolution of the great cosmic conflict which lies behind the war imagery of the Hebrew Bible (eg. Genesis 1; Psalms 104:6ff.; Job 9:13, 26:10–13; Isaiah 27:1 etc.).[30] In his English commentary of 1615, *A Revelation of the Revelation*, Thomas Brightman reads the passage in Revelation as predicting the final battle when the Jews would defeat the "dragon Turk" and the Protestants would vanquish the Roman Antichrist.[31] *Paradise Lost* (1667) opens with a report of how the "infernal Serpent" "raised impious war in heaven" (1: 34, 43), fighting the forces of Michael and Gabriel, finally to be defeated by Christ, the Messiah, in Book 6. In the poem, the war in heaven sets the stage for the fall of Adam and Eve in Eden. Blake's

Milton returns to the image of the winepress in Revelation, but now it has become War on Earth:

> This Wine-press is called War on Earth: it is the Printing-Press
> Of Los, and here he lays his words in order above the mortal brain,
> As cogs are formed in a wheel to turn the cogs of the adverse wheel.[32]

In American literature, perhaps the greatest treatment of the cosmic conflict is Herman Melville's *Moby-Dick* (1851). In the final pages of the novel, the *Pequod* is sunk by the great whale as a sailor nails to the mast a sky-hawk which has been pecking at the flag placed there as a signal:

> [A]nd so the bird of heaven, with archangelic shrieks and his imperial beak thrust upwards, and his whole captive form folded in the flag of Ahab, went down with his ship, which, like Satan, would not sink to hell till she had dragged a living part of heaven along with her and helmeted herself with it.[33]

The apocalyptic last battle is variously found in modern English literature in the writings of the Inklings. C. S. Lewis entitled the last of his Narnia stories *The Last Battle* (1956). J. R. R. Tolkien's *The Return of the King* (1955), the last volume of *The Lord of the Rings* trilogy, clearly draws on the Christian apocalyptic theme of the Second Coming and the time of chaos and destitution that precedes the final victory. Charles Williams's novel *War in Heaven* (1930) is a return to the medieval Grail legend and a quasi-realistic treatment of the apocalyptic struggle between good and evil, with overtones of the Passion narratives: the title of Chapter 15, "Tonight Thou Shalt Be with Me in Paradise," returns to Jesus' words to the penitent thief on the cross in Luke 23:43.

But twentieth-century literature begins to show a weary and cynical diversion from the biblical tradition of divine warfare, particularly after the Holocaust and under the threat of nuclear devastation. J. G. Ballard's *The Atrocity Exhibition* (1969) begins with the word "apocalypse" and trivializes the nuclear explosion by describing it as having a "carnival air" (a reference to the weird, balletic beauty of the ending of Stanley Kubrick's film *Dr. Strangelove* [1964]). For many Jewish writers, the Holocaust under Nazi Germany lies outside the narratives of history upon which the biblical perceptions of warfare are constructed. Auschwitz is, quite simply, post-biblical and beyond the boundaries of any historical scriptural theology. Thus, Elie Wiesel wrote that "the Universe of concentration camps, by its dimensions and its designs, lies outside, if not beyond, history,"[34] while for Steven T. Katz, the immensity of the Holocaust intrudes upon and even overtakes for the Jew the theology and promise of the Bible: "Auschwitz has become an inescapable *datum* for all Jewish accounts of the meaning and nature of covenantal relation and God's relation to man."[35]

If Auschwitz represents a radical break in the biblical tradition, other poets, from Wilfred Owen to the Australian emigré Peter Porter, react to mass slaughter and the nuclear threat with rage and irony. God no longer cares or promises ultimate victory to those who love him. He has become incapable of anything effective and is at best an irrelevance. In his poem "Your Attention Please" (1962–63), Porter describes the call to the fallout shelters in the face of a nuclear rocket strike with chilling irony:

> All flags are flying fully dressed
> On Government buildings – the sun is shining.
> Death is the least we have to fear.
> We are all in the hands of God,
> Whatever happens happens by His Will.
> Now go quickly to your shelters.[36]

More famously, in his poem "The Parable of the Old Man and the Young" (1918), Owen rewrites the Akedah, the story of the sacrifice of Isaac in Genesis 22. This story is usually read in the Christian tradition as an indication of Abraham's obedience, while God's reprieve of the boy through replacing him as a sacrifice with a ram is typologically interpreted as an anticipation of the Passion, with Isaac a type of Christ himself. In Owen's version, Abraham represents the generals who do not heed the angelic call to save the lad (and the young men dying in their millions in the trenches), sacrificing instead the "Ram of Pride":

> But the old man would not so, but slew his son,
> And half the seed of Europe, one by one.[37]

The "seed" is a reference to Genesis 22:17–18: "in multiplying I will multiply thy seed as the stars of the heaven … and thy seed shall possess the gate of his enemies; And in thy seed shall all the nations of the earth be blessed."[38]

Thus we end in the twentieth century on a note of human disobedience and the helplessness of the God whom Moses and Miriam celebrated as the mighty victor in battle for his people. The "design of biblical history,"[39] a plot constructed upon the final victory of God and his people and the restoration of his fallen world, with God as the "director and guarantor of things to come,"[40] has been eclipsed;[41] the totality of the Holy War is now a human presumption and the possibility of just war increasingly merely theoretical. Literature has spawned numerous dystopias,[42] and in what Brian McHale has called the "specter of infinite regress"[43] the biblical apocalypse is replaced by the postmodern apocalypse of implosion envisioned by Jean

Baudrillard – a descent into utter nihilism in a hyperreal, war-ravaged wasteland without redemption and without God.[44]

NOTES

1. Gianni Vattimo, *After Christianity*, trans. Luca D'Isanto (New York: Columbia University Press, 2002), 93.
2. The New Revised Standard Version of the Bible is used in this chapter.
3. John Milton, *Paradise Lost* 12: 379–85.
4. The phrase has its origin in the catechism of the medieval Church, following I John 2:15–17, and is found in the Litany of the Anglican *Book of Common Prayer* (1662).
5. William Blake, *Complete Writings*, ed. Geoffrey Keynes (Oxford University Press, 1966), 749.
6. Percy Dearmer (ed.), *Songs of Praise* (1925) (enlarged edition) (Oxford University Press, 1931), 388.
7. See, for example, George Herbert's "Sunday" (1633) (George Herbert, *The Complete English Poems*, ed. John Tobin [Penguin: London, 1991], 68–70), and Milton's *Samson Agonistes* (1671), in the closing semi-chorus of which Samson becomes a type of Christ.
8. From στρᾱτός, "an army".
9. In his poem "Peace" (1650), Henry Vaughan describes the "one born in a Manger [who] / Commands the beauteous files" (Henry Vaughan, *The Complete Poems*, ed. Alan Rudrum [Harmondsworth: Penguin, 1976], 185–6: 186).
10. "New Heaven, New War," *Chapters into Verse*, ed. Robert Atwan and Laurance Wieder, 2 vols. (Oxford University Press, 1993), II: 32.
11. See also Romans 13:12 and 2 Corinthians 6:7.
12. Blake, *Complete Writings*, 481.
13. In *Gawain and the Green Knight* (late fourteenth century), Gawain goes out to meet his foes protected by a Shield of Faith (ll. 619–65). The preeminent knight of Arthurian legend is Sir Galahad.
14. R. T. Davies (ed.), *Medieval English Lyrics* (London: Faber, 1963), 272.
15. Chaucer's description of the Knight in the Prologue to *The Canterbury Tales* (c.1387), l. 72.
16. David Gascoyne, "Ecce Homo," *The Faber Book of Religious Verse*, ed. Helen Gardner (London: Faber, 1972), 333–5. See also Geoffrey Hill, "Canticle for Good Friday," *For the Unfallen* (London: André Deutsch, 1959), 39.
17. Wilfred Owen, "At a Calvary Near the Ancre," *The Complete Poems and Fragments*, ed. Jon Stallworthy, 2 vols. (London: Chatto & Windus, The Hogarth Press, Oxford University Press, 1983), I: 134.
18. Quoted in David Lyle Jeffrey (ed.), *A Dictionary of Biblical Tradition in English Literature* (Grand Rapids, MI: Eerdmans, 1992), 508.
19. *Henry V* 2.3.9–10; Luke 16:23.
20. Laurence Olivier's 1944 film of *Henry V* was a deliberate piece of patriotic spirit-raising during the dark days of the Second World War.
21. *Henry V* 4.7.59–64.
22. Possibly an allusion to Judith 9:7.

23. See further Roland de Vaux, *Ancient Israel: Its Life and Institutions*, trans. John McHugh (London: Darton, Longman & Todd, 1973), 258–61.
24. John Bunyan, *The Pilgrim's Progress* (Harmondsworth: Penguin, 1965), 87.
25. Quoted in Jeffrey, *Dictionary of Biblical Tradition*, 509.
26. Both hymns were included in Percy Dearmer's *Songs of Praise*, "a national collection of hymns for use in public worship" (Dearmer, *Songs of Praise*, v). In a letter to Osbert Sitwell of July 4, 1918, Wilfred Owen bitterly employs such Passion imagery to describe his training of soldiers for the front, citing himself as Judas: "For 14 hours yesterday I was at work – teaching Christ to lift his cross by numbers ... With a piece of silver I buy him every day, and with maps I make him familiar with the topography of Golgotha" (Wilfred Owen, *Collected Letters*, ed. Harold Owen and John Bell [Oxford University Press, 1967], 562).
27. Quoted in James D. Hart (ed.), *The Concise Oxford Companion to American Literature* (Oxford University Press, 1986), 36.
28. See Elena Volkova, "Visions of Heaven and Hell," *The Oxford Handbook of English Literature and Theology*, ed. Andrew Hass, David Jasper, and Elisabeth Jay (Oxford University Press, 2007), 793–809.
29. See M. R. James, *The Apocryphal New Testament*, rev. J. K. Elliott (Oxford: Clarendon, 1993), 505–24.
30. The "time of the angels" has a place in late twentieth-century fiction in Iris Murdoch's 1966 novel of that name.
31. Quoted in Jeffrey, *Dictionary of Biblical Tradition*, 818.
32. Blake, *Complete Writings*, 513.
33. Herman Melville, *Moby-Dick, or The Whale* (New York and Toronto: The New American Library, 1961), 535.
34. Elie Wiesel, "Now We Know," *Genocide in Paraguay*, ed. Richard Arens (Philadelphia: Temple University Press, 1976), 165.
35. Steven T. Katz, *Post-Holocaust Dialogues* (New York University Press, 1983), 142. See also A. Dirk Moses, "Conceptual Blockages and Definitional Dilemmas in the 'Racial Century': Genocides of Indigenous Peoples and the Holocaust," *The Holocaust: A Reader*, ed. Simone Gigliotti and Berel Lang (Oxford: Blackwell, 2005), 448–62.
36. Peter Porter, "Your Attention Please," *The Oxford Book of War Poetry*, ed. Jon Stallworthy (Oxford University Press, 1984), 339–40.
37. Owen, *The Complete Poems and Fragments*, 1: 174.
38. The King James Version of the Bible is used here as it was clearly the origin of Owen's imagery of "the seed of Europe."
39. M. H. Abrams, *Natural Supernaturalism: Tradition and Revolution in Romantic Literature* (New York and London: Norton, 1973), 32–7.
40. Abrams, *Natural Supernaturalism*, 36.
41. Hans W. Frei, *The Eclipse of Biblical Narrative* (New Haven, CT and London: Yale University Press, 1974).
42. E.g. William Burroughs, *The Wild Boys* (1971), Russell Hoban, *Riddley Walker* (1980), Margaret Atwood, *The Handmaid's Tale* (1986).
43. Brian McHale, *Postmodern Fiction* (London: Routledge, 1987), 114.
44. Jean Baudrillard, *Simulacra and Simulation*, trans. Sheila Faria Glaser (Ann Arbor: University of Michigan Press, 1994), 1–28. See also Robert Detweiler, "Apocalyptic Fiction and the End(s) of Realism," *European Literature and*

Theology in the Twentieth Century, ed. David Jasper and Colin Crowder (London: Macmillan, 1990), 153–83.

FURTHER READING

J. Cheryl Exum, *Tragedy and Biblical Narrative: Arrows of the Almighty* (Cambridge University Press, 1992).

Andrew Hass, David Jasper, and Elisabeth Jay (eds.), *The Oxford Handbook of English Literature and Theology* (Oxford University Press, 2007).

David Jasper and Colin Crowder (eds.), *European Literature and Theology in the Twentieth Century: Ends of Time* (London: Macmillan, 1990).

Regina M. Schwartz, *The Curse of Cain: The Violent Legacy of Monotheism* (University of Chicago Press, 1997).

Ulrich Simon, *Pity and Terror: Christianity and Tragedy* (Basingstoke: Macmillan, 1989).

7

L. V. PITCHER

Classical war literature

Introduction

The central text of Greco-Roman literary culture, the *Iliad* (*c.*750 BCE), is a poem of battle, and warfare was a constant of political and civic life in antiquity. Perhaps the most famous speech to come down from classical Greece, one of those which Thucydides puts into the mouth of the politician Pericles, is a Funeral Oration for the Athenian fallen of the Peloponnesian War.[1] At Rome, the *comitia centuriata*, the assembly of the Roman people that elected senior magistrates, met in military order outside the sacred boundary of the city, even though it had ceased to mirror the disposition of actual army units early in the history of the Republic.

The prevalence of war as a theme in classical literature is therefore unremarkable. Equally unsurprising is the impact of classical war literature upon subsequent writing. The modes of engagement between modern and ancient treatments of war are, however, more sophisticated and various than is sometimes supposed. It is true that the most famous moves to appropriate ancient war literature in the service of its contemporary equivalent are also, perhaps, the most straightforward. Such, for example, are the impulses that lead a battle to be dubbed a second Marathon,[2] or, on the other hand, Wilfred Owen to rebut the Horatian claim that it is a sweet and becoming thing to die for one's fatherland in "Dulce et Decorum Est."[3]

Nonetheless, there is more to the relationship between classical and later war literature than the simple assertion or denial of parallelism between ancient and modern warfare. The writers of classical antiquity were amongst the first to grapple with the problem of *how* to depict war and its effects. This was a problem not just moral – what attitude and reactions warfare should evoke – but also formal and technical. How can words best evoke the experience of war? Which literary tropes are effective, and permissible? Which, by contrast, are to be decried, as generating the inappropriate effect?

The engagement between postclassical war narratives and similar productions from the ancient world has the potential, therefore, to work on several levels. As in other contexts, reference to the antique may just impart a specious luster to the contemporary. On the other hand, some modern visions of how warfare should be written define themselves most sharply through their relationship to ancient war literature.

"Ancient war literature" is itself a capacious category. Just as war was hard to avoid in the ancient world, so depictions of warfare crop up across the diverse literary activity of Greece and Rome. Even the ancient Greek novels, traditionally and not altogether unfairly classed as escapist fantasies, routinely took the opportunity to insert a siege narrative, often with historical resonances. Scholars have noted the possible similarities between the fictional sieges of Tyre and Syene found in the novels of Chariton and Heliodorus (?first century BCE and ?fourth century CE respectively) and the historical sieges of Tyre by Alexander the Great (332 BCE) and Nisibis by the Parthians (350 CE).

For our present study, however, the treatment of war in three areas is especially important: epic; lyric, iambic, and elegiac poetry; and historiography. This is not to deny that other genres might produce individual works of equal significance. Such a denial is refuted by a look at the subsequent fortunes of Euripides' tragedy *Trojan Women* (415 BCE), staged in different productions of the 1980s to suggest parallels with the experiences of Hiroshima, Vietnam, and Libya.[4] Nonetheless, these three categories explored par excellence ways of talking about war that would have a profound impact in their later reception.

War in epic

The importance of Homer's *Iliad* to the literature of the classical world has already been mentioned, and wars continued to be a staple of subsequent epic poetry. Vergil's poem of Rome, the *Aeneid* (late first century BCE), is the best-known of these successors and perhaps the only one that can rival the *Iliad* in terms of its postclassical influence. It is worth remembering, too, that martial epic did not restrict itself to the time of myth. Historical epic likewise flourished. Much of this is now lost; much that survives, such as Silius Italicus' first-century CE epic on the Hannibalic War, is more interesting to classicists than students of reception, but Lucan's *Bellum Civile* or *Pharsalia* (the exact title is a long-disputed question) stands as an exception. This epic of the Neronian era concerning the conflict between Julius Caesar and Pompeius Magnus in the first century BCE works out with unparalleled thoroughness the notion, later influential, of war as visual entertainment.[5]

Epic martial poetry is particularly interesting for our purposes because it addresses, from the beginning of the Greco-Roman tradition, the importance of the artist in memorializing deeds of valor and how subject matter contributes to literary prestige. The crucial part the poet played in assuring the immortal fame of his warriors was a common theme in classical antiquity. Cicero reports a story that Alexander the Great declared of Achilles, "o fortunate young man, since you found Homer as the herald of your valor,"[6] and Horace makes play of the theme that brave men lived before Agamemnon: "in vain they schemed, in vain they bled. / They had no poet, and are dead."[7]

Great martial deeds needed a poet. But it might equally be argued that a poet needed great martial deeds. In the classical hierarchy of poetic achievement, epic held a largely undisputed primacy. Warfare was such a part of epic that in Rome *bella* ("wars") could stand as a convenient shorthand for the genre.[8] The entanglement of subject matter, genre, and prestige might have ideological implications. A refusal to do epic could mean a refusal to do warfare, or vice versa. This tension is exploited by the first-century BCE Latin love elegists (Propertius, Tibullus, Ovid), whose substitution of *militia amoris* (the soldiery of love) for interest in warfare mirrored their writing of short poems in elegiac couplets rather than hexameter martial epics.[9]

Apart from this nexus of war, memorialization, and artistic prestige, classical epic is significant to later military literature because of the formal features by which it organizes its narrative. From Homer downwards, it tackles the problem of how to reconcile the scale of martial operations with the immediacy of individual human experience. War involves a lot of people – that is one of the factors which makes it a war instead of a fight. Its narratives therefore run the risk of impersonality and anonymity, as well as information overload on both narrator and audience. Homer calls into focus the "inability of the epic narrator to remember – or even to get to know – all he needs to tell, and his consequent appeal to the Muses to remember or tell it for him."[10]

Impersonality and anonymity are not necessarily defects. Indeed, they can help make a point about the primacy of duty and official role over personality. This is what the Elder Cato seems to have done in the second century BCE by omitting the proper names of all military leaders from his *Origines*, the first history of Rome written in Latin.[11] If this effect is not intended, however, the problem of reconciling martial scale with individual achievement and suffering is acute.

Homer and his successors counter this problem through persistent synecdoche. The narrator recounts the duels of particular, named warriors, to which the remainder of the fighting acts as a backdrop. The struggles of these characters plot the trajectory of their armies' fortunes while keeping the triumphs and the disasters of individual people firmly in focus. Moreover, the narrator picks out the fates of named minor characters as well. Granted narrative importance only at the moment of death, these unfortunates exemplify the fates of those less glamorous than an Achilles or a Hector. Of such a kind are Kebriones, who lies "in a swirl of dust, mightily in his might, forgetful of his horsemanship" when slain by Patroclus,[12] or Antores, who is "laid low by a wound meant for another; and looks at the sky and remembers sweet Argos as he dies" in Vergil's account of war in Latium.[13]

In Homer, this synecdoche works on another, deeper level. It is not just the case that the fortunes of individuals encapsulate the wider battle. The *Iliad* itself, in terms of strict chronology, covers only a period of fifty or so days in the tenth year of the Trojan War, but the patterning of the narrative turns this period into a microcosm of the whole conflict.[14] Calchas' prophecy of a ten-year war is recalled in Book 2; the duel between Menelaus and Paris in Book 3 replays the causes of the war; and the lamentation at Hector's death in the antepenultimate book is compared to that which would be raised at the burning of the city.[15]

Such synecdoches are not the sole prerogative of epic poetry in the Greco-Roman tradition. The narrative of the great battle of Kurukshetra in the *Mahabharata* (date uncertain) likewise resolves itself at many points into duels: Arjuna against Bhishma, Drona against Dhristadyumna. However, it is ultimately from the *Iliad* and its successors that war writing in English has most often derived its notions of how a martial text mediates questions of synecdoche and scale.

A good demonstration of this is *War Music*, Christopher Logue's remarkable "Account of Books 16 to 19 of Homer's ILIAD." The author's introduction makes it clear how important such questions were in his decisions about which passages from the poem to represent in his own work:

> [M]y choosing these passages derives from the advice of Carne-Ross. "Book 16, or *Patrocleia*," he said, "might be described as a miniature version of the *Iliad*. It has a quarrel, a making-up, a concession, several battles, the death of a famous leader (Sarpedon), disagreement in Heaven, a human cheeking the Gods, and, as a result of that human's death, an irreversible change."[16]

In the Greco-Roman tradition, such questions about the structure and architectonics of war writing arise first in martial epic. Engagement with them in subsequent texts often takes its terms from these originals.

War in lyric, iambic, and elegiac poetry

What classical epic poetry did not allow was much modulation in the relationship between the poetic narrator and his subject matter. This is not to say that the epic narrator could not express attitudes to the content of the poem. The penchant of the Homeric narrator for apostrophizing certain characters or for declaring incapacity to do justice to his subject matter is well known. In later epic, such as Lucan, the narrator can assume almost as much personality as his protagonists.[17] However, a certain degree of impersonality remains the norm. As far as the narrator was concerned, the place for "I" in "epic" was subject to strict formal limitations.

The lyric, iambic, and elegiac poetry of the ancient world had no such restraints. So much is clear from some of the earliest exponents of these genres: Archilochus (seventh century BCE); Tyrtaeus (seventh century BCE); and Alcaeus (late seventh century to early sixth century BCE). In their works, the abstracted "I" of the epic narrator could on occasion be replaced by the "I" of the citizen-soldier, as when Archilochus' narrator cheerfully admits to abandoning his shield at an engagement.[18]

Later poetry in these genres, as noted above, also made great play with the symbiotic link between epic and war. An unusual perspective on the one could imply an unusual perspective on the other. Moreover, martial imagery might be redeployed to other ends so as to make this point all the more strongly. Such poetry provided models for post-antique writers seeking room for maneuver in their depiction of warfare.

A particularly sophisticated example of this in action is presented by Henry Reed's Second World War poem "Lessons of the War" (1946–70). The epigraph to this work is taken from the work of the Roman poet Horace (65–8 BCE), the individual most responsible for introducing the complex possibilities for the poetic voice offered by Greek lyric poetry into Latin. Reed introduces his work by quoting the opening of Horace *Odes* 3.26, but with the substitution of the word "duellis" for "puellis" in the phrase "vixi puellis nuper idoneus / et militavi non sine gloria" ("I have lived up until recently fit for the girls / and I have served not without distinction").

In Horace's original, the second line appropriates the language of warfare ("I have *served*") for the amatory arena ("fit for the girls"). Reed's epigraph replaces "fit for the girls" with "fit for the wars." This substitution reverses Horace's original trope and turns the metaphorical warfare of the original poem back into reality. The ironic distance which the earlier writer places between his own enterprise and the proper poetry of warfare is ostentatiously collapsed. The epigraph thus sets the scene for a poem that crosscuts the dry instructions of military training ("And tomorrow morning / We shall have what to do after firing") with the lyrical evocation of gardens in spring ("The early bees are assaulting and fumbling the flowers").[19] It adumbrates the themes of the ensuing work by pointing up the generic tensions behind Horace's lyric enterprise.

War in classical historiography

The different classical genres of poetry, then, offered various expressive possibilities to subsequent war literature. The impact of ancient historiography was more direct. From the first, the history writing of the ancient world had a strong association with narratives of warfare. The opening of the *Histories* of Herodotus (mid-fifth century BCE), announces as its theme "both other matters and through what cause they [the Greeks and the Persians] made war on each other." Thucydides, writing somewhat later (late fifth century BCE), justifies the theme of his own historical undertaking, the Peloponnesian War, with the somewhat specious claim that it was "the greatest upheaval that befell the Greeks and a portion of the barbarians, virtually the majority of humanity."[20] The link between historiography and warfare was such that Tacitus, writing in the second century CE about the reign of Tiberius, laments that he offers nothing to compare with the subject matter of those who had written about the earlier deeds of the Roman people: "they described huge wars, the sacks of cities; the routing and capture of kings."[21] Tacitus himself has (or so he disingenuously claims) nothing as exciting to relate.

Ancient historiography's principal gift to its later counterparts was, perhaps, its methodological anxieties. Classical historiographers wrestled continuously with problems that resonate to the present. The second-century BCE historian Polybius, for example, frequently articulates such themes: the unreliability of partisan accounts of conflicts; the usefulness of history to the reader; the importance of experience and autopsy on the part of the historian himself; the complexities of producing an expressive verbal mimesis of traumatic events.[22] Ancient theoretical discussions of this last subject can have a particularly modern ring. Polybius on the legitimacy or otherwise of emotive depictions of the consequences of military action bears comparison with later discussions of the ramifications of representing war in words.[23]

It is unsurprising that the theme of historiography's practical usefulness to men of affairs has featured prominently in the reception of such works. Thus Thomas Hobbes, the philosopher of *bellum omnium contra omnes* ("war of all against all") who first translated Thucydides into English from Greek (1629), notes that this historian contains "profitable instruction for Noblemen, and such as may come to haue the mannaging of great and waighty actions."[24] Isaac Casaubon's 1609 preface to Polybius asserts the ability of history to transform uncouth men into statesmen and generals.[25]

Practical applicability aside, Greco-Roman historiography could be invoked in various fashions by writers intent upon the depiction of armed conflict and its consequences. In formal terms, it offered a convenient paradigm for certain categories of collective violence: in particular, civil war. Antiquity, as we have already noted, could lend prestige to a text at an important point in its narrative development. At the same time, however, ancient history could be deployed to achieve something subtler than new wine in old bottles.

All of these motifs are shown by an important text in the historiography of war, the *History of the Rebellion and Civil Wars in England* by Edward Hyde, First Earl of Clarendon (first published 1702–4). Book 11 of that work, which sees the execution of Charles I, concludes thus:

> So ended the year of one thousand six hundred forty-eight;[26] a year of reproach and infamy above all years which had passed before it; a year of the highest dissimulation and hypocrisy, of the deepest villainy and most bloody treasons, that any nation was ever cursed with or under; a year in which the memory of all the transactions ought to be rased out of all records, lest, by the success of it, atheism, infidelity, and rebellion should be propagated in the world, and of which we may say, as he [the historian] said of the time of Domitian, *sicut vetus aetas vidit quid ultimum in libertate esset, ita nos quid in servitute, adempto per inquisitiones et loquendi audiendique commercio etc.*; or, as the same writer says of a time not altogether so wicked, *is habitus animorum fuit, ut pessimum facinus auderent pauci, plures vellent, omnes paterentur.*[27]

Clarendon's two Latin quotations here are from Tacitus. The former ("just as the days of old saw how far liberty could go, so we have seen how far slavery can, since through spying even the exchange of speaking and listening has been taken away") is from the beginning of the Roman historian's biography of his father-in-law, the general Agricola.[28] The latter ("the disposition of spirits was such that a few dared the worst deed, more desired it, and all suffered it") comes from the account of the brief reign of the emperor Galba in his *Histories*.[29] At the simplest level, the solemn citations of Rome's greatest writer of history and student of civil strife assist the closural force of the paragraph. Clarendon rounds off his eleventh book with an explicit statement of narrative closure ("So ended the year of one thousand six hundred forty-eight"). The two quotations lend gravity to this conclusion.

The references to Tacitus are more than narrative garnish, however. Clarendon enacts a pointed historiographical paradox. In the very act of memorializing 1648 (by putting it in his history), he declares it "a year in which the memory of all the transactions ought to be rased out of all records, lest, by the success of it, atheism, infidelity, and rebellion should be propagated in the world." Then, to bring out the horror of the year, he quotes from the example of an analogous time, the reign of Domitian, something that he can only do because that time *was* memorialized by a previous historian.

Moreover, the passage quoted brings out the declension of that age into servitude through contrast with a yet further past ("just as the days of old saw how far liberty could go"). While ostensibly making a plea for forgetfulness and deletion, Clarendon subtly emphasizes why memorialization, even of bad times, is necessary: it supplies a basis for comparison and contrast.

Clarendon also refines his picture by bringing in a period that he carefully notes was "not altogether so wicked." This is the reign of Galba, whom Sir Henry Savile, in the preface to his 1591 translation of Tacitus,[30] used as a type of the "good prince" led astray by poor counsel – a failing which Clarendon has just noted as characteristic of the executed Charles I.[31] What seems a simple recourse to Latin tags proves on closer inspection, then, to be something more subtle. Through quotation, Clarendon brings into focus the resources and responsibilities of the historiographer, whether in Imperial Rome or seventeenth-century England, and also suggests with memorable compression a view of 1648 consonant with both Tacitean moralizing and his own nuanced picture of Charles's fall.

Conclusion

The door between classical and modern war literature, then, can swing in either direction. Just as the literary endeavors of Greece and Rome offered formal possibilities and intriguing perspectives to later writers on military themes, so experience of the wars of later ages has informed postclassical approaches to the conflicts of antiquity. The most famous case here is perhaps that of Edward Gibbon, who notes in his autobiography the usefulness of his militia experience in the creation of his *magnum opus*: "The discipline and evolutions of a modern battalion gave me a clearer notion of the Phalanx and the Legion, and the Captain of the Hampshire grenadiers (the reader may smile) has not been useless to the historian of the Roman Empire."[32]

Less well known is the contribution of the Second World War and other twentieth-century conflicts to scholarly readings of ancient wars. Thus, the authoritative twentieth-century commentary on the whole of Thucydides could use the analogy of the Second World War French commander Maxime Weygand to convey the qualities of the Athenian general Nicias,[33] while the relationship between modern war journalism and the conflicts which it describes has been deployed to illuminate the nature of ancient battle narratives.[34] On a grander scale, the organization of Sir Ronald Syme's *The Roman Revolution*, first published on the eve of war in 1939, explicitly takes its cue from contemporary events: chapter headings include "*Dux*" and "The First March on Rome," while the work as a whole is dedicated *PARENTIBVS OPTIMIS PATRIAEQUE* ("to my precellent parents and my country").[35]

In summary, then, classical war literature's legacy to Britain and America is multifarious, and goes beyond the simple analogizing of modern conflicts to ancient. The military writing of the Greco-Roman world developed formal structures and motifs upon which subsequent writers have often drawn, as well as initiating methodological concerns of ongoing significance. And in the sphere of war literature, as elsewhere, the classical world continues to provide a useful foil for contemporary themes and preoccupations.

NOTES

1. Thucydides, *The History of the Peloponnesian War* 2.35–46.
2. For examples, see Emma Bridges, Edith Hall, and P. J. Rhodes (eds.), *Cultural Responses to the Persian Wars: Antiquity to the Third Millennium* (Oxford University Press, 2007).
3. Horace, *Odes* 3.2.13.
4. Edith Hall, "Introduction: Why Greek Tragedy in the Late Twentieth Century?" *Dionysus Since 69: Greek Tragedy at the Dawn of the Third Millennium*, ed. Edith Hall, Fiona Macintosh, and Amanda Wrigley (Oxford University Press, 2004), 1–46: 19–20.
5. Matthew Leigh, *Lucan: Spectacle and Engagement* (Oxford: Clarendon, 1997), 234–46.
6. Cicero, *Pro Archia* 24.
7. Horace, *Odes* 4.9.25, translated by Alexander Pope.
8. Vergil, *Eclogues* 6.3; Horace, *Ars Poetica* 73; Ovid *Amores* 1.1.
9. Tibullus 1.1.75; Propertius 1.6.30; Ovid, *Amores* 1.9.
10. Christina Shuttleworth Kraus, "Caesar's Account of the Battle of Massilia (*BC* 1.34–2.22): Some Historiographical and Narratological Approaches," *A Companion to Greek and Roman Historiography*, ed. John Marincola (Malden, MA and Oxford: Blackwell, 2007), 371–8: 373, citing Homer, *Iliad* 2.485–93.
11. Pliny, *Natural History* 8.11.
12. Homer, *Iliad* 16.775–6.
13. Vergil, *Aeneid* 10.781–2.
14. Tim Rood, "The Development of the War Monograph," Marincola, *A Companion to Greek and Roman Historiography*, 147–58: 153.
15. Homer, *Iliad* 22.410–11.
16. Christopher Logue, *War Music* (London: Faber, 1988), viii.
17. Cf. Leigh, *Lucan*, 307–10.
18. Archilochus fr. 5 in M. L. West (ed.), *Iambi et elegi graeci ante Alexandrum cantata* (Oxford: Clarendon, 1989–92).
19. Henry Reed, *Collected Poems*, ed. Jon Stallworthy (Oxford University Press, 1991), 49.
20. Thucydides, *The History of the Peloponnesian War* 1.1.2.
21. Tacitus, *Annals* 4.32.
22. Unreliability of partisans: Polybius 1.14; usefulness of history: 1.1.2; experience of the historian: 12.28.1.

23. Polybius 2.56–63. Quintilian, in his training programme for orators, uses the sack of cities as an example of the point of narrative vividness (Quintilian 8.3.67–70).
24. Thomas Hobbes, *Eight Bookes of the Peloponnesian Warre written by Thucydides the Sonne of Olorus* (London, 1629), "The Epistle Dedicatorie."
25. Isaac Casaubon, *Polybii Lycortae F. Megalopolitani Historiarum libri qui supersunt* (Paris, 1609), prefatory material.
26. At the time of Charles I's execution, the New Year began in March. Hence, his death on January 30, 1649 is often recorded (as here) as happening in 1648.
27. Clarendon, *The History of the Rebellion and Civil Wars in England begun in the Year 1641*, ed. W. D. Macray, 6 vols. (Oxford: Clarendon, 1888), Book 11: 268 (IV: 511).
28. Tacitus, *Agricola* 2.
29. Tacitus, *Histories* 1.28.
30. Sir Henry Savile, *The End of Nero and the Beginning of Galba. Four Books of the Histories of Cornelius Tacitus. The Life of Agricola* (London, 1622 [1591]), prefatory material, 3–4.
31. Clarendon, *The History of the Rebellion*, Book 11: 241 (IV: 490).
32. Edward Gibbon, *Memoirs of My Life*, ed. G. A. Bonnard (London: Nelson, 1966), 117.
33. A. W. Gomme, A. Andrewes, and K. J. Dover, *A Historical Commentary on Thucydides*, 5 vols. (Oxford: Clarendon, 1970), IV: 462.
34. A. J. Woodman, *Rhetoric in Classical Historiography* (London: Croom Helm, 1988), 17–19.
35. Sir Ronald Syme, *The Roman Revolution* (Oxford: Clarendon, 1939), dedication.

FURTHER READING

Emma Bridges, Edith Hall, and P. J. Rhodes (eds.), *Cultural Responses to the Persian Wars: Antiquity to the Third Millennium* (Oxford University Press, 2007).
V. H. Hanson, *Why the West has Won: Carnage and Culture from Salamis to Vietnam* (London: Faber, 2001).
R. Jenkyns, *The Victorians and Ancient Greece* (Oxford: Blackwell, 1980).
M. Leezenberg, "From the Peloponnesian War to the Iraq War: A Post-Liberal Reading of Greek Tragedy," *Classics in Post-Colonial Worlds*, ed. Lorna Hardwick and Carol Gillespie (Oxford University Press, 2007), 265–85.
Tim Rood, *The Sea! The Sea! The Shout of the Ten Thousand in the Modern Imagination* (London: Duckworth, 2004).
Lawrence Tritle, *From Melos to My Lai: War and Survival* (London and New York: Routledge, 2000).
P. Wilson, "Homer and English Epic," *The Cambridge Companion to Homer*, ed. Robert Fowler (Cambridge University Press, 2004), 272–86.

PART THREE

Poetics

8

CORINNE SAUNDERS

Medieval warfare

War, a powerful and enduring cultural force in the medieval West from the early Middle Ages to the fifteenth century, played a shaping role in the imaginative literature of the period. In England, warfare was a constant. The establishment of Roman Britain probably involved some degree of war against the Celts, who in turn fought along with Roman Britons against the invading Saxons, perhaps with the help of a *dux bellorum* in whom King Arthur finds his origins. Anglo-Saxon England was devastated by the raids of the Vikings, and finally conquered by the Normans, whose own territory of Normandy was conquered by the French king, Philip Augustus (1202–4). Conflict between France and England endured from Philip's rivalry with King John over Flanders onwards. From 1294 until 1485, from the reign of Edward I to Henry VII, England was almost constantly at war with France and France's ally, Scotland. The Hundred Years War (1337–1453) was only a continuation of age-old rivalries. Not all wars were fought against other countries: civil war ended the reigns of five medieval kings. The Wars of the Roses (1455–87) demonstrate especially well the prevalence of violence in this period: an aristocratic struggle escalated into violent factionalism, and finally into civil war, peaking in the Battle of Towton (1461), the largest battle ever fought on British soil, in which some 28,000 men died.

Early medieval battles were, as far as is known, fought with a mixture of cavalry and infantry, and with relatively small numbers. With the development of new technology, however – in particular the stirrup – the figure of the mounted warrior came to dominate the medieval military world. From the ninth century onwards, these *milites*, *chevaliers*, or knights, as they were variously known, were placed in a lord's household and taught the noble arts, including horsemanship. In the later Middle Ages, such knights would be armed and equipped by the lord and fight for him. Medieval courtly literature and culture were profoundly influenced by the ideals of *chevalerie* that bound the great feudal lords and the knights who served them. With the growth of a more sophisticated kind of warfare, which used both knights and archers, came new systems of defense and expansion, in particular the construction of castles as military strongholds. Siege warfare became the norm and weapons such as the *trebuchet* (a siege engine with a catapult-like function) were invented. When wars were not conducted around cities or castles, they took the form of the *chevauchée* or raid. Armies could be large: expenditure records suggest that Edward III led 30,000 men. In the fourteenth century, war changed its character again – notably after the French cavalry was cut down by waiting infantry in a battle against the Flemings in 1302. As the power of infantry was recognized, much larger armies were employed and battles became bloodier. The use of gunpowder grew more widespread and the cannon was developed, marking the difference between the Battle of Agincourt (1415) and the Siege of Orleans (1428–29), in which Joan of Arc took part. The French victory at Castillon, which resolved the Hundred Years War, was the result of cannon, and cannon also enabled Mehmed II the Conqueror to take the city of Constantinople. These two battles of 1453 marked the end of medieval warfare.

The late medieval period saw new interest in the theory of war, with the production of treatises on different aspects of the art and customs of war (elaborating the widely circulated *De re militari* of Vegetius [late fourth/early fifth century BCE]), and serious philosophical discussion of the justification for war. Some of the earliest edicts of the Church (for instance, those issued by Hippolytus, Tertullian, and Lactantius) had condemned the involvement of Christians in war, but St. Augustine's endorsement of war undertaken for the good of society and with the aim of peace was widely accepted.[1] The conditions for "just war" were elaborated by St. Thomas Aquinas and echoed by many thinkers.[2] Chivalry, with its complex code of honor, was to some extent transferred to war: the ideals of loyalty, courage, and service were crucial. The tournament, popular from the twelfth century, provided training for the knight, and challenges of honor and single combat played a serious part in warfare.

But there was another side to war. Chivalric custom was not always observed: in the Battle of Agincourt, for instance, Henry V ordered many of his French prisoners to be killed. Battles could have high death tolls, as at Agincourt and Flodden (1513); the infection and disease that accompanied war took many more lives. Pillage and raids such as those of the fifteenth-century *Ecorcheurs* were devastating not only to the population but also to crops, buildings, and villages. The end of war was deeply problematic, for companies were not disbanded once they were paid off, but left to roam and pillage. Christine de Pisan's *Le Livre des faits d'armes et de chevallerie* (1410) offers a counterpoint to standard treatises by characterizing warfare as a final, deplorable course of action, which leads only too readily to material and spiritual evils.

The practices of chivalry, the figure of the knight errant, the ideals of the Crusades, the pageantry and honor of knighthood: all these must to some extent be detached from the reality of the history of war. Yet, at the same time, they played crucial roles in making glamorous the blood, sweat, and tears of warfare and in the creation of the medieval warrior. It was medieval literature most of all that shaped the ideals of warfare, even while it questioned them.

In Anglo-Saxon as in classical writing, war is both fundamental to the heroic mode and a realistic concern. The writings attributed to King Ælfred and his circle are necessarily colored by the repeated warfare that marked his reign and frequently convey nostalgia for a golden age of peace. Writers were keenly aware of the prominence of war in biblical history, episodes of which were retold in sermons and rewritten in poems such as the Old English *Genesis* and *Exodus* (?late seventh century), and *Judith* (early tenth century).[3] Later prose writers, most strikingly Bishop Wulfstan in his *Sermo Lupi Ad Anglos* (*Sermon of the Wolf to the English*) (1014), interpreted the repeated Viking raids as tokens of God's anger at the sinful English and signs of the coming apocalypse. Frequent warfare meant that Europe was scattered with ruins, menacing reminders of death and the passing of time: Anglo-Saxon poets eerily refer to the Roman remains in their landscape as "enta geweorc" (the work of giants). In *The Wanderer* (?late eighth century), the poet looks on a "splendid lofty wall, adorned with shapes / Of serpents," perhaps a Roman stone bas-relief, which he sees as a sign of the impending destruction of civilization.[4] In *Beowulf* (?late eighth century), the poet uses the same topos to describe the passing of the tribe of the Geats: a man contemplates a deserted wine hall – "a wind swept resting-place bereft of joy" – where all sleep in their graves.[5]

Beowulf contrasts monstrous and human enemies, moral battle and feud, heroism and societal disorder, and ultimately questions the viability of the fabric and ideals of a society that defines itself through heroic battle. The first half of the poem opens onto a mythic world of good versus evil, as the triumphant young warrior defends the aged king. For Beowulf, the battle against the Grendel-monsters is a venture of courage: "mightiest among mankind in that day" (196–7), he decides to seek out king Hrothgar of the Danes, whose hall is under attack, and his arrival on the ring-prowed ship with his troop of glittering, armor-clad warriors is described on an epic scale. Beowulf is defined by his boasts, to which only he can fit his actions, and the poem emphasizes his stoicism. The savage violence of his battle with Grendel is emphasized, its drama partly situated in the equal matching of the pair, who fight hand to hand: the poet employs the same term, "aglæca" (the fearful combatant or awesome one) (893, 2952), for both man and monster.

Between Beowulf's battles with Grendel and his mother is placed the most chilling historical digression in the poem, the story of the fight at Finnsburh, also contained in a separate poetic fragment. The poet recounts the marriage of the Frisian king Finn to a Danish princess, Hildeburh, who is to weave peace between feuding tribes. While her brother Hnaef and his men are staying with Finn, however, simmering enmities erupt and in the ensuing battle Hildeburh's brother and son are killed. A truce persuades the remnant of the Danes to stay on as Finn's men but after a winter, they rise up, kill Finn, and take Hildeburh back to the Danes. There seems to be no right or wrong in this story: no reason is given for the first battle and Finn's sincerity in making the treaty is emphasized, but the poet also vividly maps the ancient enmities and loyalties that twice result in the contravention of the guest–host relationship.

The volatility of heroic society is more immediately evident in the second part of the poem, which leaps over fifty years to recount the end of Beowulf's kingship. The defeat and death in battle of Beowulf's king, Hygelac, functions as a leitmotif and the poet circles back again and again to different episodes in the wars between the Geats and the Swedes. Beowulf is placed as just one of a series of great kings who have died tragic, unnecessary deaths, his rule part of a continuing process of feud, raid, revenge, and violence. At the end of the poem, his slaying of the dragon preserves his people but opens the way for further Swedish invasions and the eventual destruction of the tribe of the Geats. Impending doom is reiterated in the prophecies of the woman who laments at Beowulf's funeral pyre: "she sorely feared days of lamentation for herself, a multitude of slaughters, the terror of an army, humiliation and captivity" (3152–5). In this society, to express grief is a feminine action: the lamenting woman's voice also occurs in the Finnsburh passage, with Hildeburh grieving at the funeral pyre – "the woman mourned, chanted a dirge" (1117–18) – and in the poems known as *The Wife's Lament* and *Wulf and Eadwacer* (?late eighth century).

For war to be portrayed positively, the mythic quality evident in Beowulf's battles with the monsters seems necessary. Warfare in religious poetry can take up the same triumphant theme of the victory of good over evil: thus in the *Dream of the Rood* (?seventh century), Christ becomes the glorious warrior as he willingly climbs upon the Cross to defeat death, and returns with his glorious armies, liberated from hell, on Judgment Day. In the Old English *Judith*, Judith's beheading of Holofernes similarly asserts divine over demonic power, and the victory of the Israelites is conveyed in a great epic battle at the end of the poem. This is ideal warfare, in which heroism and moral victory coincide, and the poet revels in the tropes of glorious battle. Judith is a triumphant leader, the handmaiden of the Lord who becomes his warrior and exhorts her troops in his name, to be presented with the spoils of war at the end of the poem.

It is striking that the latest Old English heroic poems both depict English battles described in the *Anglo-Saxon Chronicle*. The tenth-century poem *The Battle of Brunanburgh* celebrates the victory in 937 of the West-Saxon king Athelstan and his brother Edmund (aged sixteen) over a combined force of Scots, Picts, Welsh, and Vikings, and employs the traditional images of battle to do so. The poet emphasizes the nobility and heroism of the Anglo-Saxons, the grim battle-play, the breaking of the shield-wall of the enemy, the day-long pursuit and terrible slaughter (including of the Scottish King Constantine's young son), and the presence of the beasts of battle feasting on the bodies. This is a confident, patriotic, victorious war song, in which the heroes achieve "eternal glory" (3) through their actions. The questioning of these values occurs only in the mind of the later reader, who is likely to recall imminent and less successful battles, and the defeat of the Anglo-Saxons just over a century later.

By contrast, the late tenth-century *The Battle of Maldon* offers a mournful and ambiguous celebration of heroism in its narrative of the defeat of the English by the Vikings in 991. Here, the tropes of battle – the boasts of warriors, the play of shield and sword, the song of war – are deeply problematized, for through his "ofermod" (overconfidence or pride), the East-Saxon leader Byhrtnoth (ealdorman of Essex) allows "too much land" to the Vikings who wait on the island at the end of a causeway over the river Blackwater (89–90). For the sake of heroic battle, with a proto-British sense of fair play, he renounces the advantage of position by letting the Vikings cross to the shore. Though Byhrtnoth and his warriors fight heroically, he is killed, perhaps as a result of malicious fate, perhaps as a punishment for his pride, and many flee in the belief that their leader has deserted. Those of Byhrtnoth's household who remain speak in turn to urge vengeance and honorable death, ending with the words of the aged retainer Byrhtwold: "Mind must be harder, spirit must be bolder, / And heart the greater, as our might grows less" (312–13). The inspiring and tragic image of the heroic last stand, evocative of all that is best and worst in warfare, resonates through later culture, particularly associated with battle in a narrow place – a bridge, a causeway, a doorway, a wall.

War plays an inevitable part in the shame–honor culture and battle is the fundamental means by which a man proves himself. Old English gnomic verses emphasize the definitive role of war in the making of masculine identity: "Noble companions must urge on the prince / While young to battle ... / Warrior must be valiant" (14–16). Yet these verses also warn against rather than celebrate the endless struggle, "army with army, foe against another": "Ever the prudent man must think about the fighting in this world" (52, 54–55). It is only through honor in action and resignation to fate that a man may gain a glorious reputation and the soul may be judged well, but Old English poetry does not mask the grief, loss, and tragedy that war may bring. As pagan ideals are overlaid by Christian, Anglo-Saxon writing also looks towards a celestial reward that endures beyond fleeting earthly glory.

In post-Conquest English literature, warfare remains a prominent trope, with many of the same emphases, again spanning and merging the real, the legendary, and the mythic, as heroism becomes more consistently interwoven with Christian idealism. The chroniclers of the period – most famously Jean Froissart, who recounts the deeds of Edward III and the Black Prince in epic style – celebrate "proesce" or martial virtue. The knights whose exploits they record become chivalric heroes, fulfilling the ideals of heroism similar to that of Anglo-Saxon literature, but adding to these courtly, Christian qualities: so Froissart characterizes English chivalry as marked by respect for female chastity (1346).[6] Violation of chivalry becomes the sign of the enemy; honor, both physical and spiritual, defines the ideal knight. In hagiography, the saint may become the enemy, but he or she may also lead armies against the nations, and the figure of the *miles Christi* functions on both a literal and a symbolic level across devotional writing. Romance, the most influential genre of imaginative literature in the Middle Ages, both sustains and adapts the tradition of epic narrative poetry. The knight-hero of romance, like the Anglo-Saxon warrior, is proven through his prowess in war, but also by individual chivalric deeds: his making of an identity can correspond with that of a nation, but tends also to go beyond this. Yet war is not necessarily celebrated, even when it is presented as justified, and it can be undercut. In the works of Chaucer and Malory, in particular, the matter of legendary history, both classical and Arthurian, proves individual heroism and preserves nationhood, but also opens up profoundly existential questions.

The earliest (French) romances retold classical epics, reflecting new interest in the individual, in courtly values, and in chivalry, but retaining war as a central theme. Thebes, Troy, and the exploits of Alexander would offer popular story matter throughout the Middle Ages. Romance writers also took up earlier twelfth-century *chansons de geste* (songs of arms/battle), which treated subjects of French history, in particular the battles of Charlemagne and the Crusades (the *Chanson de Roland* [mid-twelfth century] was especially influential). These *romans d'aventure* tended to narrate a series of individual exploits achieved by a particular French historical hero within the context of military conflict between Christians and Saracens, while a more courtly type of romance also developed, which drew on the "matter of Britain" and, in particular, on legends of the heroic exploits of King Arthur and the Round Table.

The earliest English romance, *King Horn* (*c*.1225, based on an Anglo-Norman romance), engages with the wars of the pre-Conquest period. The eponymous hero is set adrift as a boy after his father, king of Sudene, a southern kingdom, has been killed by Saracens (perhaps to be aligned with Vikings). The focal point of the story is Horn's right to kingship, which he proves through a series of ritualized battles – against the Saracens to rescue the king of Ireland; to preserve his beloved Rymenhild from enforced marriage; and finally to regain his kingdom. This movement from disorder to order, in which battle plays a crucial part, is typical of romance, as is demonstrated by the work with which *Horn* is often paired, *Havelok the Dane* (written about fifty years later and also with an Anglo-Norman source).[7] Whereas *Horn* takes place in the timeless world of romance, marked only by vague hints at a dynastic English past, the marriage at the end of the more realistic *Havelok* unites England and Denmark. The identity of the exiled Havelok as son of the Danish king is miraculously proven both by the kinglight that shines from his mouth and by his marvelous strength in battles of different sorts. This romance too promotes the model of the good king, whose defense of law, justice, and nation is actively pursued in warfare against the unrighteous.

English romances also treat the historical material of the Crusades, often again in broadly mythologizing terms: Christian against Saracen, good against evil. The fragmentary *Sege of Melayne* (*c*.1400) sets empty pagan belief against the power of the Christian supernatural, as God repeatedly manifests himself in response to heathen destruction. Christian right is affirmed through violence when, miraculously preserved, the four knightly protagonists, "clenly thorow Goddis grace," kill all the Saracens.[8] The narrative sets the ancient battle of good and evil within the context of continental history: heroic feats are celebrated, but the focus is most of all the transformative power of Christian faith. The late fourteenth-century alliterative *Siege of Jerusalem* employs many of the same motifs, but also exploits the horrific violence and suffering of siege warfare, which reaches its height when a starving Jewish mother consumes her child.[9]

In the romances of *Guy of Warwick* and *Beves of Hampton* (both included in the celebrated fourteenth-century Auchinleck manuscript, but based on earlier Anglo-Norman works), English dynastic material is combined with the history of the Crusades, as their protagonists fight both in England and abroad. These narratives of English heroes reflect a growing sense of nationalism, but also rely on the broad mythic appeal of romance (*Beves* was particularly popular on the Continent). The violent opposition between good and evil at the start, enacted in the adultery of Beves's mother, whose lover ambushes and kills Beves's father, is echoed in the conflict between pagan and Christian when the exiled Beves finds himself in the Saracen kingdom of Armenia. The crusading landscape of the East is realistically evoked: trade, culture, and civilization intersect with religious warfare and individual pilgrimage. When Beves, disguised as a palmer, is asked "Whar is pes and whar is werre?" (2258), he lists various crusading territories; he also visits Jerusalem in order to consult the patriarch.[10] There is no suggestion that he is engaged in the Crusades, but his battles, often undertaken in service to his lady, the converted Saracen princess Josian, are repeatedly depicted in terms of the opposition of Christian and Saracen. Beves's role as Christian avenger is most explicit when, in Damascus, he kills a priest who has been leading a crowd of Saracens in sacrifice to "Mahoun," his actions echoing Christ's anger at the money changers in the temple.

Guy of Warwick similarly combines an emphasis on prowess with concern for the spiritual. The first part of this romance is secular, its focus Guy's pursuit of the lady Felice, who repeatedly refuses him her hand in marriage until he proves himself worthy through a sequence of battles. The second, briefer section treats Guy's wedding and swiftly following conversion. His newfound spirituality is pursued in battles in defense of Christian justice, which culminate in his encounter with the giant Colbrond. Guy's battles against both monsters and Saracens clearly reenact the ancient war between good and evil: the black giant Amoraunt seems "a devel fram helle" (st. 95), while Colbrond's amour is "blac as piche" (st. 257).[11] Guy's strength is endorsed by the Christian supernatural: he is provided with a marvelous sword discovered through divine vision, and in battle resembles an angel (st. 188). His arrival is messianic: King Athelstan, his lords, and clerics fast for three days, praying to find "A man that were douhti of hond" to fight Colbrond (st. 234), and Athelstan is instructed by an angel to await Guy. The physical qualities of battle are never forgotten, however: although Guy calls upon Mary to help the English, when his sword breaks he rushes to seize one of Colbrond's battle-axes and kills him with his own weapon. Although Guy eventually dies a saintly death, he, like Beves, remains the epic English hero.

Alongside English and continental material, classical subjects were retained, and the matter of Troy took pride of place among these. While Homer was not known until the rediscovery of Greek texts in the Renaissance, alongside Vergil's *Aeneid* were circulated the late classical histories of Dares and Dictys, which claimed to be eyewitness narratives of the Trojan War. Troy held a special interest for English historians as the source of English civilization: Aeneas, fleeing Troy, founded Rome; his son Ascanius begot Brutus, who defeated the giants of Albion to found Britain. Geoffrey of Monmouth notes that Brutus' capital, built on the banks of the Thames, was originally called

"Troia Nova," and the possibility of renaming London "Troynovant" was seriously discussed in the 1380s; Chaucer's contemporary John Gower refers to London as the "toun of newe Troye."[12] Dares' history was expanded by the English historian, Joseph of Exeter, in *De bello Troiano* (c.1185), on which Chaucer draws for his *Troilus and Criseyde*. In the mid-twelfth century, the French writer Benoît de Sainte-Maure produced a lengthy romance of Troy, and the story of Troilus and Briseida was retold in misogynistic terms by the thirteenth-century Sicilian writer Guido de Columnis of Messina. Benoît's romance is the primary source for the early fourteenth-century English metrical poem, *The Seege or Batayle of Troy*, which also draws on a Latin prose history (*Excidium Troiae*).[13] The poem offers a brief, selective narrative that focuses on military exploits and heroes rather than love and moral questions. The late fourteenth-century English *Gest Historiale of the Destruction of Troy*, by contrast, is an extended alliterative translation of Guido's work: the poet places his subject among "sothe stories" rather than "feynit" and "false accounts," and at once celebrates and criticizes pagan heroism.[14] The *Laud Troy Book* (c.1400) also offers an extended version of Guido's text, but shifts the emphasis to Hector, while the 30,000 lines of John Lydgate's *Troy Book* (1412–20) add extensive moral comment.[15] The *Gest Historiale*, the *Laud Troy Book*, and Lydgate's *Troy Book* all question, to different extents, the role of force in desiring Helen's abduction by Paris, and engage with the political ramifications of seizing a queen. The resulting overthrow of a great society forms a powerful and disturbing subject.

War is both absent and present in Chaucer's great Trojan romance, *Troilus and Criseyde* (?1382–86), which translates and adapts, partly through the philosophical lens of Boethius' *Consolation of Philosophy* (c.524), Giovanni Boccaccio's extended romance of Troilus and Criseida, *Il Filostrato* (*The One Prostrated by Love*) (c.1340). Chaucer's poem, set largely within the walls of the houses, gardens, and chambers of Troy rather than on the battlefields beyond, engages intensely with the private space and emotional predicament of the lovers rather than with epic warfare. Yet it is also structured by the opposition of public and private, and hence the themes of love and war are inextricable. It is crucial that Troilus is the great Trojan prince and warrior, presented at the start as "this fierse and proude knyght ... a worthy kynges sone," and first seen by Criseyde proudly armed on his bay steed.[16] The point is that even so great a warrior is susceptible to love, to the unmaking and remaking of the self. War is aligned in the poem with destiny and the audience is always aware of the tragic fall of Troy to come. More immediately, the events of the war occasion the loss of Criseyde when she is exchanged for Antenor, who will betray Troy and eventually cause Troilus' death.

In the *Canterbury Tales* (late fourteenth century), Chaucer brings together legendary and contemporary warfare in the figure of the Knight and his tale. The General Prologue lists the Knight's many crusading battles – against the Muslims in Spain, North Africa, and the Near East; and with Teutonic knights against pagans in the Baltic. The description is carefully realized: Chaucer refers to Christian alliances with sympathetic pagans in order to keep supply lines open in the eastern Mediterranean, and to the Prussian custom of the table of honor, a feast held for the crusaders. There is also ambiguity: no knight could have fought in all the battles; at least one (in Tramyssene, now Algeria) may never have occurred; and the sack of Alexandria was well known even at the time to have been anything but chivalric. Terry Jones has argued that the Knight's tattered and stained clothes reflect his imperfections and the flawed nature of the Crusades, but Chaucer seems rather to present the "verray, parfit gentil knyght" (72) as the ideal embodiment of chivalry.[17] As with the tale told by the Knight, ambiguity, especially that created by the opposition between ideal and actual war, is left for the reader to tease out.

The *Knight's Tale* adapts Boccaccio's *Teseida* (*c.*1340), which uses as a backdrop Statius' *Thebaid* (late first century CE), the epic narrative of the war between two brothers for the throne of Thebes. The tale opens as Theseus, Duke of Athens, makes war on Thebes: he is "the noble conquerour" (998) who reasserts honorable social order through just battle. The narrative is constructed around the traditional romance motif of winning the woman through combat. Theseus has conquered "with his wysdom and his chivalrie" "al the regne of Femenye," the country of the Amazons, to bring back the queen, Hippolyta, as his bride (865–66). The Knight recounts the lengthy rivalry of two captured Theban knights, Palamon and Arcite, for the hand of Emilye, Hippolyta's sister. Although Theseus restores chivalric order to their savage battle by transforming it into a tournament, the competition ends in Arcite's tragic death: the principle of might is right does not yield the desired happy ending. Chaucer raises profound questions concerning the silencing of women within the military ethic and the inefficacy of that ethic within the larger context of destiny.

Whereas later war narratives may probe the fear of the hero, this is not the case with medieval writing. Ambivalence towards warfare, however, does recur, and is strikingly apparent in the other great matter of romance, Arthurian legend. The fourteenth-century Alliterative *Morte Arthure* is firmly situated within the historical tradition, drawing on chronicles of Arthur rather than on the French prose romances. Particularly striking is the realism of the descriptions of warfare: traditional motifs of challenge, boast, and heroic exploit are interwoven with details of foot soldiers and archers as well as of knights and kings, prisoners and ransoms, banners and trumpets. Battles are recounted with graphic violence – the rivers of red blood, the precise nature of wounds and death, the great encounters where thousands are hewn down, and the destruction by siege-engines of the city of Metz. There are remarkable details of place, from continental Europe to the lands of the Amazons and of Prester John. Just war and conquest seem to be celebrated and yet, as Arthur presses on in his imperialistic initiative, questions are raised concerning the limits of pride and ambition, the destructiveness of warfare, the dangers of excessively heroic tactics that detach knights from their followers, and, ultimately, the fall of the mighty as Fortune's wheel turns, Mordred usurps the throne, and Arthur himself is conquered. The narrative is nowhere more masterful than in the account of the death of Gawain, the epic hero of the work. He ventures in by galley as Arthur and his ships wait offshore, his few knights performing heroic feats against thousands, but is eventually killed when his knife slips on Mordred's armor:

> He [Gawain] shockes out a short knife shethed with silver
> And sholde have slotted him in but no slit happened;
> His hand slipped and slode o-slant on the mailes
> And the tother slely slinges him under;
> With a trenchand knife the traitour him hittes
> Through the helm and the hed on high on the brain;
> And thus Sir Gawain is gone, the good man of armes.[18]

For a moment, even Mordred weeps. The passage captures the vivid, realistic mode of the poem, the violence of warfare and the fragility of human life, as one slip of the hand brings about the fall of the great knight. The motif of tragic loss occasioned by extreme heroism recalls *The Battle of Maldon*, while the poem also conveys a message concerning the dangers of imperialist expansion at the expense of the realm and the savagery of war.

Unease is also key to Malory's *Morte Darthur*. Malory's imprisonment, during which he wrote his great Arthurian history, may have been directly occasioned by the turbulent politics of the Wars of the Roses, and the work emphasizes the enduring and practical value of stable kingship, nationhood, and chivalry, which uphold peace in the realm. It both translates and dramatically adapts material from the thirteenth-century French *Prose Vulgate* cycle of Arthurian romances. The first part recounts Arthur's succession to the throne and his unifying of a divided Britain through battle against the country's eleven kings. Malory achieves verisimilitude by naming actual places such as Dover and Trent, and presenting Merlin as a military tactician who guides Arthur's army through the back ways of Sherwood Forest. Such realism, alongside the epic qualities of the battles, contributes to Malory's historical emphasis on Arthur as the rightful ruler of Britain. After defeating rival powers within Britain, Arthur must prove himself on the Continent: Malory takes from the end of the Alliterative *Morte Arthure* the episode of the Emperor Lucius' desire for tribute and the ensuing war, using it to mark the climax of Arthur's rise to power. Defeat of the Roman Empire is balanced by Arthur's battle against the giant of Mont Saint Michel, whose savage acts of rape and murder render him the archetype of the antichivalric, monstrous forces of the untamed natural world.

The core of the *Morte Darthur* concerns the achievements of individual knights in upholding the values of the oath of chivalry sworn every year at Pentecost.[19] The oath (not found in Malory's sources but closely echoing knightly oaths of his own time) presents chivalry in practical terms of mutual support and of service to king, lady, and fellow-knight, and establishes a pattern for behavior that defines the quests of individual knights, in particular Launcelot, Gareth, and Tristram. Their battles repeatedly prove that right is might: honor wins over dishonor and the defeated tend to be those who contravene the principles of chivalry. But the central books of the *Morte* are dominated by a sense of battle as game and play, as knights repeatedly seek to assert their prowess through quest and adventure and in tournaments, described in considerable and realistic detail by Malory.

The final part of the work circles back to warfare on a larger scale. The slander and hatred of Agravain, Mordred, and their brothers leads to the taking of Launcelot with the queen and hence the final rift in the fellowship of the Round Table. Once the affair is made public, the order of a shame culture is under threat: despite Arthur's sorrow at the destruction of the Round Table ("quenys I myght have inow, but such a felyship of good knyghtes shall never be todydirs in no company" [20.9, 1184]), he is bound to avenge dishonor. Similarly, Launcelot is honor-bound to rescue the queen once she is condemned to death by fire. At this point in the *Morte*, the tensions inherent in the military ethic of chivalry are evident, as Launcelot finds himself the victim of a clash of loyalties: "I woll feyght for the quene, that she ys a trew lady untyll her lorde. But the kynge in hys hete, I drede, woll nat take me as I ought to be takyn" (20.5, 1171). Chance or malicious destiny intervenes to move the story further towards tragedy when, in the battle that takes place as Guinevere is led out to the fire, Launcelot fails to recognize and so kills the two best-loved of Gawain's brothers, Gareth and Gaheris, who, unwilling to fight against Launcelot, have gone unarmed into the press. This misfortune seals the fate of the Round Table. Gawain has previously taken Launcelot's part and stayed away from the battle; now the extreme ethic of revenge that has defined Gawain and his brothers across the work (to the extent that they kill their own mother for her adultery) is turned against Launcelot himself: "for the deth of my brothir, sir Gareth," says Gawain, "I shall seke sir

Launcelot thorowoute seven kynges realmys, but I shall sle hym, other ellis he shall sle me" (20.10, 1186).

Gawain's implacable desire for vengeance forces Arthur to take his army to the Continent. Battle takes the form of repeated single combat between Gawain and Launcelot, who is consistently depicted as unwilling yet bound by chivalric conventions to accept Gawain's challenges. The absence of the king opens the way for Mordred to seize the English throne, an episode that recalls the civil war of Malory's own time. Discord on the highest level – within the fellowship – leads to discord amongst the people, who support Mordred against their king and whom Malory condemns for their fickleness. In these last books, Arthur and Launcelot are presented as victims of fortune as well as human frailty, and the hope for a different outcome is retained until the end.

This is most evident in the narrative of Arthur's last battle, for which Malory turns again to English sources, in particular the late fourteenth-century English Stanzaic *Morte Arthure*, to set malevolent fortune against beneficent providence. Arthur is warned in a dream vision not to fight, yet through the ill chance of a knight drawing his sword to kill an adder the battle begins:

> And never syns was there seyne a more dolefuller batayle in no Crysten londe, for there was but russhynge and rydynge, foynynge and strykynge, and many a grym worde was there spokyn of aythir to othir, and many a dedely stroke.
>
> …
>
> And thus they fought all the longe day, and never stynted tylle the noble knyghtes were layde to the colde erthe. And ever they fought stylle tylle hit was nere nyght, and by than was there an hondred thousand leyde dede uppon the downe. (21.4, 1235–6)

Malory conveys a sense of figures moving, only half-seeing, in the events surrounding "this unhappy day," while the battle also recalls that fought at Towton in his lifetime. Like the chroniclers of that battle, Malory describes the looters who prey on the bodies of the fallen. His narrative draws much of its dramatic power from its understated tone of realism: as well as the heroic deeds of the great Arthurian knights, it makes plain the waste, confusion, and loss of warfare. The last pages of the work treat a world from which chivalric glory has passed. Like the medieval literature and culture that precede and shape it, the *Morte* weaves together actual, legendary, and mythic notions of war to celebrate heroism, but also to convey tragedy and suffering.

NOTES

1. Book 1 of Augustine's *De libero arbitrio* (*Concerning Free Will*) (426–27 CE) treats preemptive self-defense. The themes of war, peace, and divine law, including the

notion of preventive war, recur across his *De civitate Dei* (*Concerning the City of God*) (416–22 CE): see especially Book 4.15 on the "stern necessity" of war.

2. See Aquinas's *Summa Theologiae* 2.2, qu. 40, *de bello* (*c*.1270).

3. Old English poetry is notoriously difficult to date: the four major poetry manuscripts date to the late ninth or early tenth centuries, but the poetry they contain was composed from the mid-seventh century onwards.

4. *The Wanderer, A Choice of Anglo-Saxon Verse*, trans. Richard Hamer (London: Faber, 1970), l. 98. All other Old English poems instanced here, with the exception of *Beowulf*, may be found in this selection; subsequent references to these are from this translation, cited by line number.

5. *Beowulf*, ed. and trans. Michael Swanton (Manchester University Press; New York: Barnes and Noble, 1978), ll. 2456–7. Subsequent references to *Beowulf* are from this translation, cited by line number.

6. See Sir John Froissart, *The Chronicles of Froissart*, trans. John Bourchier, Lord Berners, 6 vols. (London: David Nutt, 1901–3): I: cxxiiii, 284.

7. For both *King Horn* and *Havelok the Dane*, see *Middle English Verse Romances*, ed. Donald B. Sands (Exeter University Press, 1986), 15–54 and 55–129.

8. *The Sege of Melayne, Six Middle English Romances*, ed. Maldwyn Mills (London: Dent, 1973; Rutland, VT: Tuttle, 1992) 1–45: l. 495.

9. See *The Siege of Jerusalem*, ed. Ralph Hanna and David Lawton, Early English Text Society ES 320 (Oxford University Press, 2003).

10. *The Romance of Sir Beues of Hamtoun*, ed. Eugen Kölbing, Early English Text Society ES 46, 48, 65 (London: Kegan Paul, Trench, Trübner & Co., 1885, 1886, 1894), l. 2258. Subsequent references to *Beves of Hampton* are from this edition, cited by line number, and use slightly modernized spelling. See further Carol F. Heffernan's discussion in *The Orient in Chaucer and Medieval Romance* (Cambridge: D. S. Brewer, 2003), 15–16.

11. *The Romance of Guy of Warwick: The First or 14th-century Version*, ed. Julius Zupitza, Early English Text Society ES 42, 49, 59 (London: Kegan Paul, Trench, Trübner & Co., 1883, 1887, 1891), ll. 1660–6. Subsequent references to *Guy of Warwick* are from this edition (Auchinleck MS unless otherwise stated), cited by line or stanza number. The second section of *Guy of Warwick* is written in rhymed stanzas instead of couplets in the Auchinleck manuscript cited here; Gonville and Caius College, Cambridge MS 107 is also printed in Zupitza's edition.

12. John Gower, *Confessio Amantis, The English Works of John Gower*, ed. G. C. Macaulay, Early English Text Society ES 81, 82, 4 vols. (Oxford University Press, 1900), I: Prologue, l. 37.

13. See *The Seege or Batayle of Troye: A Middle English Metrical Romance*, ed. Mary Elizabeth Barnicle, Early English Text Society OS 172 (Oxford University Press, 1927).

14. *The "Gest Historiale" of the Destruction of Troy: An Alliterative Romance*, ed. George A. Panton and David Donaldson, Early English Text Society OS 39, 56 (London: N. Trübner, 1869, 1874), ll. 11, 18.

15. See *The Laud Troy Book: A Romance of About 1400 A.D.*, ed. J. Ernst Wülfing, Early English Text Society OS 121 (London: Kegan Paul, Trench, Trübner & Co., 1902) and John Lydgate, *Lydgate's Troy Book*, ed. Henry Bergen, Early English Text Society ES 97, 103, 106, 126 (London: Kegan Paul, Trench, Trübner & Co., 1906–35).

16. Geoffrey Chaucer, *Troilus and Criseyde*, *The Riverside Chaucer*, ed. Larry D. Benson, 3rd edn. (Oxford University Press, 1988), 471–586: ll. 225–6. Subsequent references to Chaucer's works are from this edition, cited by book and line number.

17. See Terry Jones, *Chaucer's Knight: The Portrait of a Medieval Mercenary* (London: Weidenfeld & Nicolson, 1980).

18. Alliterative *Morte Arthure*, *King Arthur's Death: The Middle English Stanzaic Morte Arthur and Alliterative Morte Arthure*, ed. Larry D. Benson (Exeter University Press, 1986), 115–238: ll. 3852–8.

19. Sir Thomas Malory, *The Works of Sir Thomas Malory*, ed. Eugène Vinaver, rev. P. J. C. Field, 3rd edn., 3 vols. (Oxford: Clarendon, 1990), I: 3.15, 120. Subsequent references to Malory's *Morte Darthur* are from this edition, cited by book, section, and page number.

FURTHER READING

Andrew Ayton, *Knights and Warhorses: Military Service and the English Aristocracy Under Edward III* (Woodbridge: Boydell, 1994).

Philippe Contamine, *War in the Middle Ages*, trans. Michael Jones (Oxford: Blackwell, 1984).

Maurice Keen, *Chivalry* (New Haven, CT: Yale University Press, 1984).

The Laws of War in the Late Middle Ages (London: Routledge, 1965).

Medieval Warfare: A History (Oxford University Press, 1999).

Hans-Henning Kortüm (ed.), *Transcultural Wars from the Middle Ages to the 21st Century* (Berlin: Akademie Verlag, 2006).

Andrew Lynch, *Malory's Book of Arms: The Narrative of Combat in "Le Morte Darthur"* (Cambridge: D. S. Brewer, 1997).

John H. Pratt, *Chaucer and War* (Lanham, MD: University Press of America, 2000).

Corinne Saunders, Françoise Le Saux, and Neil Thomas (eds.), *Writing War: Medieval Literary Responses to Warfare* (Cambridge: D. S. Brewer, 2004).

Matthew J. Strickland, *War and Chivalry. The Conduct and Perception of War in England and Normandy, 1066–1217* (Cambridge University Press, 1996).

Malcolm Vale, *War and Chivalry: Warfare and Aristocratic Culture in England, France and Burgundy at the End of the Middle Ages* (London: Duckworth, 1981).

9

PHILIP WEST

Early modern war writing and the British Civil Wars

Early modern war writing was neither transparent nor impartial, but in many ways a continuation off the field of the battles begun on it. Whether a professional soldier, gentlemen volunteer, or nobleman from the very elite of Europe's aristocracy, an early modern war writer mustered whatever rhetorical muscle he could in order to shape his military memoirs, experiences of battle, or views on strategy into a persuasive whole. Demand for war writing grew throughout the sixteenth and seventeenth centuries and publishers increasingly cared more about the vividness of a report than they did about its accuracy. Eyewitness accounts were valued, but phrases about "the thundering shot of the canon [which] calleth me to my place" were no guarantee that the writer had actually been present at events.[1] The newly founded grammar schools taught sixteenth-century schoolboys that powerful language was part and parcel of great military command: it enabled success on the battlefield by commanding respect and it gave the victor means to commemorate his victory and tactics. Julius Caesar was idolized as the greatest commander and orator of the ancient world, his *Commentarii de bello gallico* (*Commentaries on the Gallic War*) (58–52 BCE) becoming a fixture on the Elizabethan school curriculum. Admiration for Caesar and warrior-orators like him forms part of the cultural background to the warrior-heroes of Marlowe's and Shakespeare's 1590s drama – men like Tamburlaine and Henry V, who fought as eloquently as they spoke and whose eloquence was integral to their command.[2] This chapter considers early modern war writing in two sections: the first focuses on the sixteenth century, the second on the British Civil Wars.

Sixteenth-century war writing

"A Just, and Honourable Warre, is the true *Exercise*," noted Francis Bacon in his essay "Of the True Greatness of Kingdoms and Estates" (1612), and in contrast with the twentieth century, very few early modern recorders of war

98

saw their goal as discrediting war or its aura of glory.[3] Like Bacon, they may have come increasingly to accept Machiavelli's notorious statement in *The Prince* that a ruler should have no other objective or concern than the theory and practice of war. Certainly pacifism or quietism found few champions until the Quakers of the 1660s, with the notable exception of the influential humanist Erasmus. In essays such as "Dulce bellum inexpertis" ("War Is Sweet to Those Who Know It Not") (1515), Erasmus dared to speak out against the cherished idea of holy war, pointing out that the devil, not God, had invented the "arts" of war and that Christian warfare was essentially spiritual and metaphorical. Yet Erasmus's words (and those of Sir Thomas More in *Utopia* [1516]) were no match for two widely held beliefs – that war was divinely ordained, as punishment or deliverance, and that it was the theater of glory where nobility most showed itself. Against these entrenched beliefs, even Erasmus could do little. Much more successful at swaying opinion were Machiavelli's views of the necessity of forming national or civic militias, and his argument for justifying war by "reason of state," as developed in his *Art of War* (1521) and *The Prince* (1513; published 1532).

On his accession in 1509, Henry VIII saw war with France as essential to his image as a warrior-king, but to his daughters Mary and Elizabeth, such self-fashioning was evidently impossible. Mary took sound military counsel, but militarily her reign was significant for the loss of Calais, England's last overseas territory, in 1558. Unlike many of her courtiers and advisors, Elizabeth hated the expense and danger of war and resisted it wherever possible – a legacy taken up after 1603 by James I, who refused to be drawn into the Thirty Years War and pursued an unpopular peace agenda with Spain. For the first five years of his reign, Charles I attempted to instigate the interventions his father had refused, but a series of underfunded expeditions ended in complete retreat from war during the 1630s. As well as wars against continental neighbors, England tried repeatedly to invade and colonize Ireland throughout this period. Ireland had acknowledged Henry VIII as king in 1541, but uprisings and rebellions led many of Elizabeth's courtiers to seek a decisive military conquest, much to the horror of the queen.[4] The poet Edmund Spenser was among those who believed that total military defeat of Ireland was required. He had gone to Ireland as secretary to the Lord Deputy and so would have been close at hand as the rebellions were put down in 1580, including at the infamous Smerwick massacre in October of that year. His treatise *A Present View of the State of Ireland* (written before 1596) chillingly calls for a squad of elite troops from England to suppress the Irish rebels once and for all.

In the early sixteenth century, European monarchs were still likely to take an active part in fighting, since feats of arms performed in the theater of war constituted the greatest possible opportunity for a monarch to gain glory. When monarchs could not attend the field, their courtier-commanders could benefit from the opportunity to show their valor. In September 1513, Henry VIII was forced to send the Earl of Surrey to face the Scottish force gathered at Flodden, since he was busy fighting in France. The odds seemed against Surrey. As a prose account written after the battle noted, the Scots had advantages including "the hyghe Hylles and mountaynes a great wynde with them and sodayne rayne all contrary to [our] bowes and Archers."[5] Furthermore, they were led by the charismatic James IV, a monarch seen by many as the epitome of the Renaissance warrior-prince, immersed in learning, chivalry, and feats of arms.[6] In the end, Henry missed his chance to lead the most decisive sixteenth-century battle on "British" soil, as Surrey commanded his forces to a staggering victory, killing the king and most of the nobility, as well as ten thousand of their men. His victory was duly celebrated by English poets, including an anonymous gentleman of the north west, whose poem "Scottish Field" is one of the last surviving works in alliterative meter.[7] John Skelton, probably in France with Henry VIII at the time of the battle, cobbled together "A Ballade of the Scottysshe Kynge" before the facts had become clear, taunting James IV with defeat in the entirely erroneous belief he was a prisoner at Norham Castle.[8] His second attempt, "Agaynst the Scottes," was written two weeks later and shows a much greater familiarity with established details of the battle.[9]

Henry Howard, Earl of Surrey, was the grandson of Flodden's victorious commander. Widely admired as both *vir armatus* and *vir togatus*, a man who combined Roman military achievement with civic duty and courtly accomplishment, he sought in his life and writing to embody a high conception of honor and nobility, turning to epic poetry when he found it lacking in the court of Henry VIII and inventing in the process the iambic pentameter as an English form that could express high conceptions of Roman honor. In the first of two surviving books of Surrey's translation of Vergil's *Aeneid* (2 and 4) (published 1554 and 1557 respectively), Aeneas relates to Dido both the inexpressible slaughter of Troy and his recognition among the flames of the city that "manhod oft times into the vanquisht brest / Returnes."[10] The word "manhood" here is the equivalent of Vergil's *virtus* (manly courage and nobility), and in many ways Surrey's life's project can be seen as an attempt to revitalize conceptions of honor in the dangerous world of the Henrician court. Military disaster lay ahead, however. In 1546 Surrey was placed in command of the king's defense of Boulogne and was accused of fleeing from battle at St. Etienne. The scapegoat for Henry's defeated honor, he was accused of treason by his former friends and executed. The publication of his *Aeneid* translation and lyric poetry during the 1550s (the latter in *Tottel's*

Miscellany [1557]) saw the revival of his reputation as the epitome of nobility. Even after the Restoration, John Aubrey could still refer to him in terms that the Earl's life and works had sought to uphold: "a man equally celebrated *tam Marti quam Mercurio*" ("as much for Mars as for Mercury").[11]

The title page of George Gascoigne's *Posies* (1576) expresses his claim on the soldier-courtier's twin skills of arms and eloquence in the same motto, *tam Marti, quam Mercurio*. Announcing his loyalty to Surrey's ideals, Gascoigne was also declaring his availability for service to the queen and state. During the 1570s he had fought in the Netherlands, and his early war writing foregrounded his eyewitness status as well as his familiarity with contemporary military literature. Reading his alternating passages of detailed poetic narrative and explanations and justifications of campaigns, it can sometimes appear that Gascoigne was championing a new realism in war recording. For instance, in *The Fruites of Warre, written uppon this Theame, Dulce Bellum inexpertis* (1575), he opposes his narrative of war in the Netherlands with, on the one hand, those poets and painters whose representations of war have been a "faine to farre," and, on the other, war reports whose testimony is unreliable and "light." The reader is encouraged to think of him as a reliable witness:

> In this retyre three English miles we trodde,
> With face to foes and shot as thicke as hayle,
> Of whose choyce men full fiftie soules and odde,
> We layed on ground, this is withouten fayle,
> Yet of our owne, we lost but three by tale.[12]

Here Gascoigne stresses not only his reliability ("withouten fayle"), but even his numerical accuracy, stating the precise number of miles marched and stressing that the losses are calculated "by tale," that is, by "telling" or counting individuals. Yet as plain and factual as Gascoigne often appears, his intention is not to write a transparent report of events. *The Fruites of Warre* is a rhetorical defense of his surrender at Valkenburgh, an action that led to accusations of treachery by the Dutch. Weight of detail acts as a kind of seal of authenticity for the poem and its author: Gascoigne has a vested interest in seeming to tell the truth.[13] In the last year of his life he published another eyewitness account, this time of the Siege of Antwerp. His prose records how Spanish soldiers continued to massacre Walloons after the siege was long over and emphasizes that the author himself came close to death several times. In England "these and other barbarous factes" from Gascoigne's harrowing record were eagerly taken up as evidence of Spanish atrocities, forming the basis for a play, *A Larum for London* (c.1602). Gascoigne's emphasis in *The Spoyle of Antwerp* (1577) is on the delinquency of the common Spanish: "Men wyll boast of the Spanierds that they are the best & most orderlye Souldiours in the world: but sure, if this be their order, I had rather be coumpted a *Besoigner*, then a brave Souldiour in such a bande."[14]

Sir Philip Sidney was heir to the Earls of Leicester and Warwick and a rising star in Elizabeth's court in the 1570s. His desire to see action in the Netherlands was palpable for many years, and Elizabeth's reluctance to send him reflects not only her general resistance to military engagement but also an awareness of Sidney's fiery, unstable temperament. Denied his opportunity with the sword, Sidney took up the pen, producing the literary-theoretical *An Apology for Poetry* (*The Defence of Poesy*) around 1582–83. Like Surrey, Sidney had a humanist education in rhetoric and literature, but he was also well-read in contemporary works of statecraft, including Machiavelli. Profoundly interested in how words could move and shape virtuous actions, Sidney defends poetry in his *Apology* as "the companion of the camps," holding that songs and poems of war are unequalled in their ability to inspire emulation in soldiers. After all, Alexander the Great had "left his schoolmaster, living Aristotle, behind him, but took dead Homer with him [because] he well found he received more bravery of mind by the pattern of Achilles than by hearing the definition of fortitude."[15]

Also written during the 1580s, *The Faerie Queene* (published 1590, 1596) of Sidney's client Edmund Spenser offered a particularly provocative and ambitious image of military life under Elizabeth. Spenser drew heavily on the chivalric traditions the queen had adapted as part of her Accession Day Tilts, but his poetic images of battle seek to remind his monarch of the virtue of the real military engagements she resisted. Book 1 allegorizes the Red Cross Knight's exhausting battles with the dragon of Roman Catholicism, while Book 2 finds Sir Guyon on a quest to destroy the enchantress Acrasia and her Bowre of Bliss, in which knights are led into a state of idle, sensual indulgence. Guyon sees the youth Verdant asleep in the Bowre and, in an image of emasculation, observes "his warlike Armes, the ydle instruments / Of sleeping praise ... hong vpon a tree" (2.7.80).[16] Acrasia recalls the Homeric figure of Circe, who changes Odysseus' men into pigs; the warning against inaction and neglect of military honor thus remembers one of the classical texts whose heroes provided early modern literature with its archetypes of warrior cunning and bravery.

Sidney died in October 1586 from wounds received at the Battle of Zutphen, Elizabeth having finally acceded to his desire for action. In *The Life of the Renowned Sir Philip Sidney* (written by 1612, published 1652), his close friend Fulke Greville commemorated the war hero as "a true modell of Worth; A man fit for Conquest, Plantation, Reformation, or what Action soever is greatest, and hardest among men."[17] Greville's *Life* sustained Sidney's reputation as both "a generall *Maecenas* of Learning" and "a man so honoured among soldiers that no man thought he marched under the true Banner of *Mars* that had not obtained [his] approbation."[18] In Greville's later work, war is viewed more skeptically. Greville's sonnet sequence *Caelica* (published 1633), begun in friendly rivalry with Sidney's, accuses war of "sin[ning] / In blood, [and] wrong[ing] liberty," and ends on a note of cryptic skepticism about martial glory:

> Yet what strength those be [there is in them] which can blot out fear,
> And to self-ruin joyfully proceeds,
> Ask them that from the ashes of this fire,
> With new lives still to such new flames aspire.[19]

Greville's exact contemporary Sir Walter Ralegh left his mark on war writing as well as on the image of the courtier-warrior. After fighting as a volunteer for the Huguenots, he served Lord Grey in Ireland, overseeing the massacre at Smerwick in 1580. As the queen's favorite, he maintained a strong interest in England's defenses and pursued wide reading in political theory, with the work of Machiavelli a particular fascination; many of his works, including the *Discourse of the Original and Fundamental Cause of ... War* (published 1650), have close verbal parallels with Machiavelli's *Discourses on Livy* (written 1513–17, published 1531). Under James I, Ralegh was refused military command, but he continued to try to influence royal policy, addressing *A Discourse Touching War with Spain* to the new monarch shortly after his accession. The failure of his second expedition to Guiana in 1616–18, in which he used military force contrary to his directions from the Privy Council, led to his eventual trial and execution.

In 1596, Ralegh had commanded part of the Earl of Essex's fleet bound for Cadiz and as such was briefly the commander of the poet and later Dean of St. Paul's, John Donne. Two verse letters emerged from Donne's expedition as a gentleman volunteer, in which he expresses the accidents of war in a mixture of military and philosophical registers. "The Storme" (1596) evokes a violent tempest that seized Donne's ship, the poem's prosody stretching and rolling with the vessel, whose "Mast / Shak'd with this ague, and the Hold and Wast / With a salt dropsie clog'd, and all our tacklings / Snapping, like too-high-stretched treble strings."[20] Letters written on his return to England suggest that he had been in the brunt of the storm and are valuable for their details of the expedition's military organization.[21] "The Storme" was popular with contemporary readers eager for its glamorous combination of eyewitness account and vigorous, "masculine" verse style found in the rhythmical strength and daring of its syntax. A companion piece, "The Calme" (1596), records the lack of winds that delayed Ralegh's fleet on its way to join with Essex, and lingers over the details of intense tropical heat which turned Donne's swimming comrades into "parboyl'd wretches."[22]

London theatergoers had already begun to witness dramatizations of war – and its literature – by the time Donne sailed. At its best, Elizabethan drama delved deep into the ideological intermeshing of words and swords that characterized sixteenth-century views of war. Marlowe's pioneering *Tamburlaine* plays (performed 1587) used the story of the fourteenth-century Tartar Timur-i-leng to dramatize the problems of military command and to examine popular assumptions about war as divine punishment or deliverance. Both Marlowe and Shakespeare drew on "arts of war" books published in the 1570s, 1580s, and 1590s, and the connections between their theatrical works and the world of war were intimate and far-reaching.[23]

Shakespeare was interested not only in the language of war, but in the way it is shaped by the aftermath and the telling of stories about the events of war. As early as the Marlowe-influenced *Titus Andronicus* (first performed *c.*1592), he began to explore the military hero's struggles to return to civic life that became the great theme of *Coriolanus* (1608), while the inheritance of classical warfare provided the basis for *Julius Caesar* (1599), *Troilus and Cressida* (1602), and *Antony and Cleopatra* (1606). Of Shakespeare's sources, Plutarch's *Parallel Lives of the Greeks and Romans* (75 CE) was especially influential in the period, with its central concern for the heroic acts of great men. Thomas North's translation, which appeared in 1579, was itself instrumental in his gaining service in both Ireland and the Netherlands.

Shakespeare's ten English history plays are where he engaged most profoundly with the experience and recording of early modern warfare. The first tetralogy (*1, 2, 3 Henry VI* and *Richard III*) traces the later Wars of the Roses up to Henry VII's accession, while the second tetralogy (*Richard II; 1, 2 Henry IV; Henry V*) goes further back in time to deal with events from the deposition of Richard II to Henry V's victory at Agincourt. *Richard II* (1595) investigates the figure of the warrior-king by splitting it down the middle, giving eloquence to Richard and military command to his usurper Bolingbroke (the future Henry IV). Richard's departure for war in Ireland at the end of Act 2, Scene 1 provides Bolingbroke's opportunity for the beginnings of his military coup, while false rumors of Richard's death cause the Welsh to join the rebellion, precipitating the collapse of Richard's hope in Act 3, Scene 2. The two parts of *Henry IV* (1596, 1598) and *Henry V* (1599) together make perhaps the most encompassing vision of war to be found in all of early modern English literature. Crucially it is a vision which draws into the experience of war the means of its representation and recording, as at the start of *2 Henry IV*, when the figure of Rumor, "painted full of tongues," announces her false reports of the death of Hal. The *Henry IV* plays dramatize different ideas of what it means to be a soldier, commander, and king, pitting the chivalric Hotspur against Falstaff, who rejects honor as an illusion, and against the Machiavellian dissimulation of both Hal and his brother John, who in *2 Henry IV* uses verbal trickery to persuade the rebels (4.1) to disband their army before swiftly arresting and condemning their leaders. As *Henry V* alternates between the choruses, the king's military victories, and the comic subplots, so the conventional view of Agincourt as a simple tale of glory, honor, and *virtus* becomes a complex, contingent, and difficult set of events that the audience must interpret as best they can. In the play's most brilliant war scene (4.1), Henry disguises himself in order to pass unseen through the ranks, observe his men, and elicit their views of the campaign. He hears and approves the Welsh Captain Fluellen appeal to ancient authority regarding the conduct of the English camp (4.1.66–74), and the audience also witnesses Ancient Pistol following correct military procedure as set out in contemporary literature (albeit in comic vein). By contrast, Henry may even be showing "unprofessional conduct" by deserting his command post on the night before battle in order to console himself.[24]

Interpretations of Henry's actions in the play have varied hugely as the play has come in and out of fashion, variously championed and derided as jingoistic propaganda. Adapted as part of celebrations for George III's coronation in the eighteenth century, the play was much vaunted as patriotic spectacle by the Victorians before becoming increasingly read as a satire or criticism of Henry (or hortatory leaders like him) after the First World War.[25] Laurence Olivier's 1944 film was so popular in Britain in the years after its release that patriotic interpretations were for a time the only ones possible, and the play was viewed as demonstrating the justness of Britain's participation in the Second World War.[26]

The British Civil Wars

The wars that shook England, Wales, and Scotland from 1642 to 1648 were unparalleled in the history of the three kingdoms and forced those who attempted to write about them to rethink existing forms of expression or create new ones. With the theaters shut down by Parliament, it was left to poetry and prose to try to come to terms with the staggering social disruption caused by the six hundred or more battles and sieges of the first Civil War, the eighty thousand dead, and the thousands of buildings rendered ruined or uninhabitable.[27]

Printed news was increasingly important as a form of war recording from its beginnings at the end of the sixteenth century, and during the 1640s it became the only way that writing could keep up with the speed of events. The first European-wide newsbook, *Mercurius Gallo-Belgicus*, had been printed at Cologne twice a year since 1594, but not even the most gullible reader looked to it for clear and unbiased reporting; Donne even averred in an epigram that it would be "sin to do, / In this case, as thou wouldst be done unto, / To believe all."[28] Newssheets in English began to appear from around 1620, responding to what was evidently a growing demand; but the events they recorded were exclusively foreign, since it was illegal to print domestic news. With the breakdown of censorship in 1641, the printing press finally became an adjunct of political conflict, and domestic news of "England's troubles" began to be consumed in great quantities. Parliament and Charles I both realized the power of news in creating and shaping a public sphere of opinion, and gave their backing to news producers. Though newsbooks were cheaply produced and short (at eight pages), and had limited print runs of a thousand or fewer copies, they were quickly and widely disseminated, and often shared and read aloud.[29] Reporting of battles could be highly partial – the Royalist *Mercurius Aulicus* did not appear after the defeat of Marston Moor, for instance – but the speed of report quickened over time so that London heard fairly accurate news of Parliament's victory at Marston only six days after the battle two hundred miles to the north.[30] Readers were well aware of the political affiliations of newsbooks but often read them regardless of their private views, so that different reports could be compared and accounts called into question.

Abhorrence for news as something dirty and ephemeral is a feature of much courtly poetry of the 1630s. With the Thirty Years War at its height and war breaking out in France and the Netherlands, English poets of that decade increasingly recorded war by its absence, as perhaps most famously in Sir Richard Fanshawe's "Ode Upon occasion of His Majesties Proclamation in the yeare 1630":

> Now warre is all the world about,
> And everywhere *Erynnis* raignes,
> …
> Onely the Island which wee sowe,
> (A world without the world) so farre
> From present wounds, it cannot showe
> An ancient skarre.[31]

Invited by his friend Aurelian Townshend to mourn the death of the Protestant King Gustavus Adolphus of Sweden in 1653, the courtier-poet Thomas Carew instead wrote a hymn to "the benefit / Of peace and plenty, which the blessed hand / Of our good King gives this obdurate Land."[32] The proper subject for English poetry, Carew advised Townshend, is "harmeless pastimes."[33] With an uneasy inversion of the generic priorities so dear to Sidney and Spenser, Carew ends his poem averring that if continental poets had "securitie like ours" they would "hang their Armes up on the Olive bough, / And dance, and revell then, as we doe now."[34] The lines ambiguously recall both the emasculated knights of Spenser's Bowre of Bliss and the singing of the captive Hebrews in Psalms 137:2 ("We hanged our harps upon the willows").

As civil war divided England and Wales, poets on both sides of the conflict began to adapt their writing to changed conditions. In 1643, the prodigious Abraham Cowley, who had published Carew's recommended "pastimes" poetry while still in his teens, joined the Royalist court at Oxford and began writing *The Civil Warre*. This was an audacious attempt to fuse epic poetry with the unfolding story of the hitherto successful Royalist campaign, but Cowley discontinued the poem when the king's fortunes turned sour. The Preface to his *Poems* (1656) excuses his not publishing the poem on the grounds that "it is so uncustomary, as to become almost *ridiculous*, to make *Lawrels* for the *Conquered*," but he was also motivated by a desire to make peace with Cromwell's Protectorate.[35]

A greater poetic record of the effects of war is found among the poems of Andrew Marvell. In an early panegyric to Richard Lovelace's *Lucasta* (1649), Marvell reveals a Royalist nostalgia for the 1630s and disdain for the "barbèd censurers" and "grim consistory" of Puritan critics.[36] But in his poems in praise of Parliament's two great military commanders – Oliver Cromwell and Thomas, Lord Fairfax – Marvell registers as perhaps no one else the impact of war on political and literary life in England. Written after the brutally efficient victories of summer 1650, "An Horatian Ode upon Cromwell's Return from Ireland" at once reaches out to the Horatian renditions of Royalist poets like Fanshawe and retreats from them in its evocation of Cromwell as a new force in nature. Composed a year later, "Upon Appleton House, To My Lord Fairfax" is ostensibly a poem in praise of the former commander of Parliament's armies who had controversially retired to his Yorkshire estates rather than assent to the king's trial. The poem wants to celebrate peace and retreat, but war haunts its figurative language throughout, from the "shining armour white" of the nuns who formerly occupied Appleton to the "sweet militia" of the garden laid out by Fairfax "in the just figure of a fort."[37] The poem's speaker asserts that he has retreated from war into the safety of a wooded grove, but his very language – he has "encamped his mind" – brings him back out into the danger of the meadow where "lowness is unsafe as height" and the reapers kill indiscriminately.[38]

If Marvell's poetry sought to acknowledge and encompass the new realities of war and peace, the Welsh poet Henry Vaughan sought to denounce them. Proud of his loyalty, Vaughan fought in the first Civil War in Wales in 1645/46 and wrote elegies for Royalist friends slain in both the first and the second Civil Wars. The sheer difficulty of obtaining accurate news provides an emotionally explosive opening to his elegy for "Mr. R. W. slain in the late unfortunate differences at *Routon* Heath" (1651), in which it is revealed that Vaughan had to wait "a full years griefe" to learn that his friend had indeed died.[39] "An Elegie on the death of Mr. R. *Hall*, slain at *Pontefract*, 1648" (1651) commemorates its subject as a warrior-scholar, echoing the high ideals of sixteenth-century war writing in its description of Hall's "*bookish feat*" as serving not as an emasculating force but rather "as the light unto thy *heat*."[40] Vaughan himself seems to have been reluctant to draw blood, though he was becoming deeply perturbed by the events of the wars themselves. A spiritual crisis in 1648–49 led him to dedicate his writing to God and to resist the Parliamentarian victory that he saw as a sign of the imminent Last Days prophesied by Christ. To signal his new fierceness he adopted the title "Silurist," the name of a British tribe in Tacitus who occupied Vaughan's south-eastern area of Wales in Roman times and who successfully resisted the occupying forces.

Vaughan's devotional imagination was gripped by warfare, both actual and spiritual. "Peace" (1650) evokes a heavenly army so incomprehensible and strange – the infant Christ is guarded by "a winged Centrie / All skilfull in the wars" at the head of "beauteous files" of angels – that earthly powers must pale by comparison.[41] Only by laying down the physical arms of warfare in the face of divine power and leaving the "foolish ranges" of this world can man reach true safety in God's "fortresse." Vaughan's most profound scriptural meditations on Christian warfaring come in the second edition of *Silex* (1655). Rejecting utterly the millenarian vision that inspired Cromwell's army, his poems weave a beguiling tapestry of biblical proof texts against violence, drawing on the Gospels of Luke and John and on that most revered of millenarian texts, the book of Revelation. Parliament's armies are implicitly aligned with the soldiers who crucified Jesus, as Vaughan takes up the Sword of the Spirit – a biblical metaphor for the Bible – and opposes it to the sword martial. "The sword wherewith thou dost command," he tells Christ, "Is in thy mouth, not in thy hand."[42]

In 1659, with Cromwell dead and his son Richard deposed by the English army, it was another army officer, Sir George Monck, whose military and political maneuvers paved the way to the Restoration of Charles II in May 1660. This indicated the new importance of the army and was an early sign that "enlarged machinery of state, both military and bureaucratic ... was an undoubted product of the revolutionary years."[43] Indeed, it was probably to Monck that the poet and former servant of the Republic, John Milton, addressed a letter later published as *The Present Means and Brief Delineation of a Free Commonwealth* (1660). Milton was in hiding after 1660 and spent time in the Tower for his defense of the regicide and involvement in the Commonwealth government. His composition of *Paradise Lost* in the years 1658–63 was thus carried out against a backdrop of continuing military involvement in civil affairs.

Milton had been reflecting on the relationship between war, ethics, and society for many years, as witnessed by his commonplace book entries for "War," "Civil War," and "Of Military Discipline."[44] In Book 9 of *Paradise Lost*, Milton's narrator famously argues that wars, "hitherto the only argument / Heroic deemed," are not the only proper subject for epic, but that "the better fortitude / Of patience and heroic martyrdom / Unsung" will be his subject.[45] Milton's pamphlets of the 1640s had echoed contemporary parliamentary praise of the army as saints fighting a holy war, though his rhetoric was never as fervent as that of the army chaplains. In *Paradise Lost*, by contrast, it is only the fallen angels who see military victory as determining right; the faithful angels who fight under Michael in Book 6 cannot even win the battle. What is important is their faithful conduct in the war; thus the moment of supreme importance is not, as traditionally, Michael's victory over Satan in single combat, but rather the appearance of the Messiah in his chariot. This prefigures the apocalyptic appearance of Christ prophesied in Revelation – chapter 7 of which provided Milton with the scriptural basis for the war in heaven – in order to emphasize that Christian warfare is an ongoing spiritual battle against Satan in the world at large.[46] In his last works, Milton's view of virtue moved even further away from the image of the armed Christian warrior and towards individual spiritual warfaring. The pacific tone of *Paradise Regained* (1673), in which Christ is tempted in the desert, may have been influenced by Milton's Quaker friends and shows Jesus specifically rejecting the glory of war, "fragile arms, much instrument of war ... battles and leagues, / Plausible to the world, to me worth naught."[47] Armies, once the pride of Renaissance war writing and the engine of the English Republic, are now rejected as "cumbersome / Luggage ... argument / Of human weakness rather than of strength."[48]

NOTES

1. Quoted in H. S. Bennett, *English Books & Readers 1558–1603* (Cambridge University Press, 1965), 235.
2. See Henry J. Webb, *Elizabethan Military Science: The Books and the Practice* (Madison: University of Wisconsin Press, 1965).

3. Sir Francis Bacon, *The Essayes or Counsels, Civill and Morall*, ed. Michael Kiernan (Oxford: Clarendon, 1985).
4. Colm Lennon, *Sixteenth-Century Ireland: The Incomplete Conquest* (Dublin: Gill and Macmillan, 1994), 155–9.
5. *Hereafter ensues[s] the trewe encountre or … batayle* [STC 11088.5] (London: R. Faquest, 1513).
6. William A. Sessions, *Henry Howard, the Poet Earl of Surrey: A Life* (Oxford University Press, 1999), 38–9.
7. See Emrys Jones (ed.), *The New Oxford Book of Sixteenth-Century Verse* (Oxford University Press, 2002), 67–73.
8. John Skelton, *The Complete English Poems*, ed. John Scattergood (Harmondsworth: Penguin), 113–15, 420–2.
9. Ibid., 115–20, 420–4.
10. Emrys Jones (ed.), *Henry Howard: Earl of Surrey* (Oxford: Clarendon, 1964), 47.
11. Sessions, *Henry Howard*, 293.
12. George Gascoigne, *The Complete Works of George Gascoigne*, ed. John W. Cunliffe, 2 vols. (Cambridge University Press, 1907), I: 173.
13. On Gascoigne, see Yuval Noah Harari, *Renaissance Military Memoirs: War, History, and Identity, 1450–1600* (Woodbridge: Boydell, 2004), 98–100.
14. Gascoigne, *The Complete Works of George Gascoigne*, I: 597.
15. Geoffrey Shepherd and R. W. Maslen (eds.), *An Apology for Poetry (or The Defence of Poesy)* (Manchester University Press, 2002), 105.
16. A. C. Hamilton, Hiroshi Yamashita, and Toshiyuki Suzuki (eds.), *Spenser: The Faerie Queene*, rev. 2nd edn. (Harlow: Longman, 2007), 284.
17. Fulke Greville, *Sir Fulke Greville's Life of Sir Philip Sidney* (Oxford: Clarendon, 1907), 33.
18. Ibid.
19. Fulke Greville, *Selected Poems*, ed. Thom Gunn (London: Faber, 1968), 138.
20. John Donne, *The Satires, Epigrams and Verse Letters*, ed. W. Milgate (Oxford: Clarendon, 1967), 56–7.
21. R. C. Bald, *John Donne: A Life* (Oxford: Clarendon, 1970), 87–8.
22. Donne, *The Satires, Epigrams and Verse Letters*, 58.
23. See Nina Taunton, *1590s Drama and Militarism: Portrayals of War in Marlowe, Chapman and Shakespeare's* Henry V (Aldershot: Ashgate, 2001); Nick de Somogyi, *Shakespeare's Theatre of War* (Aldershot: Ashgate, 1998).
24. Taunton, *1590s Drama and Militarism*, 177.
25. Emma Smith (ed.), *King Henry V* (Cambridge University Press, 2002), 16–17.
26. Ibid., 53.
27. John Morrill, "The Civil Wars," *The Oxford Illustrated History of Tudor and Stuart Britain*, ed. John Morrill (Oxford University Press, 1996), 367.
28. Donne, *The Satires, Epigrams and Verse Letters*, 53.
29. Joad Raymond, *The Invention of the Newspaper: English Newsbooks, 1641–1649* (Oxford: Clarendon, 1996), ch. 1.
30. Charles Carlton, *Going to the Wars: The Experience of the British Civil Wars, 1638–1651* (London and New York: Routledge, 1992), 231.
31. Sir Richard Fanshawe, *The Poems and Translations of Sir Richard Fanshawe*, ed. Peter Davidson, 2 vols. (Oxford: Clarendon, 1997), II: 55–6.

32. Thomas Carew, *The Poems of Thomas Carew with his Masque* Coelum Britannicum, ed. Rhodes Dunlap (Oxford: Clarendon, 1949), 75.
33. Ibid., 77.
34. Ibid., 77.
35. Abraham Cowley, *Poems* (London: for Humphrey Moseley, 1656), sig. (a)4r.
36. Andrew Marvell, *The Poems of Andrew Marvell*, ed. Nigel Smith (London: Longman, 2003), 21.
37. Ibid., 224.
38. Ibid., 235.
39. Henry Vaughan, *The Works of Henry Vaughan*, ed. L. C. Martin (Oxford: Clarendon, 1957), 49.
40. Ibid., 58.
41. Ibid., 430.
42. Ibid., 517.
43. Derek Hirst, *Authority and Conflict: England 1603–1658* (London: Arnold, 1986), 357.
44. John Milton, *Complete Prose Works of John Milton*, ed. Don M. Wolfe *et al.*, 8 vols. (New Haven, CT: Yale University Press, 1953–82), I: 491–501.
45. 9.28–33. Text from Milton, *Paradise Lost*, ed. Alastair Fowler (London: Longman, 1998).
46. For a detailed account of this argument see Stella Purce Revard, *The War in Heaven*: Paradise Lost *and the Tradition of Satan's Rebellion* (Ithaca, NY and London: Cornell University Press, 1980), ch. 4.
47. 3.388, 392–3. Text from Milton, *Complete Shorter Poems*, ed. John Carey (London: Longman, 1997).
48. 3.401–2. Text from Milton, *Complete Shorter Poems*.

FURTHER READING

Martyn Bennett, *The Civil Wars Experienced: Britain and Ireland, 1638–1661* (London: Routledge, 2000).
J. R. Hale, *Renaissance War Studies* (London: Hambledon, 1983).
Yuval Noah Harari, *Renaissance Military Memoirs: War, History, and Identity, 1450–1600* (Woodbridge: Boydell, 2004).
Nick de Somogyi, *Shakespeare's Theatre of War* (Aldershot: Ashgate, 1998).
Nina Taunton, *1590s Drama and Militarism: Portrayals of War in Marlowe, Chapman and Shakespeare's* Henry V (Aldershot: Ashgate, 2001).

10

GILLIAN RUSSELL

The eighteenth century and the romantics on war

All literary production in the "long" eighteenth century (1688–1832) was, to varying degrees, engaged with the subject of war. Most of the major writers of the period in the British Isles and Ireland, ranging from Swift to Austen, from Pope to Barbauld, addressed the topic of war, either directly or indirectly. Beyond what is now recognized as the literary canon, the preoccupation with war is even more striking. This is apparent in Roger Lonsdale's groundbreaking *New Oxford Book of Eighteenth Century Verse* (1984), which highlighted the representation of battle and the experiences of the military and their dependents as persistent themes in what Lonsdale described as a "submerged" tradition – the work of minor poets and contributors to newspapers and journals.[1] The major conflicts of the period were registered by an outpouring of such verse, which supplemented the role of official dispatches and private communications to constitute the "news" of war for readers at home. M. John Cardwell has noted the importance of an "explosion" of such literature – "ballads, ephemeral verse, prose satire and prints" – in the shaping of public opinion during the Seven Years War (1756–63), while Betty T. Bennett located 1,360 texts for her edition of the war poetry of the French Revolutionary and Napoleonic Wars (1793–1815).[2] Earlier conflicts were not exceptional in this respect: the Duke of Marlborough's successes in the War of the Spanish Succession (1700–13) were commemorated in more than forty poems. These polite texts, designed for middling and elite audiences, were linked with a vital popular tradition of ballad and chapbook literature that circulated stories and songs of the heroism, suffering, and loss of soldiers and sailors and their families. Until the nineteenth century, popular song constituted the only significant textual record of the war experience of the lower orders.[3]

Such engagement with the subject of war was not confined to poetry and song. Throughout the period the theater was an important forum for the mediation of war across the whole range of genres and theatrical forms – tragedy and comedy, pantomime and farce, stage pageants, topical prologues and epilogues, and, towards the turn of the nineteenth century, new genres such as melodrama. Soldiers and sailors of all ranks formed an important section of the theater audience, as the rituals of theatergoing, combined with the shows of war on stage, reinforced the theatricality of military culture as a whole, ranging from parade-ground display at home to synchronized bodies in battle both on land and at sea.[4] The prose fiction of the period is less obviously saturated with the subject of war, though even here the impact of Britain's conflicts is pervasive, in texts such as Defoe's *Memoirs of a Cavalier* (1720) and Swift's *Gulliver's Travels* (1726, 1735), as well as mid-century novels such as those of Smollett and Sterne, culminating in the Napoleonic War fiction of Austen and Scott. Samuel Richardson's monumental story of a rape and its aftermath, *Clarissa* (1748), may initially appear to have little to do with war, but on closer scrutiny even that text can be seen as subject to the incursion of wartime. As M. John Cardwell has shown, *Clarissa* adapts the long-standing metaphorical association between sexual aggression and war. Richardson amplifies the significance of the struggle between Clarissa and the rake Lovelace in the context of contemporary European geopolitics, particularly the War of the Austrian Succession (1740–48). Cardwell argues that Lovelace's ingenious and relentless persecution of Clarissa is analogous to the cruelty and élan of aristocratic war in this period, exemplified by the contemporary warrior prince, Frederick II of Prussia. As Cardwell emphasizes, *Clarissa* is "not a simple political allegory," but a novel that illustrates how war was embedded in all aspects of eighteenth-century life.[5] A reconsideration of *Clarissa* and other canonical texts as "war writing" therefore enables us to view them in new, revelatory ways, which literary history has previously ignored or forgotten. This chapter does not aim to be a comprehensive account of war in eighteenth-century and romantic writing, but to outline some of the contexts and developments in the representation of war in this period and to consider their enduring impact on how war continues to be conceived and interpreted.

Perpetual war

War was a ubiquitous presence in literature because it was an inescapable fact of life for Britons in the eighteenth century. By 1815, Britain had established itself as a global power as a result of, according to Jeremy Black, a military system based on "multiple capability."[6] The globalization of goods, products, and ideas that scholars have identified as distinctive of eighteenth-century modernity was, above all, promoted and sustained by military conflict. Soldiers and sailors, of all ranks, were "men of the world," familiar with the forests of North America, the baking heat of the Deccan Plateau in India, as well as the English Channel or the killing fields of the Scottish Highlands after the 1745 rebellion. Of the many wars of the long eighteenth century – Black notes 194 major battles – some were epochal. The Seven Years War established Britain as a global empire, extending from North America to the Indian subcontinent, while the American Revolutionary War was profoundly important because of its status, in British eyes, as a civil conflict, a struggle within the imperial family of greater Britain. The successful rebellion of the American colonists administered a profound shock to British national identity and confidence that resonated for many years afterwards.

The long eighteenth century of war culminated in the French Revolutionary and Napoleonic Wars, notable as the first "war of civilizations" and, in Britain's case, directed as much against the fear of revolution within as the antagonist without. Historians continue to debate questions such as how and when eighteenth-century warfare became "modern" and to what extent the concept of "total war" is applicable to the French Revolutionary and Napoleonic Wars. The dominant view is that wars in this period were comparatively limited in scale, fought for dynastic or commercial rather than ideological reasons by an aristocratic officer class, for whom soldiering was merely part of the natural role of a gentleman. This aristocratic war of elites sought to avoid the catastrophic magnitude and intensity of the religious wars of the previous two centuries that had devastated Europe. This was a "civilized" theater of war, as much a forum for display and ritualized performance as the actual theater in which officers and their subordinates were so conspicuous. But the theatricality could not remove the facts: even "limited" war was shocking in its brutality, with 24,000 dead in one day at the Battle of Malplaquet in 1709.

The French Revolutionary and Napoleonic Wars required soldiers and sailors to fight, not as automata or actors in a show directed by monarchs, but as the nation embodied in a more transparent theater of war. In order to counter the threat of the French Revolution and, later, Napoleonic imperialism to the institutions of the crown, church, and state, it was essential for the soldier and sailor to be ideologically committed to the cause in which they were fighting and, conversely, for the civilian population to have faith in the military as its surrogate, or extension of the patriotic will.

More than ever before, war after 1793 needed to be made imaginatively "real" to the majority of the British population: in particular, ordinary soldiers and sailors emerged from anonymity or suspicion to become the focus of public curiosity because of their roles as sons and brothers of the national "family." This imaginative identification with Britain's armed forces was largely achieved through print culture, the outpouring of writing about war that has only recently been acknowledged by scholars of British romanticism. But there is a danger in exaggerating the watershed significance of the French Revolutionary and Napoleonic Wars, in the same way that the view of limited war as an aristocratic pastime is an oversimplification. "Modern" war in the British context can be dated, not to the long process of technological change in weaponry and strategy known as the "Military Revolution," but to the lapse of the Licensing Act in 1695, which removed government censorship and stimulated the development of the print trade. Later legislative measures, particularly changes to the copyright law after 1774, eventually created what William St. Clair has described as a "take-off" in reading and textual production, comparable in its scale and effects to the impact of the Industrial Revolution.[7] The emergence of a sophisticated reading public and a market for British books extending across the globe was linked with the rise of Britain as a global military power. The status of twenty-first-century wars as complex multimedia events has a precedent in the way in which eighteenth-century print culture configured the wars of that era as reading experiences, imaginatively connecting the coffeehouses or drawing rooms of Britain with the bloody fields of Malplaquet or Waterloo.

The literature of war

Some of the implications of this connection are apparent in John Philips's "Blenheim: A Poem," published in 1705 to commemorate the Duke of Marlborough's famous victory. The poem is notable for its graphic depictions of the horrors of battle, a response to the heroic euphemisms of Joseph Addison's *The Campaign* (1705), which trumpeted Marlborough's successes as a modern "Iliad," a glorious hunt accomplished with spears rather than cannon and musketry.[8] Philips's Blenheim is a vision of hell, illuminated by "Horrible flames, and turbid streaming Clouds / Of Smoak sulphureous" in the midst of which "globous Irons" dispatch:

> Surprizing Slaughter; on each side they fly
> By Chains connext, and with destructive Sweep
> Behead whole Troops at once; the hairy Scalps
> Are whirl'd aloof, while numerous Trunks bestrew
> Th'ensanguin'd Field; with latent Mischief stor'd
> Show'rs of Granadoes rain, by sudden Burst
> Disploding murd'rous Bowels, Fragments of Steel,
> And Stones, and Glass, and nitrous Grain adust.[9]

Philips represents the battlefield as a spectacle of entropy, a maelstrom of bits of flesh, metal and sulphur – the contents or "bowels" of grenades merging with the innards of the soldiers they destroy. This is the opposite of the image of eighteenth-century battle as choreographed encounters between disciplined and, above all, intact bodies. However, "Blenheim" is not a wholly antiwar poem: such grotesque horror is a sign of what Marlborough is capable of delivering against Queen Anne's enemies in the name of preserving Britain as a land of peace. Philips came from a Royalist family, and the trauma of the British Civil Wars and knowledge of the European religious wars of the previous centuries inform his construction of "Albion" as a country blessedly free of war at its most extreme:

> Remote thou hears't the dire Effect of War,
> Depopulation, void alone of Fear,
> And Peril, whilst the dismal Symphony
> Of Drums and Clarions other Realms annoys.[10]

"Blenheim" concludes with a vision of war ultimately being banished to "*Mauritania* ... the *Bactrian* Coasts, / Or *Tartary*" in order that the "Arts / Pacifick" may "flourish" in Europe as a whole.[11] Philips's poem is historically important in articulating many of the preoccupations of later war writing: the emphasis on viewing battle as a grotesque spectacle; a fascination with war as a corporeal experience, written on and through the body of the soldier; and a desire to see Britain as "remote" from the wars that preserved its liberty and peace, at the same time recognizing the contradictions in maintaining peace by exporting war's horrors abroad. It is no accident that the construction of British national identity as a "home front" that had to be protected from wars that were necessary for her existence and survival took place at the same time as the development of print culture and the growth of the reading public. Such an idea of the nation necessitates some kind of virtuality, a way of mediating war's horrors, transforming actual "hairy scalps" into text or image.

The fiction that the horrors of war could be concealed was always a precarious one, however, mainly because the military system, and war itself, were often close at hand. Not only did the invasion of England by Jacobite forces in 1745 revive memories of the civil wars of the previous century, but war exerted its presence in the form of recruiting parties and naval press gangs, in the spectacle of parades and war games, and often most forcefully, in the military's role as a form of police. More soldiers were deployed in the north of England to quell the Luddite disturbances of 1811–12 than were then fighting in the Iberian Peninsula. Throughout the period, the army was viewed by all political persuasions as a potential tool of tyranny that could be used to enslave the people; individual soldiers and sailors were often regarded as disruptive, licentious and alienated from home and society, their commanding officers seen as either callow youths fresh from Eton or as seasoned, corrupt rakes. Warfare also made its presence felt in the more pathetic spectacle of veterans displaying wounds or lost limbs in an appeal for charity, often accompanied by wives and children who may have followed them on their campaigns. The plight of the old soldier or the destitute widow was a persistent theme in the now "submerged" tradition of war poetry and popular ballads: in the 1790s it became more acutely politicized in a critique of the Pitt government's prosecution of the war against Revolutionary France. Poems such as Robert Merry's "The Wounded Soldier" (1795) represented the individual combatant as a cog in the war machine of kings: on the soldier's return from the wars, "mangled" and broken, his wife dies in shock at the sight of him.[12] The truth of war, Merry suggests, cannot be admitted to hearth and home, nor can those at home confront the destruction wrought in their name. Attitudes towards the armed forces in eighteenth-century Britain were therefore profoundly ambivalent: soldiers and sailors, of all ranks, were regarded as objects of both sympathy and suspicion, idealization and revulsion.

The tension in how the military was regarded is apparent in George Farquhar's 1706 comedy, *The Recruiting Officer*, an enduring text in the British literary canon and theater that is still performed today. An actor-playwright turned lieutenant in the Grenadiers, Farquhar based his play on his own experience of recruiting in Shropshire, where the action is based. Shrewsbury in the play stands for "Fortress Middle England," a stable and secure social community able to distance itself from the wars fought in its name. But even here, war is able to penetrate in the form of Captain Plume and his agent, the wily and ruthless Serjeant Kite. Farquhar contrasts the fixity of the Shrewsbury community with Plume's sphere of maneuver, which, as Kite makes clear, extends from "the banks of the Danube" (the site of the Battle of Blenheim) to the river Severn.[13] The space of the stage, in standing for both Shrewsbury and Plume's larger freewheeling domain, signifies the extent to which these two "theaters of war" are inextricable. *The Recruiting Officer* deals not with the horrific, grotesque reality of the battlefield, but with how and why men become soldiers in the first place. It figuratively attaches the anonymous "hairy scalps" of Philips's "Blenheim" to bodies with names and local identities – specifically Thomas Appletree and Costar Pearmain, two Shropshire lads who are "persuaded" by Kite and Plume to take the Queen's shilling. Farquhar shows how dependent military culture is on performance, as Kite's chicanery and Plume's class assurance combine in an irresistible double-act. Moreover, the play refuses to sentimentalize the outcome for Pearmain and Appletree, making it clear that they are exchanging independence for a life of military slavery and probable death. The theatricality of Plume and Kite also has an eroticism that links war to the performance of masculinity and vice versa: Plume's seduction of a servant girl on a previous visit to Shrewsbury results in a child, the responsibility for which he disposes on Kite while he conducts an affair with a more eligible gentle-woman, Silvia Balance. As in *Clarissa*, the taking of a town, whether in recruiting or in battle, is made synonymous with sexual conquest. The play ends normatively with the "taming" of Plume in the form of marriage to Silvia, but the captain's resolve to quit the "recruiting trade" to "raise recruits the matrimonial way" accentuates rather than obscures the blurring of boundaries between military and civilian worlds in the play as a whole.[14]

The Recruiting Officer's linking of war with the making of new life antici-pates Laurence Sterne's *The Life and Opinions of Tristram Shandy, Gentleman*. Published during the Seven Years War, with a dedication to William Pitt, the prime minister who had led Britain to victory, Sterne's novel is haunted by a conflict of over sixty years before – the Williamite wars of 1688–97. The eponymous hero's uncle, Toby Shandy, received a wound in an "unmentionable" place (suggesting castration) fighting at the 1695 siege of Namur, an experience recapitulated in the damage inflicted on Tristram's nose during his birth and later in a "delicate" accident involving a falling window. Accompanied by his servant, the loyal Corporal Trim, Uncle Toby constructs a miniature Namur in the grounds of Shandy Hall and becomes an expert in the technology and jargon of siege warfare, in an attempt to comprehend the "place" of his wounding. It is only relatively recently, with the developing interest in reenactment, that Uncle Toby's significance as the first military hobbyist in literature has been recognized.[15] In its depiction of Uncle Toby's compulsive desire to reenact his wounding, and the impossibility of truly recovering that moment, *Tristram Shandy* is a kind of trauma fiction which addresses a recurring issue in the representation of war: how can words or images adequately convey what is unspeakable? What have been described as the proto-modernist or postmodernist aspects of *Tristram Shandy* – the rambling narrative which cannot come to a point or conclusion, the lapses into silence signified by dots or a blank page – can be ascribed to the difficulty of writing and speaking about the personal suffering of war and its aftermath. This difficulty was complicated by the success of the Seven Years War in extending and consolidating Britain as a global empire, which only intensified the ambivalence articulated by Philips in "Blenheim": that is, how to distance oneself from war's horrors while using it to maintain peace and profit at home. Public opinion was increasingly divided between the view that the progress of civilization would render war redundant, conflict being incompatible with the free intercourse of people and goods that under-pinned a polite and commercial society, and a conviction that bellicosity was what made Britain "great" as both an imperial and a commercial power. Sterne addresses the conceptual difficulties of this latter position in Uncle

Toby's defense of his attachment to war, which he mounts in spite of the suffering he has endured as a consequence of it. What made it possible to balance these apparently contradictory positions was the capacity for feeling: the pursuit of glory and the public good by means of war could be legitimate if it was heartfelt and also combined with the capacity to sympathize or identify with the victims of war (including oneself). War could therefore be both pleasurably virtuous and morally responsible. Sterne's novel exemplifies an important shift in attitudes towards war around the mid-century that began to transform the soldier of all ranks from a suspect figure of rampant, immoral virility, to the soldier as the "man of feeling."[16] Moreover, by emphasizing identification and reflection in the response to war, texts such as Sterne's encouraged the development of what Mary Favret has described as "war literacy" and the reciprocity of the military system and the reading public: to be a "good" soldier was to be a "good" reader of war (and vice versa).[17]

The expansion of print culture and the boundaries of the political nation allowed greater scope for women to participate in Britain's wars, not merely in sexualized terms as prospective mothers of soldiers and sailors, but as patriotic subjects in their own right. The logical consequence of this – whether or not the soldier could truly embody an idea of the national that included women as subjects – is explored in Anna Seward's *Monody on Major Andrè* (1781).[18] John André, a British officer, was involved in one of the most notorious events of the American Revolutionary War when he was hanged as a spy by the Americans. He was a friend of Seward, one of her circle based in the English Midlands town of Lichfield, making the poem an intensely personal as well as a public work, addressing the national significance of the American war. Its status as a monody – an elegy sung by an individual rather than the chorus in Greek tragedy – reflects Seward's attempt to express the voice of private grief within the context of collective sorrow over the loss of the American colonies. Seward's Major André represents the transformation of the military officer from attractive rake to romantic hero. The poem is supplemented by personal letters from André to the author that demonstrate his prowess in the arts of conversation and polite sociability. His virtue as a warrior, Seward suggests, is essentially a projection of his domestic character. Seward mourns André as the ornament of the Lichfield social circle who goes to fight in America after his rejection by Honora Sneyd, the object of Seward's own devotion. When taken prisoner by the Americans, André had tried to retain his connection with Honora by concealing a miniature painting of her in his mouth, an incident which Seward represents in terms of an erotically charged saintliness:

> Quick to his mouth his eager hand removes
> The beauteous semblance of the Form he loves.

That darling treasure safe, resign'd he wears
The sordid robe, the scanty viand shares;
With chearful fortitude content to wait
The barter'd ransom of a kinder fate.[19]

The miniature of Honora Sneyd functions as André's shield or talisman, his "inner femininity" that affirms his virtue as a warrior. Seward thereby attempts to imagine war in terms that avoid the identification of conflict with predatory male sexuality as well as the emphasis on women as vessels for the reproduction of soldiers. The *Monody* also tries to deal with the question of how to reconcile the contradiction between the maintenance of domestic peace and civility through the pursuit of war by imagining the ideals of private life being translated into a kind of modern chivalry. Instead of bringing war "home," then, Seward projects "home" into war, enabling women in particular to play a role as militant patriotic subjects in their own right. However, the poem shows that a feminized war in these terms is impossible: not only is the knight André never ransomed, but the manner of his death, by hanging, denies both his personal integrity and his honor as a gentleman. André's death, foreshadowing a war of covert operations and the strategic killing of hostages, combined with the complexities of the American Revolutionary War to make Seward's vision of modern chivalry untenable, even as it was being articulated. The poem was of long-term significance, however, in consolidating the idealization of the military officer as a man of feeling. Major André ultimately paved the way for figures such as Viscount Nelson and Jane Austen's Captain Wentworth, romantic heroes whose domestic virtues, indistinguishable from their military strength, enabled women to see themselves as proper actors in the national theater of war.[20]

"Romantic" war

The war writing of the French Revolutionary and Napoleonic Wars, rather than representing a radical break or innovation, is therefore part of a continuous tradition that can be traced back to the development of print culture after 1695, or even further, to the experience of the British Civil Wars. What is notable about this phase is the magnitude and diversity of textual engagement with war. The representation of war became more urgent and complex because of the evolving significance of the struggle with France, which, according to political perspective, began in the 1790s either as a defense against the threat of revolutionary infidelity to the core values of the British state or as a counterrevolution designed to defeat the will of the people both at home and abroad. After the rise of Napoleon, the wars took on the more familiar character of a struggle against French tyranny and imperial expansionism, though the radical critique of war endured and Napoleon remained a hero to writers such as William Hazlitt. Unanimity against France only began to emerge after the beginning of the Peninsular War (1807–14), in which British forces, led by the Duke of Wellington, were viewed as acting to liberate the people of Spain and Portugal from French oppression. Though there was no mass conscription comparable to what happened in the twentieth century, the armed forces were considerably expanded and a body of volunteers recruited to defend the country in case of invasion – a level of "national mobilization," according to J. E. Cookson, "quite unprecedented in its scale and intensity."[21] The mobilization of bodies had its parallel in the mobilization of texts, as all kinds of discursive matériel – songs, graphic satire, newspaper poetry, pamphlets, theatrical entertainments – galvanized the public against Napoleon. Antiwar literature also proliferated in scale and impact, deploying figures such as the wounded soldier or the grieving widow to criticize the campaign against France. Robert Southey, William Wordsworth, and Samuel Taylor Coleridge all produced antiwar poetry and polemic in their radical youth in the 1790s.

A number of trends make war writing of this period distinctive. The pressure of the wars led to the increasing valorization of the army and navy as professions of intrinsic worth to the nation. As discussed, this change in status was already underway before 1793, and soldiers and sailors did not completely lose their dubious or stigmatized status (the Duke of Wellington reputedly described his rank and file as "the scum of the earth").[22] But it is undoubtedly the case that the nation's affective bonds with its armed forces were intensified and strengthened. This development was manifested in two significant ways. Firstly, writers such as Sir Walter Scott sought to legitimate the valor of the officer and the honor of war by means of metrical romances and historical fiction that interpreted contemporary war in terms of a heroic, chivalric past.[23] Secondly, the period witnessed the emergence of the military author, a sign of the legitimation and respect accorded to the profession and interest in the personal experience of the soldier and sailor. There was an outpouring of military memoirs after 1815 that has largely gone unrecognized in literary history. Among these voices were those of the rank and file, the equivalent of Farquhar's Pearmain and Appletree. Publications such as the *Journal of a Soldier of the Seventy-First* (1819), detailing the experience of a Scottish soldier in the Peninsular War, signified how the development of print culture and the valorization of Britain's armed forces had granted a visibility to an experience and a class hitherto marginalized in eighteenth-century literary culture.[24]

However, the admission of such voices to the category of professional authorship and the spread of news of war in ever-increasing circles were potentially problematic: who was entitled to "speak" for war and at what point did knowledge of what was happening in the people's name become destructive in its own right? There was a risk that war would lose the virtuality that was necessary to keep the truth of its horrors from the domestic population. Hence a recurrent theme in romantic war writing is the role of the print media and of war "news." In "Fears in Solitude" (1798), Samuel Taylor Coleridge claimed that war had become an entertainment and commodity – "all read of war, / The best amusement for our morning meal!" – stimulating an unhealthy, even savage, bellicosity based on ignorance of war's reality:

> Thankless too for peace,
> (Peace long preserved by fleets and perilous seas)
> Secure from actual warfare, we have loved
> To swell the war-whoop, passionate for war![25]

Coleridge's fear was that Britain would reap the whirlwind of what had been perpetrated in its name, not only in this but also in previous wars:

> From east to west
> A groan of accusation pierces Heaven!
> The wretched plead against us; multitudes
> Countless and vehement, the sons of God,
> Our brethren![26]

"Fears in Solitude" can therefore be seen as an anxiety-of-empire poem, consistent with Philips's "Blenheim" of nearly a hundred years before. Underpinning it is the same deep-rooted historical consciousness that Britain had not always been "secure from actual warfare" and that devastation could be visited on her again. However, Coleridge's critique is ultimately designed not to dismantle the *cordon sanitaire* between home and the battle-field, but to shore it up by elevating the role of the poet as mediator of the "actual" horror of war, shocking the reading public out of its complacency and mobilizing the people in manly defense of a patriotism based on love of humanity. In this way, "Fears in Solitude" recasts Uncle Toby's argument that bellicosity is legitimate as long as it is sensitive to war's distresses and is heartfelt. Moreover, it promotes a distinctive role for the poet as a necessary filter between the actuality of war and the reading public, ensuring that the latter would be alerted but not alarmed.

Just as soldiers and sailors became authors, so poets could become warriors in defense of the structures of ideas and feelings that made war possible. Coleridge defines this role in gendered terms as the particular responsibility of men, but it also applied to women writers who were able to use the emphasis on patriotic duty as an exercise in feeling to validate a role for women and, indirectly, writing itself as a profession comparable to the national value of the army and navy. Jane Austen's fiction, previously regarded as incurious about war, is particularly notable in this respect.[27]

A different kind of strategy is apparent in Anna Laetitia Barbauld's poem *Eighteen Hundred and Eleven* (1812). Like "Fears in Solitude," this text addresses the role of print culture in publicizing war and the consequences of "war literacy":

> Frequent, some stream obscure, some uncouth name
> By deeds of blood is lifted into fame;
> Oft o'er the daily page some soft-one bends
> To learn the fate of husband, brothers, friends,
> Or the spread map with anxious eye explores,
> Its dotted boundaries and penciled shores,
> Asks *where* the spot that wrecked her bliss is found,
> And learns its name but to detest the sound.[28]

Instead of blunting the British public's sense of the actuality of war, print, Barbauld suggests, only brings war home more acutely, enabling the reader to give a name and location to pain and loss. This reflects the poem's general claim that war has become uncontainable, no longer capable of being defined by contemplation of battle alone: as if addressing Philips, Barbauld writes that "war's least horror" was "the ensanguined field."[29] Like Coleridge, she suggests that the consequences of war will be visited on its perpetrators – "Thou who hast shared the guilt must share the woe" – but whereas "Fears in Solitude" ultimately affirms that the imperial mission can be reinvigorated, *Eighteen Hundred and Eleven* emphasizes the inevitability of decay, prophesying the eclipse of the British Empire by a nascent America.[30] *Eighteen Hundred and Eleven* was dismissed as the foolish effort of a "lady-author," an attack that led to Barbauld's self-imposed silence and the end of her literary career. The poem had threatened the very foundations of a long-established mode of thinking and writing about war that had sought to acknowledge its horrors and its global consequences, but not to the extent of making it no longer possible. Barbauld's silencing as a writer was a consequence of the impasse that she had exposed, highlighting the investment of literary culture and the privileged role of the imaginative writer as "culture warrior" in keeping war within bounds. It is this latter fact which may account for why the presence of war in eighteenth-century and romantic writing has been hidden from view for so long and why this period is relevant to how war continues to be perceived and represented today.

NOTES

I am grateful to Neil Ramsey for research assistance in the preparation of this chapter, which has also benefited from many discussions with Neil about romantic war and representation.

1. Roger Lonsdale (ed.), *The New Oxford Book of Eighteenth Century Verse* (Oxford University Press, 1984), xxxix.
2. M. John Cardwell, *Arts and Arms: Literature, Politics and Patriotism during the Seven Years War* (Manchester University Press, 2004), 51; Betty T. Bennett, "British War Poetry in the Age of Romanticism 1793–1815," available at www.rc.umd.edu/editions/warpoetry/supp_bibliography.html (accessed January 2009).
3. See Roy Palmer, *The Sound of History: Songs and Social Comment* (London: Pimlico, 1996), 272–99.
4. See Gillian Russell, *The Theatres of War: Performance, Politics and Society, 1793–1815* (Oxford University Press, 1995).
5. Cardwell, "The Rake as Military Strategist: *Clarissa* and Eighteenth-Century Warfare," *Eighteenth Century Fiction* 19.1&2 (2006–7), 153–180: 180.
6. Jeremy Black, *Britain as a Military Power, 1688–1815* (University College London Press, 1999), 5.
7. William St. Clair, *The Reading Nation in the Romantic Period* (Cambridge University Press, 2004), 14.
8. Joseph Addison, *The Campaign, A Poem to His Grace the Duke of Marlborough* (London: Jacob Tonson, 1705), 3.
9. John Philips, "Blenheim: A Poem, Inscrib'd to the Right Honourable Robert Harley, Esq.," *The Works of Mr. John Philips* (London: J. Tonson and T. Jauncy, 1720), 40–1.
10. Ibid., 55.
11. Ibid., 59.
12. Robert Merry, "The Wounded Soldier" (London: Ballard, 1795); also available at www.rc.umd.edu/editions/warpoetry/1799/1799_12.html (accessed January 2009).
13. George Farquhar, *The Recruiting Officer*, ed. Michael Shugrue (Lincoln: University of Nebraska Press, 1965), 13.
14. Ibid., 125.
15. See Jonathan Lamb, "Sterne, Sebald, and Siege Architecture," *Eighteenth-Century Fiction* 19.1&2 (2006–7), 21–41; and Simon During, "Mimic Toil: Eighteenth-Century Preconditions for the Modern Historical Reenactment," *Rethinking History* 11.3 (2007), 313–33.
16. See Carol Watts, *The Cultural Work of Empire: The Seven Years' War and the Imagining of the Shandean State* (Edinburgh University Press, 2007).
17. Mary A. Favret, "War Correspondence: Reading Romantic War," *Prose Studies* 19.2 (1996), 173–85: 181.
18. Seward's title has a grave accent on the final "e," but the standard spelling is with an acute accent, which is that adopted in this text.
19. Anna Seward, *Monody on Major Andrè* (London: J. Jackson, 1781), 18.

20. See Kate Williams, "Nelson and Women: Marketing, Representations and the Female Consumer," *Admiral Lord Nelson: Context and Legacy*, ed. David Cannadine (London: Palgrave Macmillan, 2005), 67–89.
21. J. E. Cookson, "War," *An Oxford Companion to the Romantic Age: British Culture 1776–1832*, ed. Iain McCalman (Oxford University Press, 1999), 26–34: 29.
22. Quoted in A. D. Harvey, *Collision of Empires: Britain in Three World Wars, 1793–1945* (Hambledon: Continuum, 2003), 153.
23. See Simon Bainbridge, *British Poetry and the Revolutionary and Napoleonic Wars: Visions of Conflict* (Oxford University Press, 2003).
24. *Journal of a Soldier of the Seventy-First, or Glasgow Regiment Highland Light Infantry, from 1806 to 1815* (Edinburgh: William and Charles Tait, 1819).
25. Samuel Taylor Coleridge, *The Oxford Authors: Samuel Taylor Coleridge*, ed. H. J. Jackson (Oxford University Press, 1985), 95.
26. Ibid., 93–4.
27. See Gillian Russell, "The Army, the Navy and the Napoleonic Wars," *A Companion to Jane Austen*, ed. Claudia Johnson and Clara Tuite (Oxford: Blackwell, 2008).
28. Anna Laetitia Barbauld, *Eighteen Hundred and Eleven* (Oxford: Woodstock, 1995), 3–4.
29. Ibid., 3.
30. Ibid., 4.

FURTHER READING

Simon Bainbridge, *Napoleon and English Romanticism* (Cambridge University Press, 1995).

David A. Bell, *The First Total War: Napoleon's Europe and the Birth of Modern Warfare* (Boston, MA: Houghton Mifflin, 2007).

John Brewer, *The Sinews of Power: War, Money and the English State, 1688–1783* (New York: Knopf, 1989).

Linda Colley, *Britons: Forging the Nation 1707–1837* (New Haven, CT: Yale University Press, 1992).

Mary Favret, "Coming Home: The Public Spaces of Romantic War," *Studies in Romanticism* 33.4 (1994), 539–48.

"Everyday War," *English Literary History* 72.3 (2005), 605–33.

David McNeil, *The Grotesque Depiction of War and the Military in Eighteenth-Century English Fiction* (London: Associated University Press, 2000).

Philip Shaw, *Waterloo and the Romantic Imagination* (London: Palgrave Macmillan, 2002).

(ed.), *Romantic Wars: Studies in Culture and Conflict, 1793–1822* (Aldershot: Ashgate, 2000).

11

EDWARD LARKIN

American Revolutionary War writing

It can be easy to forget that the American Revolution included a long and difficult armed conflict. Scholars of the period, in both historical and literary studies, have focused almost entirely on the ideas that drove the American colonists to resist British imperial rule and underpinned the new form of government they adopted in that process, the so-called experiment in democracy. The contrast to the historical memory of the American Civil War is instructive. The symbols and images of the Civil War are for the most part specifically related to the bloodshed of war: battlefields such as Gettysburg and Petersburg and events such as the burning of Atlanta and Richmond have become the enduring emblems of the conflict that divided the states. Although battlefields are not entirely absent from the memorializing of the Revolution, the national imagination has been captured more by political sites such as Independence Hall, Mount Vernon, Monticello, and documents such as the Declaration of Independence, the United States Constitution, and the Bill of Rights. Moreover, images such as the signing of the Declaration of Independence (disseminated widely as a popular engraving), the Liberty Bell, and the Boston Tea Party focus attention on the political motivations for independence and push the war into the background, as if the war were incidental to the Revolution and not essential to its success. War, in other words, remains at the center of the cultural memory of the Civil War, whereas it has been pushed to the margins of the story of the American Revolution.

Even the term "American Revolution" calls attention to the broader ideological questions underwriting the "patriot" point of view. A descriptor such as "The War of American Independence," for example, gives an entirely different sense of the conflict because it ascribes a specific political and material goal to the war. Revolution speaks to a larger process that cannot be pinned down to a specific end (the independence of the thirteen colonies from Great Britain), but instead implies a more sweeping series of social, political, and cultural transformations. Thus, American Revolutionary War writing only rarely addresses the violence and bloodshed of the conflict with

Britain. The most stunning example of this elision is Benjamin Franklin's memoirs. Franklin drafted the first part of his *Autobiography* in 1771, but later returned to the manuscript, adding three more sections:[1] although the events recorded only cover his life up to the early 1760s, the paucity of references to the Revolution is remarkable given the major role he played. Critics have long speculated on the reasons why Franklin may have chosen to omit a thorough account of his participation in the Revolution, but his *Autobiography* actually seems more characteristic of American writing in the 1780s and 1790s precisely because it does not directly engage with the Revolution as such.

Most of the writing produced in the United States between 1775 and 1781, when the last major battle of the war was fought at Yorktown, debated the merits of the Revolution and, in the process, often overlooked the war. Indeed, for many of the advocates of independence, especially early on, playing down the difficulties of the war was an essential part of their effort to persuade Americans to join their ranks. Rhetorically, this strategy made perfect sense: Americans generally considered the British military to be the most powerful force on earth. The idea that their volunteer army could defeat the professional British redcoats was difficult to imagine. Consequently, American Revolutionary War writing tended to emphasize the questions of rights and the ideals at stake in the political conflict with Britain rather than the viability of the military campaign. Thomas Paine, the foremost advocate for the Revolution, captures this sentiment perfectly in the "Introduction" to the second part of *Rights of Man* (1791) when he reflects, "The independence of America, considered merely as a separation from England, would have been a matter but of little importance, had it not been accompanied by a revolution in the principles and practise [*sic*] of governments."[2] Paine's words not only distill the views of his contemporaries, but also set the tone for how the Revolution would be viewed by subsequent generations.

Surprisingly, Paine's loyalist opponents do not play on fears about the foolhardiness of going to war with the British. From the historical vantage point of knowing that the Americans actually managed to repel the British military's attempts to reassert the Crown's authority, it can be easy to forget how unlikely such an outcome would have seemed in 1776. Loyalist pamphlets such as *Plain Truth* (1776) and *The True Interest of America* (1776) only reluctantly address the logistical questions about the military viability of securing American independence, and instead focus on Paine's attacks on the behavior of the British government and on his ideas of the proper role of government in general.

The debates between Paine and the loyalists in Philadelphia were only the most spectacular version of such discussions about the future of the thirteen colonies. Similar debates occupied the newspapers across the colonies as a mostly ambivalent population of European immigrants to British North America tried to decide which side to support. For much of American history the mythology of the Revolution has presented independence as a foregone conclusion. However, most Americans were deeply torn between their allegiance to Britain and their frustration with recent imperial policy. John Adams's calculation of the "divisions among the people of America" set the proportions at "one third ... averse to the revolution," an "opposite third" for it, and a "middle third, composed mainly of the yeomanry" who wavered in their allegiances.[3] Most of the canonical literature, such as it is, of the American Revolution, has not only emphasized the patriot point of view, but has almost invariably written the loyalists out of the narrative. More importantly, many of the figures who have been celebrated as patriot authors endorsing an unambiguously patriotic account of the American cause were often deeply ambivalent about the Revolution, and in some cases even loyalists themselves.

The most remarkable case of a loyalist who has been appropriated as a patriot for nationalist cultural aims is the career of J. Hector St. John de Crèvecoeur. Crèvecoeur's *Letters from an American Farmer* (1782) has often been cited as one of the foundational texts for the exceptionalist narrative of the origins of a distinct American identity at the time of the Revolution. This reading ignores a crucial detail: Crèvecoeur was a loyalist who fled the colonies in the Revolution's early phases. His novel's semi-autobiographical protagonist, Farmer James, rejects the Revolution, fleeing instead to the Western backcountry to build a new life among the Native Americans. Through a variety of creative misreadings, critics have often managed to avoid the problems posed by Crèvecoeur's loyalism and his hero's abnegation of the Revolution, not only to make his text fit their patriotically motivated narrative, but also to ascribe to it a leading role in that story. If Crèvecoeur represents the most extreme case of this problem, early American literature is full of authors with loyalist sympathies whose texts reflect their confused allegiances. Among these writers are Susanna Rowson, William Dunlap, Washington Irving, and James Fenimore Cooper.

Thus far this chapter has focused mostly on texts by writers who sought to incite or resist the cause of political independence. But even setting aside overtly political texts such as the Declaration of Independence, the Articles of Confederation, the United States Constitution, and *The Federalist*, the vast majority of texts that scholars and popular histories alike associate with the Revolution are ones that attempt to interpret or codify its meaning. This interpretative effort was virtually contemporaneous with the event. Thomas Paine was urging the American Congress to commission an official history of the Revolution as early as 1781, concerned that if too much time passed the real story would be lost to later historians. Paine would have been well aware that histories of the Revolution were already being written. He objected in particular to the Abbé Raynal's interpretation of the recent course of events in British North America, which had been translated into English and published in 1782 under the title *The Revolution in America*. Paine quickly published his *Letter to the Abbé Raynal* (1782), a response to what he perceived as significant misrepresentations of the true causes and aims of the Revolution. In addition to Raynal's early history, a number of American authors produced narratives of the Revolution in the decades immediately following the conclusion of the war. These works include those by participant observers such as David Ramsay (*History of the American Revolution* [1789]), Mercy Otis Warren (*History of the Rise, Progress, and Termination of the American Revolution* [1805]), and the loyalist Peter Oliver, who circulated his *Origin and Progress of the American Rebellion* (1961)[4] in manuscript form among like-minded friends.

Another popular genre for writing about the Revolution was the biography of George Washington. The two most famous biographies of the leader of the Continental Army and first president of the United States were published in the first decade of the nineteenth century by John Marshall, then Chief Justice of the Supreme Court, and Mason Locke Weems, a book peddler turned author. Marshall's five-volume *Life of Washington* (1805–7) was clearly aimed at an elite audience, whereas Weems's much slimmer and more colorful *The Life of Washington* (1800) was intended for mass consumption. Weems's text captured the popular imagination with its tale of young George and the cherry tree, which would be redacted in nineteenth-century school textbooks and become part of Washington's legend. The mythology of George Washington encapsulates the very same phenomenon surrounding the Revolution that this chapter has discussed: although he first distinguishes himself as a military leader, he comes to symbolize the primacy of the ideals of the Revolution over its achievements on the battlefield. Washington would still be strongly associated with his role as commander in chief of the revolutionary forces, but it is his laying down of arms to become a farmer (emblematized by the figure of Cincinnatus with whom he was so strongly associated) and then a civilian president after the war that cements his legacy as the "father" of the country.

The most famous early interpretation of the Revolution and its implications was not written for publication – at least, not explicitly. The decades-long correspondence between John Adams and Thomas Jefferson remains an influential source for contemporary understandings of the Revolution. Although their correspondence was ostensibly a private exchange between two very different political actors, it is difficult to read the letters and not feel that they are each attempting to persuade not only one another, but also future readers, about their interpretations about the Revolution and early United States. Adams raises the possibility explicitly in a 28 June 1813 letter to Jefferson: "If, one hundred years hence, Your Letters and mine should see the light, I hope the Reader will hunt up this Address and read it all." Less than a month later, Adams returns to the topic with a general comment on the frequent publication of private correspondence between significant participants in the Revolution: "Correspondences! The Letters of Bernard and Hutchinson, and Oliver and Paxton etc. were detected and exposed before The Revolution. There are I doubt not, thousands of Letters, now in being, but still concealed, (from their Party to their Friends,) which will, one day see the light ... Private Letters of all Parties will be found analogous to the Newspapers Pamph[l]ets and Historians of the Times."[5] Although in this particular exchange Jefferson expresses dismay that his privacy has been violated through the exposure of a private correspondence, it is worth remembering that he had invented a machine to make copies of his letters so that he could keep a record of them. In this context, the Adams–Jefferson exchanges about the ways in which certain events, decisions, and statements related to the course of the Revolution and early republic may be interpreted by future generations – what they call "posterity" – take on greater urgency. They are responding to the same concerns that Paine had expressed to the Congress decades earlier: the long-term impact of the Revolution depends in part on how future generations interpret the causes and aims of the era.

John Adams is also a participant in the other great epistolary exchange of the Revolution – the body of letters between him and his wife Abigail Adams. Whereas his correspondence with Jefferson provides a strong perspective on the events of the Revolution after the fact, the dialogue with Abigail Adams reacts to events as they were unfolding. Abigail and John reflect not only on the philosophical and political implications of the Revolution, but on the strain it puts on their family and friends. They constantly weigh the personal cost of the events against the larger goals of the cause. At the same time, Abigail Adams's letters have become a crucial document to critics attempting to assess the role of women and understandings of gender in the early United States. In perhaps her most famous letter (March 31, 1776), she writes:

> I long to hear that you have declared an independancy – and by the way in the new Code of Laws which I suppose it will be necessary for you to make I desire you would Remember the Ladies, and be more generous and favourable to them than your ancestors. Do not put such unlimited power into the hands of the Husbands. Remember all Men would be tyrants if they could. If perticuliar care

and attention is not paid to the Laidies we are determined to foment a Rebelion, and will not hold ourselves bound by any Laws in which we have no voice, or Representation.[6]

Adams's appeal to her husband to ensure that women are not left out of the social and political changes being undertaken by the new American government serves as one index for thinking about the possibilities and limits of freedom and equality as defined during the Revolutionary era.

John Adams's exchanges with his wife Abigail and his friend and political rival Jefferson are but two of a host of personal writings about the Revolution and its war. Historians have uncovered a rich archive of private journals and letters illuminating the impact of the Revolution on early Americans' daily lives and local communities, as well as their hopes and anxieties about the country at large. Journals by women who recorded their experiences of the Revolution include those by Milcah Martha Moore and Elizabeth Drinker. American loyalists, such as Joseph Galloway, Jonathan Boucher, and Thomas Hutchinson kept diaries, wrote letters, and published essays, tracts, and narratives about their views of the Revolution and the trials they experienced as a result of their political opinions. These texts often circulated in manuscript among the community of loyalists who relocated to Britain and Canada or remained in the United States. The violence of the Revolution often took a very personal shape in the accounts rendered by loyalist leaders, many of whom suffered detention or banishment, had their homes burned, and had their wealth dispossessed. The war feels much more present in the writings of the loyalists than it does in those of the patriots.

In addition to these forms of direct analysis and interpretation, much of the fiction of the early United States addressed itself to the Revolution and its legacy. Scholars have focused in particular on the ways in which early American novels by authors such as Hannah Webster Foster (*The Coquette* [1797]), Susanna Rowson (*Charlotte Temple* [1794]), and Charles Brockden Brown (*Wieland* [1798]) sought to come to grips with the legacy of the Revolution and displaced its violence onto domestic or local relationships. Their novels register profound anxieties about the nature of freedom and the potentialities of human agency – issues which often grew even more salient when applied to the dynamics of race and gender in the new American state, with its ideals of life, liberty, and the pursuit of happiness. Most often these issues are engaged in the context of the seduction plot. Contemporaneously with Rowson, Foster, and Brown, writers such as William Hill Brown (*The Power of Sympathy* [1789]) and Tabitha Tenney (*Female Quixotism* [1801]) also produced popular novels featuring heroines who are seduced by libertines. At the same time, Americans in the early United States consumed British seduction novels, such as Samuel Richardson's *Pamela* (1740) and *Clarissa* (1748) (often in abridged form), in large numbers. The novel of seduction, in other words, presented an especially appealing format for American readers, one in which they could think about the social and political dimensions of the Revolution without specifically discussing it.

Novels featuring seduction plots may have been especially attractive to early Americans because they dealt with the social challenges of the breakdown of the Anglo-American family, both figuratively in the metaphorical mother–daughter dynamic between Britain and her colonies, and literally in the ways the conflict divided families in America (between loyalists and patriots) and across the ocean. With the exception of Rowson's *Charlotte Temple*, none of the early American novels addressed the Revolution directly. Instead, their fictions are understood to register the cultural and political questions of the day, but always in metaphorical or allegorical terms. Perhaps the most vivid example of the parallel play between the politics and fiction of the day can be seen in Judith Sargent Murray's pseudonymous series of essays published under the title of "The Gleaner" in *The Massachusetts Magazine* (1792–94). Murray embeds a narrative about a female heroine named Margaretta to which she returns sporadically between essays on female education, early American cultural issues, and other subjects. That narrative, which has come to be known as "The Story of Margaretta," dramatizes the ideas presented in "The Gleaner" in the form of Margaretta's travails.

It would not be until the 1820s that the Revolution would begin to appear as the explicit setting for American novels. In 1821, James Fenimore Cooper published *The Spy*, which takes place during the Revolution and was inspired by the death of Major John André, a British spy who had been captured and subsequently hanged. André was well known at the time and widely admired. He represented the beau ideal of the British gentleman, an image many Americans still cherished. Poems and popular ballads were printed in American newspapers to commemorate his death and in 1798 William Dunlap seized upon the figure of André for his first play. The play, which depicted André in heroic terms, was heavily attended on opening night, but reproduced much of the original ambivalence over how to interpret the event. A measure of this ambivalence is also evident in Washington Irving's reference to André in "The Legend of Sleepy Hollow" (1820). The headless horseman, we are told, appears on the spot where André was captured. André thus haunts the early American imagination. In *The Spy*, Cooper does not attempt to revisit the André case, but the specter of André's death looms over the events of the novel. Although ultimately patriotic in its explicit political message, the novel seems skeptical of the social and cultural cost of the Revolution, much as Crèvecoeur's *Letters* had been three decades earlier.

A few years later, Lydia Maria Child would publish a much more unambiguously patriotic novel, *The Rebels* (1825), which celebrates the heroic patriots of Boston, who are seen leading the charge for independence. Navigating a position somewhere between Cooper and Child, in 1835 Catharine Maria Sedgwick published *The Linwoods*, a novel that traces its heroine's intellectual and sentimental journey from loyalist to patriot. All deeply indebted to Walter Scott's fictions, Cooper, Child, and Sedgwick's novels are especially concerned with the nature of American identity and how to find resolution and reconciliation after the damage the Revolution has inflicted on the Anglo-American social fabric. Each presents readers with an example of a family torn between patriotism and loyalism. In Cooper and Sedgwick's novels, the denouements enact such reconciliation to emphasize the desire not only to reintegrate Americans of differing political opinions, but also to recover the all-important link to a British cultural past upon which an American culture will be built.

The other major strand of writing that revisits the Revolution insistently in the nineteenth century is the literature of the disenfranchised, be they women, African-Americans, or Native Americans. The ideals of the Revolution, in the writings of Margaret Fuller or Frederick Douglass, for example, are now deployed to criticize the American state for its failure to deliver on its promises of liberty and equality. Unlike the novels by Cooper, Child, and Sedgwick, which feature battle scenes and in which the war figures centrally in the drama, these writers pull on the strand of the Revolution as ideological event. Nonetheless, the threat of violence lurks – for example in Douglass's deployment of the Revolution in famous speeches such as "What to the Slave Is the Fourth of July" (1852). The link between the ideas of the Revolution and the violence required to secure those ideas can be seen even more clearly in antislavery texts such as "David Walker's Appeal" (1829) or "The Confessions of Nat Turner" (1831). The potential for black revolutionary action, legitimized by the language of the Revolution, also looms over Leonora Sansay's *Secret History* (1808), which takes place during the Haitian Revolution. Sansay is especially effective at connecting the plight of women with the troubles of enslaved blacks, themes that converge most spectacularly in William Wells Brown's novel *Clotel* (1853), about a young enslaved woman who is a descendent of Thomas Jefferson.

Perhaps the most important writer on the challenges race poses for the Revolution, however, was the African-American poet Phillis Wheatley. Writing in late eighteenth-century Boston, Wheatley subtly explores the ironies of a patriot rhetoric of freedom that could not only tolerate but actually embrace racial slavery. In poems such as "To the Earl of Dartmouth" (1802) and "On Imagination" (1773), Wheatley strategically weaves together the rhetoric of the Revolution with images of slavery. This is precisely what the American patriots had done by identifying British imperial policies with an attempt to enslave the colonies. Wheatley cannily throws that language back at the patriots without explicitly rebuking them. Instead, her poems work to extend the freedoms of the Revolution to the truly enslaved in America. In this respect, it could be said that Wheatley inaugurated what would become a tradition of using patriotic American political rhetoric as a means to critique the injustice and inequality of the American government. This was made possible in large measure by the way the Revolution had become dissociated with war and linked instead to the triumph of a set of ideas.

NOTES

1. Franklin wrote a second segment in 1784, a third in 1788–89, and he was working on a fourth section when he died in 1790.
2. Thomas Paine, *The Complete Works of Thomas Paine*, ed. Philip S. Foner, 2 vols. (New York: Citadel, 1969), I: 354.
3. John Adams, Letter to James Lloyd of January 1815, *The Works of John Adams, Second President of the United States*, ed. Charles Francis Adams, 10 vols. (Boston, MA: Little, Brown, 1856), X: 108–14.
4. Oliver's manuscript is dated 1781, but it was not published until 1961. At least three copies of the manuscript, which was widely circulated among loyalist families, are known to have existed, two of which survived into the twentieth century.
5. Abigail Adams, John Adams, and Thomas Jefferson, *The Adams–Jefferson Letters: The Complete Correspondence Between Thomas Jefferson and Abigail and John Adams*, ed. Lester J. Cappon (Chapel Hill: University of North Carolina Press for The Institute of Early American History and Culture, 1959), 339, 349.
6. Abigail Adams, Letter to John Adams, March 31, 1776, available at www.masshist. org/adams/manuscripts_1.cfm## (accessed January 2009).

FURTHER READING

Cathy N. Davidson, *Revolution and the Word: The Rise of the Novel in America* (Oxford University Press, 1986).
Jay Fliegelman, *Declaring Independence: Jefferson, Natural Language, and the Culture of Performance* (Palo Alto, CA: Stanford University Press, 1993).
Michael Kammen, *Mystic Chords of Memory: The Transformation of Tradition in American Culture* (New York: Vintage, 1993).
Christopher Looby, *Voicing America: Language, Literary Form, and the Origins of the United States* (Chicago University Press, 1996).
Alfred Young, *The Shoemaker and the Tea Party: Memory and the American Revolution* (Boston, MA: Beacon, 1999).

12

JOHN R. REED

The Victorians and war

Introduction

Victory in the Battle of Waterloo (1815), the culmination of the wars against Napoleonic France (1803–15), bequeathed essential stability to Victorian Britain. Though fears of internal social upheaval replaced fears of invasion, Britain now had the freedom and naval preeminence to develop her vast empire. The combination of imperial expansion and ever-improving communications technology (electrical telegraphy was available at the start of the century, wireless telegraphy by the end) meant that war became at once very close to and very far away from the British public. Literature could respond to newspaper headlines (Tennyson's "The Charge of the Light Brigade" [1854] was written moments after the poet had read a report by William Howard Russell in the London *Times* from the Crimea) and there was wider public familiarity, and empathy, with the lot of soldiers. At the same time, the reduced threat of invasion and the ending of the practice of press-ganging after Waterloo diminished the personal relevance of war in many Britons' lives.

"There is no great art possible to a nation but that which is based on battle," John Ruskin told an audience of soldiers at the Royal Military Academy, Woolwich, in a lecture delivered in 1865.[1] Victorian war literature is generically varied, ranging from adventure stories to poetry to historical novels to works for children. Patriotic and imperial impulses jostle with antiwar sentiment, often within the oeuvre of a single writer. Rudyard Kipling's "The White Man's Burden" (1899) may seem simplistically supportive of Empire, but "Recessional" (1897) expresses anxiety about national triumphalism in the context of Queen Victoria's Diamond Jubilee and petitions God's mercy on the "heathen heart that puts her trust / In reeking tube and iron shard."[2]

Constructions of the man-at-war varied through the nineteenth century. Developing weapons technology – repeating rifles, machine guns, torpedo boats – continued the industrialization of warfare, with predictable results to the human body and concomitant developments both in battlefield medicine and in the perception of courage and honor. "Because you have to fight with machines instead of lances, there may be a necessity for more ghastly danger," Ruskin told his soldier audience at Woolwich, "but there is none for less worthiness of character than in olden time."[3] The Muscular Christianity movement produced in mid-century the figure of the Christian hero, a character who combined physical excellence with Christian virtues and was not averse to fighting. Exemplars can be found in Charles Kingsley's *Two Years Ago* (1857) and Thomas Hughes's *Tom Brown at Oxford* (1861); Sabine Baring-Gould wrote the hymn "Onward, Christian Soldiers" (music by Sir Arthur Sullivan) in 1871. The logical flaw in the concept did not go unremarked: "Of all conceits mis-grafted on God's Word, / A christian soldier seems the most absurd," wrote James Philip Bailey in *The Age: A Colloquial Satire* (1858): "a christian soldier's duty is to slay."[4]

Muscular Christianity was essentially the ethos of the English public school. Works such as Sir Henry Newbolt's "Vitaï Lampada" (1897), with its refrain "Play up! Play up! And play the game!,"[5] and "Clifton Chapel" (1898) connect the public school spirit of fair play with proper soldierly behavior on the battlefield – particularly in relation to the enemy – which is:

> To love the game beyond the prize,
> To honour, while you strike him down,
> The foe that comes with fearless eyes:
> To count the life of battle good.[6]

Respect for the foe also emerges in Kipling's poems, for example "'Fuzzy-Wuzzy'" (1890) and "Gunga Din" (1892). "'Fuzzy-Wuzzy'" commends the Sudanese warrior (albeit while voicing racist attitudes): "You're a pore benighted 'eathen but a first-class fightin' man."[7]

In the later nineteenth century, the muscular Christian hero was replaced by a hyper-masculine imperial adventurer, a reaction against both mid-century "feminized" realism and late-century aestheticism. H. Rider Haggard's Allan Quatermain, protagonist of *King Solomon's Mines* (1885) and other novels in the series, is the quintessential imperial hero, a big-game hunter turned fighter. Another version of masculinity was the common soldier – a determinedly unglamorous, lower-class, antiheroic figure, whose true mettle emerges in courage and fortitude shown in fraught conditions or in the face of public indifference or criticism. In this vein are the poems in Kipling's *Barrack-Room Ballads* (1892, 1896). "Danny Deever" (1890) describes the execution of a British soldier in India, while "Tommy" (1892) (originally

"The Queen's Uniform" [1890]) remarks with wry weariness the public's fickle treatment of their fighting men:

> We aren't no thin red 'eroes, nor we aren't no blackguards too,
> But single men in barricks, most remarkable like you;
> ...
> For it's Tommy this, an' Tommy that, an' "Chuck him out, the brute!"
> But it's "Saviour of 'is country" when the guns begin to shoot.[8]

The wars in which Britain engaged in the nineteenth century ranged in location from India to southern Africa, from the Crimea to France. Victorian war writing is *particularistic* – and this chapter now examines the literary responses to each major conflict in turn. It concludes with a consideration of the depiction of women in the period's war literature.

The Napoleonic Wars

The great battles of the Napoleonic Wars, culminating in Waterloo, were accorded near-legendary status in Victorian Britain. Their legacy included a gallery of military and naval heroes headed by Viscount Horatio Nelson and Arthur Wellesley, Duke of Wellington. Army and naval autobiographies were not new, but over the next fifty years, a spate of military memoirs appeared. One of the most notable was G. R. Gleig's fictionalized memoir *The Subaltern* (1825), which has been viewed as fostering two new subgenres of British fiction – the naval novel and the military novel. The naval novel is associated chiefly with Captain Frederick Marryat, author of *Frank Mildmay* (1829), *The King's Own* (1830), and *Peter Simple* (1834). Other naval writers of the period include Edward George Greville Howard (*Rattlin' the Reefer* [1838] [edited by Marryat]); Captain Frederick Chamier (*The Life of a Sailor* [1832], *The Arethusa* [1837]); and William Johnson Neale (*Cavendish, or the Patrician at Sea* [1831], *Paul Periwinkle; or, The Pressgang* [1839–41]). The military novel is identified mainly with Charles Lever, author of *The Confessions of Harry Lorrequer* (1839), *Charles O'Malley* (1841), and *Jack Hinton* (1842). Other writers in the genre were W. H. Maxwell (*Stories of Waterloo* [1829], *The Bivouac; or, Stories of the Peninsular War* [1837]) and Thomas Hamilton (*Cyril Thornton* [1827]). Most of these works include scenes of real or imagined battles on land and at sea. William Makepeace Thackeray satirized the military subgenre in *Barry Lyndon* (1844), perhaps contributing to the demise of the form. *Vanity Fair* (1847–48) refers to the Battle of Waterloo but avoids descriptions of the battlefield itself (with the exception of concluding a chapter with George Osborne lying dead with a bullet through his heart), in favor of a domestic focus on the wives awaiting news in Brussels.

As a child, Thomas Hardy was fascinated by stories of the Napoleonic Wars, which had left traces on the Wessex landscape. He refers to them in *The Trumpet-Major* (1880) (the military action is again offstage), while *Wessex Poems* (1898) contains a number of poems on Napoleonic topics: "The Sergeant's Song," "Valenciennes," "The Alarm" (all written for *The Trumpet-Major*), "San Sebastian," "Leipzig," and "The Peasant's Confession." The Napoleonic conflict is also the setting for Hardy's ultimate meditation on the universe and the human condition, his epic poem "The Dynasts" (1904–8).

The Crimean War

The Crimean War (1853–56) involved the British and French (with assistance) fighting the Russians, supposedly in defense of the Ottoman Empire, but really to prevent Russian expansionism. (The war ended disappointingly for the British public, with what amounted to a draw.) This conflict saw the beginning of modern war correspondence, with William Howard Russell sending vivid eyewitness dispatches to the London *Times*. Photography was also introduced to the theater of war: for the first time, the public back home could see, as well as read about, the reality of conflict. Initially, there was enthusiastic support for the war. Even the radical Ernest Charles Jones produced a work, *The Battle-Day and Other Poems* (1855), that is positive in its treatment of the conflict. But disillusionment swiftly set in, due to the public's unprecedented access to the realities of what was taking place. The perceived mishandling of the war by officers and authorities led to an outcry. There were reforms in the army and Florence Nightingale led a revolution in military nursing. Jones's *The Emperor's Vigil, and The Waves and the War* (1856) shows his disenchantment.

The Poet Laureate, Alfred, Lord Tennyson, evinced similar ambivalence. "The Charge of the Light Brigade" apparently presents for celebration the glory of obedient sacrifice, however futile –

> Stormed at with shot and shell,
> Boldly they rode and well,
> Into the jaws of Death,
> Into the mouth of Hell
> Rode the six hundred.[9]

– but the poem has also been read as an indictment of the same. Antiwar sentiment can also be inferred from the end of Tennyson's long poem "Maud" (1855). The speaker claims that the Crimean conflict is to be welcomed as it will purge society of greedy commercialism:

> No more shall commerce be all in all, and Peace
> Pipe on her pastoral hillock a languid note,

And watch her harvest ripen, her herd increase,
Nor the cannon-bullet rust on a slothful shore.[10]

However, this point of view is expressed by a character already shown to be unreliable and the poem's conclusion remains difficult to interpret.

The Crimean War appears in a number of novels, including Henry Kingsley's *Ravenshoe* (1861), George Alfred Lawrence's *Sword and Gown* (1859), Major Arthur Griffiths's *The Queen's Shilling* (1873), and Anne Thackeray Ritchie's *Old Kensington* (1873). The last features scenes with soldiers on the battlefield and later back in Britain being nursed. In this and other works, the Crimean War is firmly associated with individual glory and soldierly heroism, but also with administrative failure.

The "Indian Mutiny"

The "Indian Mutiny" is a disputed term for events in 1857 involving military revolts by sepoys and civilian rebellions against the ruling British East India Company. Though the appellation "First War of Independence" is often preferred, "Indian Mutiny" is used here as it was an important term in Victorian discourse. Outrage greeted the news of the mutinous sepoys when it reached Britain. Even poets otherwise unconcerned about war as a subject took up the theme. A notable example is Christina Rossetti's "In the Round Tower at Jhansi" (1862). Like Tennyson's "The Charge of the Light Brigade," Rossetti's poem was written in response to a newspaper story (in this case, inaccurate) about a husband, Captain Skene, shooting his wife and then himself. The Mutiny setting allows Rossetti to explore her characteristic preoccupation with love and death in the face of imperialized violence.

The Mutiny generated the possibility that seemingly secure colonial spaces could become threatening. Literary responses emphasized British heroism – for example, Tennyson's "Havelock" (1858) and his much later "The Defence of Lucknow" (1879), both celebrations of Sir Henry Havelock who broke the Siege of Lucknow: "Handful of men as we were, we were English in heart and in limb, / Strong with the strength of the race to command, to obey, to endure."[11] Plays about the Mutiny include the anonymous *Nana Sahib* (1857) and Dion Boucicault's popular *Jessie Brown; or, The Relief of Lucknow* (1858). Novels set in or referring to the Mutiny include George Lawrence's *Maurice Dering* (1864), James Grant's *First Love and Last Love: A Tale of the Indian Mutiny* (1868), Henry Kingsley's *Stretton* (1869), and Philip Meadows Taylor's *Seeta* (1872).

In Grant's *First Love and Last Love*, sexual violence is a central theme. As Jenny Sharpe has shown, the Mutiny changed the stereotype of "the Indian" in the Victorian British mind from the mild, effeminate Hindu to the murderous Muslim.[12] One of the most curious features of the developing "Mutiny narrative" was the recurrence of tales of rapes of Englishwomen by Indians, despite the remarkably limited factual evidence of such rapes actually taking place. The recurring figure of the raped Englishwoman, Sharpe argues, serves two purposes. Firstly, it transfers violence against British men to violence against British women, exorcising threats to ideas of masculinity through the image of the violated and dismembered female body. Secondly, the motif serves as justification for retaliation in any form. The desire for vengeance against the rebellious colonized is expressed in Charles Dickens and Wilkie Collins's "The Perils of Certain English Prisoners" (1857), in which John Peck has also detected a movement towards Christian militarism.[13] Collins's *The Moonstone* (1868) opens with an account of the storming of Seringapatam (Srirangapattana) in 1799, a major factor in consolidating British control of India. The main events of the novel take place between 1848 and 1850, when the consequences of this initial imperial violence are visited upon an English country house.

Late-century works continued to treat the Mutiny. Flora Annie Steel's *On the Face of the Waters* (1896) is a thoughtful novel placing special emphasis on the British and Indian women whose lives are caught up in the Mutiny. G. A. Henty, who made his name as a war correspondent, produced a children's tale of adventure, *In Times of Peril* (1881), and a novel for adults, *Rujub the Juggler* (1893). The basis for the detective plot of Arthur Conan Doyle's 1890 Sherlock Holmes novel, *The Sign of Four*, takes place during the Mutiny in a flashback sequence.

The Afghan Wars

Part of what the British significantly termed "The Great Game" (the ongoing competition for land and power between the British Empire and Russia), the Anglo-Afghan Wars took place in 1839–42, 1878–81, and 1919. The ostensible reason for the British invasion of Afghanistan in 1839 was to establish an ally on India's western frontier. The campaign ended with the routing of the British garrison and the iconic image of the "sole survivor," Dr. William Brydon, riding into Jalalabad. Accounts of the action emerged very quickly, among them *A Journal of the First Afghan War* (1843) by Florentia, Lady Sale, wife of the general who was second-in-command at Kabul. Such accounts stirred public anger and, like the Indian Mutiny, the First Afghan War was seen as a military disaster requiring vengeance – but it never really attained the same iconic status as the Mutiny in popular mythology.

Sir Francis Hastings Doyle's ballad "The Red Thread of Honour" was published in 1866 but referred to the first campaign. It purports to be a true story of Afghan respect for British soldiers who died in battle – a valorization, typical of the period, of courage and fair play. Thomas Hardy wrote of the First Afghan War in "The Casterbridge Captains" (1898), which begins with the familiar trope of the discrepancy between the numbers of those going out to fight and those safely returning: "Three captains went to Indian wars, / And only one returned."[14] The survivor is humbled by his companions' achievements in the battle that brought their deaths. Sir Henry Newbolt's "The Guides at Cabul" (1879) is an account of how the native guides fought on against the Afghans after their British officers were dead and the Afghans offered them a truce. Kipling's "Ford o' Kabul River" (1890) commemorates a disastrous attempt by the 10th Hussars to cross the river during the Second Afghan War, a subject recalling the futile heroism and *esprit de corps* of Tennyson's Light Brigade. The Second Afghan War is also the subject of G. A. Henty's stirring novel *For Name and Fame, To Cabul with Roberts* (1886).

Imperialist wars in Africa

The last twenty years of the nineteenth century saw increasingly aggressive imperial assaults on the African continent by European nations – the so-called "scramble for Africa." In 1879, the British invaded Zululand with the intention of ending Zulu independence. Though the Zulu army won a great victory at the Battle of Isandlwana (closely followed by the British holding out against the odds at Rorke's Drift), the Zulu were eventually defeated and the British consolidated their control over southern Africa. The reaction of the Afrikaners or Boers, long-term settlers of mostly Netherlandish descent, led to the Boer Wars. Meanwhile, Britain occupied Egypt in 1882 and took over administrative control of the country (Kitchener put down the Mahdist Rebellion in 1898). In 1885, General Charles Gordon, charged with evacuating Egyptian forces from Sudan, was killed at the Siege of Khartoum: the resulting public outrage in Britain brought down Gladstone's government. The scramble for Africa therefore produced more individual heroics for the British public. In literary terms, Africa, a still little-known continent, opened up a new arena for war writing.

The Anglo-Zulu War of 1879 is the setting for imperial adventure novels by G. A. Henty (*The Young Colonists* [1885]), Constantine Ralli (*The Strange Case of Falconer Thring* [1902]), Frederick Brereton (*With Shield and Assegai* [1900]), and Ernest Glanville (*The Lost Heiress* [1892]).[15] According to Michael Lieven, in works such as *Cetewayo and his White Neighbours* (1882) and *The Witch's Head* (1885), H. Rider Haggard mixes a "clear imperialist message" and "a nostalgic respect ... for the traditional warrior society of the Zulus."[16] The works of Bertram Mitford – including *The Curse of Clement Waynflete* (1894), *The King's Assegai* (1894), and *The White Shield* (1895) – give more complicated accounts of the "contradictions at the heart of liberal imperialism."[17]

The two Boer Wars took place in 1880–81 and 1899–1902. In literary terms, they offered a venue for disgraced men to reclaim their nobility and/or their masculinity through death. E. W. Hornung's rakish gentleman thief, Raffles, who made his first appearance in the *Strand* magazine in the 1880s, comes to a heroic end fighting the Boers in *The Black Mask* (1901). Rider Haggard's novel *Jess* (1887) deals with the First Boer War, and G. A. Henty was ready as usual with some novels for boys (the Scout Movement, begun in 1908, was inspired by the experiences of its founder, Robert Baden-Powell, at the Siege of Mafeking). Two short stories by Kipling are moderately critical of the British performance in the Second or Great Boer War – "A Sahib's War" (1901) and "The Captive" (1902) – but the criticism is voiced indirectly by a Sikh and an American respectively. Bertram Mitford produced an adventure tale entitled *Aletta: A Tale of the Boer Invasion* (1900), but the prevailing prose response, especially to the Second Boer War, was memoir or commentary in the manner of Arthur Conan Doyle's *The Great Boer War* (1900–2). Olive Schreiner's powerful antiwar allegory *Trooper Peter Halkett of Mashonaland* (1897) criticizes British expansionism in Africa, particularly the methods used by Cecil Rhodes.

The section in Thomas Hardy's *Poems of the Past and the Present* (1901) entitled "War Poems" includes a number referring to the Boer Wars. "Embarcation" (1899) notes the departure of troops to war. "Drummer Hodge" (originally "The Dead Drummer") (1899) commemorates a young Englishman losing his life in a land he does not comprehend. "A Christmas Ghost-Story" (1899) contrasts Christ's Law of Peace with the ongoing human inclination to war. "A Wife in London" (1899), "The Souls of the Slain" (1899), and "Song of the Soldiers' Wives" (1900) are in a long tradition of poems directed to the behavior and reactions of soldiers' loved ones back home. In "The Man He Killed" (1902) from *Time's Laughingstocks* (1909), a Boer War veteran reflects on killing an enemy, concluding, in a foreshadowing of Wilfred Owen's "Strange Meeting" (1918):

> Yes; quaint and curious war is!
> You shoot a fellow down
> You'd treat if met where any bar is,
> Or help to half-a-crown.[18]

Near the end of his career, Algernon Charles Swinburne published poems of a patriotic nature about war and the preparation for war in *A Channel Passage*

(1904). "A Word for the Navy" (1896) cautions about the growing sea strength of Germany and others; "The Transvaal" (1899) urges England to strike back at the Boers; and "The Turning of the Tide" (1900) and "Astraea Victrix" (1900) applaud British success against the Boers in highly figurative language.

Historical, mythological, and imagined wars

Since most of the conflicts involving the British armed forces in the nineteenth century occurred outside Britain and even Europe, military literature involving actual combat often has an "exotic" feel – for example, J. H. Amherst's play *The Burmese War; or, Our Victories in the East* (1826). Some writers found an alien location in the future. Colonel G. T. Chesney's *The Battle of Dorking* (1871) and H. G. Wells's *The War of the Worlds* (1897) were among the rash of invasion novels that appeared before the outbreak of the First World War. Chesney's work is explicitly concerned with Britain falling behind in the evolving arms race with Germany, while Wells's is the ultimate invasion fantasy: though military might fails, the earth-invading Martians are ultimately defeated by the planet itself, catching the common cold.

Other authors turned to long-past wars. Victorian interest in the medieval period, of which the Pre-Raphaelite movement was an expression, brought chivalric motifs and ethics into literature. In his Woolwich lecture, Ruskin noted:

> With Gothic chivalry, there comes back into the mind of Europe a passionate delight in war itself for the sake of war. And then, with the romantic knighthood which can imagine no other employment … art is born again.[19]

"You have vowed your life to England, give it her wholly; – a bright, stainless, perfect life – a knightly life," Ruskin went on to instruct his soldier audience, conflating contemporary gentlemanly behavior with medieval chivalry in a vision of battle that must have seemed wholly unrealistic to those lately returned from the Crimea.[20] The same union of medieval and contemporary "courtly" values takes place in the battle scenes in Tennyson's *Idylls of the King* (1859–85). William Morris also took up medieval warlike themes in *The Defense of Guenevere and Other Poems* (1858); explored Norse and Greek legends involving various battles in *The Earthly Paradise* (1868–70); and wrote other poems and prose narratives about Nordic conquests. William Cory's "War Music" (1891) is an old man's recollection of youthful ambitions set in medieval terms: "For stepping to music I dreamt of a siege, / A vow to my mistress, a fight for my liege."[21] W. E. Henley's "The Song of the Sword" (1892), dedicated to Kipling, is a first-person account by the Sword itself of its origin and its grand destiny in combat. The poem ends, before the repeated stanza from its opening, with the lines:

> Arch-anarch, chief builder,
> Prince and evangelist,
> I am the Will of God:
> I am the Sword.[22]

Women in Victorian war literature

Another far-flung location – Algeria – is used by the novelist Ouida (Maria Louise Ramé) as the setting for her work *Under Two Flags* (1867). The hero, the suitably named Sergeant Victor, an Englishman in the French Foreign Legion,[23] fights Arab rebels while the plucky heroine, Cigarette, is a mascot for the troop and wins the Cross of the Legion of Honor by taking part in battle, sacrificing herself in the process for Victor, so that he can go home to his title and marry his aristocratic true love. Cigarette's participation in battle is unusual in the literature of the period, which tends to cast women in a nursing or auxiliary role. Florence Nightingale gained a powerful public image as "The Lady with the Lamp" – a lovingly feminine nurturer figure rather than a professional with efficient organizational capacities. (A counter-example is the Scottish-Jamaican "doctress" and sutler, Mary Seacole, who was refused permission to work as one of Nightingale's volunteer nurses but made her way to the Crimea at her own cost. Her account of her own experiences of treating the wounded, *Wonderful Adventures of Mrs. Seacole in Many Lands* [1857], gives detailed insight into battlefield conditions.) Ruskin told his audience at Woolwich that "every virtue of the higher phases of manly character begins in this; – in truth and modesty before the face of all maidens; in truth and pity, or truth and reverence, to all womanhood."[24] But if war brought out men's best qualities, Ruskin thought, it arose from women's worst:

> The real final reason for all the poverty, misery, and rage of battle throughout Europe, is simply that you women, however good, however religious, however self-sacrificing for those whom you love, are too selfish and too thoughtless to take pains for any creatures out of your immediate circles.[25]

Alongside this complicated idealization-cum-accusation of women, there emerges in Victorian literature – usually endorsed by its historical setting – the medieval ballad or folklore motif of the warrior woman. In Elizabeth Barrett Browning's "The Romaunt of the Page" (1840), for example, the heroine dresses up as the hero's page in order to fight alongside him in battle, though this ends unhappily when the hero derides the idea as unwomanly and the heroine goes off to get herself killed.

In Indian Mutiny narratives, this female warrior figure is negatively personified in the evil Rani of Jhansi: British women, as already noted, are presented as defending their virtue. The brothels in India maintained by and for the military were an important influence on the Contagious Diseases Acts of 1864, 1866, and 1869, which were originally aimed at reducing sexually transmitted diseases in the armed forces and were a cause of controversy in Britain. Sexual conquests by soldiers are used as plot devices in a number of novels. Sergeant Troy dazzles Bathsheba Everdene with a display of swordsmanship in Hardy's *Far From the Madding Crowd* (1874), and Arthur Donnithorne, a captain in the militia, impregnates Hetty Sorrel in George Eliot's *Adam Bede* (1859).

Conclusion

Towards the end of the nineteenth century, though loyalty to the Empire remained strong, a note of melancholy and even doubt appeared. T. W. H. Crosland's "Slain" (1899), a saddened if approving apostrophe to a dead soldier, uses the epigraph *dulce et decorum est pro patria mori* (though not with Wilfred Owen's later bitterness). In 1885, William Watson produced a series of poems on public affairs that manifested misgivings about England's direction. "The Soudanese" laments England's involvement in Egypt's war against Sudan and ends with the line "O England, O my country, curse thy name!"[26] But "The English Dead," "Gordon," and "Gordon (concluded)" are poems in praise of fallen soldiers. A set of poems beginning with "Foreign Menace" bewails England's apparent unwillingness to challenge the menace posed by a threatening Russia. Watson complains: "I marvel that this land with heart so tame / Can brook the northern insolence and guile."[27] Published the year before the Diamond Jubilee, A. E. Housman's *A Shropshire Lad* (1896) elegizes young soldiers who have died in Queen Victoria's service.

While the fate of the common soldier touched many Victorian hearts, belief in war as politically necessary, commercially advantageous, and morally improving was slow to die. War was geographically distant from Victorian Britons, but the public had unprecedented access to the facts of conflict, a situation that resulted in an uneasy tension between glorifying individual heroics and recognizing war's cost. At the turn of the century, invasion fears, long laid to rest by Waterloo, were current again. The elegiac mood of fin-de-siècle war literature has in it a note of warning.

NOTES

1. John Ruskin, "War," *The Crown of Wild Olive. Four Lectures on Industry and War* (1866, 1873) (London: George Allen, 1895), 115–71: 116.

2. Rudyard Kipling, "Recessional," *Rudyard Kipling's Verse: Definitive Edition* (London, Sydney, Auckland, Toronto: Hodder & Stoughton, 1940, rptd 1977), 329.
3. Ruskin, "War," 164.
4. James Philip Bailey, *The Age: A Colloquial Satire* (Boston, MA: Ticknor and Fields, 1858), 17.
5. Henry Newbolt, *The Island Race* (London: Elkin Mathews, 1898), 81.
6. Ibid., 76.
7. Kipling, *Rudyard Kipling's Verse*, 400.
8. Ibid., 399.
9. Alfred, Lord Tennyson, *The Poems of Tennyson*, ed. Christopher Ricks (London: Longman, 1969), 1035.
10. Ibid., 1091.
11. Ibid., 1252.
12. Jenny Sharpe, *Allegories of Empire – The Figure of Woman in the Colonial Text* (London and Minneapolis, MN: University of Minneapolis Press, 1993).
13. John Peck, *War, the Army and Victorian Literature* (New York: St. Martin's, 1998), 83.
14. Thomas Hardy, *The Complete Poetical Works of Thomas Hardy*, ed. Samuel Hynes, 5 vols. (Oxford: Clarendon, 1982), V: 63.
15. Michael Lieven, "Contested Empire: Bertram Mitford and the Imperial Adventure Story," *Paradigm* 25 (May 1998), unpaginated, available at http://faculty.ed.uiuc.edu/westbury/paradigm/lieven2.html (accessed January 2009).
16. Ibid., unpaginated.
17. Ibid., unpaginated.
18. Hardy, *The Complete Poetical Works*, 345.
19. Ruskin, "War," 121.
20. Ibid., 164.
21. William Cory, *Ionica*, ed. Arthur C. Benson (London: George Allen, 1905), 39.
22. William Ernest Henley, *Poems* (New York: Scribner, 1926), 55.
23. Strictly speaking, Victor joins the Chasseurs d'Afrique, a light cavalry troop akin to the French Foreign Legion.
24. Ruskin, "War," 165.
25. Ibid., 169.
26. William Watson, *The Poems of William Watson* (New York: Macmillan, 1893), 151.
27. Ibid., 155.

FURTHER READING

Patrick Brantlinger, *Rule of Darkness: British Literature and Imperialism, 1830–1914* (Ithaca, NY: Cornell University Press, 1988).
Cecil Degrotte Eby, *The Road to Armageddon: The Martial Spirit in English Popular Literature, 1870–1914* (Durham, NC: Duke University Press, 1987).
Christopher Herbert, *The War of No Pity. The Indian Mutiny and Victorian Trauma* (New Jersey: Princeton University Press, 2007).

Matthew Paul Lalumia, *Realism and Politics in Victorian Art of the Crimean War* (Ann Arbor, MI: UMI Research Press, 1984).

Nancy Paxton, "Mobilizing Chivalry: Rape in British Novels about the Indian Uprising of 1857," *Victorian Studies* 36 (1992), 5–27.

Suvendrini Perera, *Reaches of Empire: The English Novel from Edgeworth to Dickens* (New York: Columbia University Press, 1991).

13

The American Civil War

No single episode in American history has spawned as much literary output as the Civil War. Indeed, it has been estimated that "more than a hundred thousand volumes"[1] have been produced on the subject. This prodigious mass of writing is all the more compelling for the problems it has continued to raise over the location and definition of the conflict, which the American novelist and historian Shelby Foote described as "the crossroads of our nation."[2] No consensus has yet been reached even as to the cause or purpose of the war. Contemporary Southern partisans such as the United Daughters of the Confederacy will argue about "the truths of history (one of the most important of which is, that the War Between the States was not a rebellion, nor was its underlying cause to sustain slavery)."[3] Thus, the war for "a new birth of freedom," as Abraham Lincoln described it in his Gettysburg Address of 1863, is by no means universally considered as such even in this century, as the founders of the neo-Confederate organization, The League of the South, make clear in their diatribe against "the heartless brigades of Abraham Lincoln's army of Northern aggression and occupation."[4] The "War of the Rebellion," the "War of Northern Aggression," the "Civil War" – such contradictory terms are only the simplest outward markers of the problems of interpretation and situation. As Jennifer James observes, "The Civil War was nothing if not a conflict rife with conflicts."[5]

That these conflicts have found their place in the imaginative literature of the American Civil War should come as no surprise. Neither should their longevity seem remarkable, for if – on the historical plane – the word "Appomattox" (where the Confederate surrender was signed) has not quite signaled a full cessation of sectional hostilities, neither have the interpretative conflicts over the war's meaning or its intelligibility ceased. In 1944, Joseph Stanley Pennell reflected on the opacity, the selectivity, of Civil War recollection in his best-selling novel *The History of Rome Hanks and Kindred Matters*. The book's narrator, trying to perceive the historical truth obscured in the recollections of Civil War veterans such as his grandfather, wonders about what is left out – "the cowering under the bluff, the smashed bodies, the rain and hail, the seas of sandy mud, the stink of their dead friends."[6] Such elision had not only been predicted with apparent equanimity by Walt Whitman in his autobiography *Specimen Days in America* (1887), but apparently encouraged by him: "Future years will never know the seething hell and the black infernal background of countless minor scenes and interiors ... of the Secession War; and it is best they should not – the real war will never get in the books."[7]

Whitman's reasoning stems from his first-hand knowledge as a wound-dresser and hospital ward-visitor. His witnessing of inevitable horrors in the aftermath of battle led him to conclude that the war's "interior history" should never be written, its "practicality, minutiæ of deeds and passions ... never even be suggested."[8] But other interpretative possibilities are opened up by this passage. Whitman may be counseling future poets not to get bogged down in chasing the details sought by historians and sectional partisans. He may be mischievously throwing down the gauntlet to those writers who might otherwise shy away from fixing myriad details of the Civil War into an intelligible narrative – or issuing a challenge to squeamish publishers and editors. Most likely he is characteristically – by the "faint indirections" he espouses in the poem, "Among the Multitude" – urging the opposite of what he implies.[9]

The conflict of detail, the tension between competing origins, aims, experiences, and interpretations, is precisely what makes for the resilience and richness of American Civil War writing. The wealth of conflict is neatly inscribed in what Richard Marius calls the first important "ideological poem" of the war, "John Brown's Body" (1861).[10] Not only is that poem's ideological position obscure (does it truly sanction John Brown's butchery on the plains of Kansas as well as the "truth" that "goes marching on" against slavery?), but its origins are as contested as those of the war itself. Either it was a rewriting of an antebellum camp-meeting hymn, as Hugh Brogan suggests; or it was composed by members of the Boston Light Infantry to honor the spot where Crispus Attucks fell in the Revolution, as W. E. B. Du Bois maintained; or it was simply an ode to an obscure Boston infantry sergeant who happened to be named John Brown.[11] The confusion surrounding the poem's genesis and the difficulties in assigning meaning to its central figure – was John Brown a terrorist or a freedom fighter, a holy martyr or a homicidal lunatic? – mirror the problems of identifying the actual beginning of the Civil War. Conventionally, historians date the start of the war to the Confederate assault on Fort Sumter on April 12, 1861; some – particularly neo-Confederate partisans – will cite the election of Lincoln in 1860 as a *de facto* declaration of war against the slaveholding South. In Herman

Melville's estimation, if "Weird John Brown" was not the instigator, he at least proved to be "The Portent," the "meteor of the war" with his raid on Harper's Ferry in 1859 in hopes of inciting a slave insurrection.[12]

However, of all the attempts to assign a primal cause for the American Civil War, two stand out for their direct, if tongue-in-cheek, indictments of literature. For Mark Twain, who condemned the Southern predilection for plantation-based feudalism and "jejune" codes of chivalry and class, the blame lay with the popularity of romantic novels in the antebellum South. The chief culprit here was Walter Scott, who, Twain claimed, "had so large a hand in making Southern character, as it existed before the war, that he is in great measure responsible for the war."[13] For Lincoln (perhaps apocryphally), it was Harriet Beecher Stowe – "the little lady who started this big war."[14] Stowe's *Uncle Tom's Cabin* (1852) certainly sparked a literary civil war, if not a martial one. In its wake came a plethora of Southern titles denouncing Stowe's attack on chattel slavery – titles such as Mary Henderson Eastman's *Aunt Phillis's Cabin* (1852) and John White Page's *Uncle Robin, in his cabin in Virginia, and Tom without one in Boston* (1853). Such tit-for-tat titles were perhaps the inevitable outcome of a much longer literary conflict that had been brewing for centuries.

Literary sectionalism

It is certainly true that writers bore a great responsibility for the creation and perpetuation of sectional identities and tension in the years leading up to the American Civil War. Mark Twain's criticism of Walter Scott was based partly on those antebellum Southern novelists who used his feudal, chivalric romances as a model for their own works – for instance, George Tucker in *The Valley of the Shenandoah* (1824), John Pendleton Kennedy in *Swallow Barn* (1832), William Alexander Carruthers in *The Cavaliers of Virginia* (1834–35), and Nathaniel Beverley Tucker in *The Partisan Leader* (1836). Such works reinforced a sense of Southern difference that manifested itself in a literary plantation cult romanticizing the codes of honor, feudalism, patriarchy, and – above all – white supremacy below the Mason–Dixon Line. It is no accident that such novels became increasingly popular as Northern abolitionists intensified their attacks on the antebellum slave system. Indeed, so powerful was the romanticization of the plantation culture that even the defeat of the South could not kill it; hence the spectacular postbellum success of Joel Chandler Harris's "Uncle Remus" tales (1881 onwards) and – dwarfing all other romantic representations of the Old South, with its chivalrous figures and grotesque caricatures of happy "darkies" in the fields – Margaret Mitchell's *Gone with the Wind* (1936).

The sense of Southern exceptionalism in literature did not develop over-night. As Richard Gray has argued, the South "has always represented itself historically as different, deviant, and (usually) in danger."[15] Since the late sixteenth and early seventeenth centuries, colonial pamphleteers seeking investment had represented the South – particularly Virginia – as a Garden of Eden, a pastoral Arcadia which, in later representation, posited itself in a binary divide against the developing Northern manufacturing culture. In terms deriving from the English Civil War, Northerners were grasping, common-sense Roundhead businessmen; Southerners were aristocratic, romantic, agrarian Cavaliers. By the mid-eighteenth century, Virginia plan-ters as influential as Thomas Jefferson had done their bit to establish what Gray calls the "primitive portraits of the Southerner and Yankee," with the former assured of a higher moral standing, closer to God and the land than any corrupt Northern city-dweller.[16]

By the mid-1850s, then, amidst the turbulence of the growing sectional schism enflamed by the Kansas-Nebraska Act, the Fugitive Slave Law, the bloodletting of proslavery and antislavery partisans on the Kansas plains, and the worldwide reception of *Uncle Tom's Cabin*, the moment had come for the South Carolina poet William J. Grayson to pen his defensive ode to the supposedly benign institution of plantation slavery, "The Hireling and the Slave" (1855). This sprawling fifty-nine-page verse diatribe argued that the lot of the Northern factory operative was considerably worse than that of the plantation slave, "brought by Providence" to America and thus benefiting from "superiority ... over the rest of his race" left behind in Africa.[17]

Grayson was not alone in romanticizing slavery and cotton. With the inauguration of Lincoln and the onset of martial hostilities, Grayson's fellow South Carolinian, Henry Timrod – soon dubbed "the Poet Laureate of the Confederacy" – produced his most famous work, "The Cotton Boll" (1861), described by Edmund Wilson as a piece of "war propaganda," "a hymn to the power of cotton and an assertion of confidence in the victory of the South."[18] Grayson and Timrod had responded to what they considered the slander and calumnies of *Uncle Tom's Cabin* and the plethora of odes to John Brown by Yankees such as Edmund Clarence Steadman, John Greenleaf Whittier, Henry David Thoreau, and Ralph Waldo Emerson. By the close of 1861, a literary war was truly being fought in parallel with the military one.

Writing disunion

Arguably, and in spite of important exceptions, the most ephemeral American Civil War writing appeared during the actual war years (1861–65). This is understandable, as the conflict's drama and its broader historical significance would not become apparent until after a period of reflection. With the battle lines drawn in the heat of sectional outrage, much wartime literary output consisted of crude partisan versifying on both sides. Whether it be Albert Pike's appropriation of the old minstrel song, "Dixie" (1861) –

> Hear the Northern thunders mutter,
> Northern flags in South winds flutter:
> Send them back your fierce defiance!
> Stamp upon the accursed alliance![19]

– or Julia Ward Howe's borrowing of "John Brown's Body" for her tub-thumping war-chant, "The Battle Hymn of the Republic" (1862) –

> I have read a fiery gospel writ in burnished rows of steel:
> "As ye deal with my contemners, so with you my grace shall deal;
> Let the Hero, born of woman, crush the serpent with his heel,
> Since God is marching on."[20]

– the propaganda value outshone all other literary considerations. War novels such as Henry Morford's series, *Shoulder Straps* (1863), *The Coward* (1863), and *The Days of Shoddy* (1864), are largely unremembered, as are the many once-popular poetry collections such as Frank Moore's *Rebel Rhymes and Rhapsodies* (1864) and Henry H. Brownell's *Lyrics of a Day* (1863).

One important aspect of the early to mid-war years was the remarkable development of writing centered on women's experience of the conflict. Louisa May Alcott's *Hospital Sketches* (1863), a fictionalized account of her brief period as a war nurse in Washington, established her literary reputation and paved the way for one of the most martial of books ever written about the Civil War's domestic front, *Little Women* (1868). More intriguing is the spate of "Female Warrior" writings – the stories of distaff soldiers (women in male disguise) – such as Madeline Moore's *The Lady Lieutenant* (1862) and Wesley Bradshaw's *Pauline of the Potomac* (1862). Such novels reflected – with varying degrees of accuracy – the officially denied fact that there were over two hundred distaff soldiers fighting in both the Union and Confederate armies.[21] These works of popular fiction were answered by the avowedly (if questionably) factual narrative of Sarah Emma Evelyn Edmonds in *Unsexed, or, The Female Soldier* (1864), retitled *Nurse and Spy in the Union Army*. An even more popular and audacious Confederate counterpart was published after the war – Loreta Velazquez's *The Woman in Battle* (1876). Elsewhere at the literary battlefront, John Greenleaf Whittier commemorated Barbara Frietchie, the defiant nonagenarian who was said to have patriotically brandished the American flag in the face of Stonewall Jackson and his Confederate troops occupying Frederick,

Maryland, in 1862. Whittier's "Barbara Frietchie" (1863) depicts the woman "Bowed with her fourscore years and ten," drawing the admiration of Jackson himself, who growls at his troops, "Who touches a hair of yon gray head / Dies like a dog!"[22]

It was immediately after the close of the war that the more complex poetic reflections began to appear, particularly in Walt Whitman's *Drum-Taps* (1865) and Herman Melville's *Battle-Pieces* (1866). In comparison with such popular Northern collections as Brownell's *War Lyrics* (1866) and Southern collections such as William Gilmore Simms's *War Poetry of the South* (1867), the concentration and development of Whitman's and Melville's reflections stand out. Early in *Drum-Taps* (eventually incorporated into *Leaves of Grass*), Whitman proposes with his typically nationalistic – and journalistic – exuberance:

> I'll pour the verse with streams of blood, full of volition, full of joy,
> Then loosen, launch forth, to go and compete,
> With the banner and pennant a-flapping.[23]

But later, in a reflection of increasing war-weariness based on his own experience as an army hospital worker, he confesses:

> (Arous'd and angry, I'd thought to beat the alarum, and urge relentless war,
> But soon my fingers fail'd me, my face droop'd and I resign'd myself,
> To sit by the wounded and soothe them, or silently watch the dead).[24]

In contrast, Melville's "Misgivings," "The Conflict of Convictions," and "Apathy and Enthusiasm" evince a more brooding poetic consciousness from the outset. With uncanny omniscience (if not through mere coincidence), Melville describes in "The Scout toward Aldie" precisely the change of character eventually confessed by Whitman:

> The Hospital Steward – even he –
> Who on the sleeper kept his glance,
> Was changed; late bright-black beard and eye
> Looked now hearse-black; his heavy heart,
> Like his fagged mare, no more could dance.[25]

Melville also demonstrated, in his "Supplement" to *Battle-Pieces*, his awareness of the consequences of victory for a Union that had forcibly reincorporated a disaffected population into its midst: "Some of us are concerned because as yet the South shows no penitence ... Certain it is that penitence, in the sense of voluntary humiliation, will never be displayed."[26]

What in fact was displayed, in both literature and the wider culture, was no less problematic, particularly for what it implied about the place of African-Americans in the reconstituted Union. For William Wells Brown, who had become the first published African-American novelist with *Clotel; or, the President's Daughter* (1853), the first step was to set the record straight and remind the world that the Civil War was, first and foremost, a war over slavery and emancipation – not Union or States' Rights. Brown revised *Clotel* to include a battlefield episode, publishing it in 1867 as *Clotelle; or, The Colored Heroine. A Tale of the Southern States*, thus becoming – as Jennifer James observes – "the first black American war novelist."[27] As many African-Americans realized, their emancipation was not wholly secured with the Confederate defeat, as much of the literary output following the Civil War clearly indicated.

The "Romance of Reunion"

In Simms's preface to *War Poetry of the South*, we can see the effects of what Nina Silber has rightly called the "romance of reunion"[28] and the means by which the formerly antagonistic parties secured a literary, as well as a national, reconstruction. This reunion was based partly on a Northern agreement of the South's "lost cause" as somewhat noble, if misguided – a perception hardly shared by millions of African-Americans for whom the cry of "States' Rights" has been nothing more than a code for the defense of slavery and segregation – and partly on a sense of the war as a shared tragedy that ultimately strengthened the American national character and its democratic purpose. As Simms explained:

> This collection is essentially as much the property of the whole as are the captured cannon which were employed against it during the progress of the late war. It belongs to the national literature, and will hereafter be regarded as constituting a proper part of it, just as legitimately to be recognized by the nation as are the rival ballads of the cavaliers and roundheads by the English in the great civil conflict of their country.[29]

Perpetuators of the romantic tragedy of Southern defeat included Abram Joseph Ryan – known as Father Ryan, "the Poet of the Lost Cause" – who invoked in "The Sword of Robert E. Lee" (1866) "the sleep of our noble slain; / Defeated yet without a stain,"[30] and, in "The Conquered Banner" (1866), drenched the Confederate defeat in pathos:

> FURL that Banner, for 'tis weary;
> Round its staff 'tis drooping dreary;
> Furl it, fold it, it is best:
> For there's not a man to wave it,
> And there's not a sword to save it,
> And there's no one left to lave it

In the blood which heroes gave it;
And its foes now scorn and brave it;
Furl it, hide it – let it rest.[31]

Other Southern approaches to defeat included Sidney Lanier's novel *Tiger-lilies* (1867), in which the arch-nemesis of the protagonist, Philip Sterling, is not a Yankee but rather a fellow Confederate, a deserter who kills Sterling's parents – as if to imply that Southerners' woes were largely brought about by themselves.

For the North, the great tragedy was the loss of the murdered Lincoln, sanctified and canonized through literature as no other American has been. His was the holy blood that cleansed the restored Union; he was, in Whitman's words, the "powerful western fallen star" and the "Captain" thanks to whom "The ship is anchor'd safe and sound, its voyage closed and done."[32] As Deak Nabors argues, Lincoln's martyrdom constituted for Whitman "the basis for an unchallengeable sectional reconciliation," which – as the civil rights struggles of the next century were amply to show – "does not resolve the conflict between the Union and the Confederacy so much as conceal it."[33]

An oft-repeated literary device was the heavy-handed symbolism of romantic reunion represented in the marriage of two characters from opposite sides of the conflict. John W. De Forest's *Miss Ravenel's Conversion from Secession to Loyalty* (1867) brings his heroine, Lillie Ravenel, gradually back into the fold of the reunited nation through her successive marriages to Confederate and Union officers. As the romance concludes: "At last Colburne had his wife, and his wife had her home. For the last four years they have sailed separately over strange seas, but now they are in a quiet haven, united so long as life shall last."[34] Thomas Dixon repeated this outcome in his pernicious novel of 1905, *The Clansman* (the basis for D. W. Griffith's *The Birth of a Nation* [1915]), in which Southern and Northern families are united through marriage in a white supremacist pact against the prospect of black empowerment under Reconstruction – "the challenge of race against race to mortal combat."[35] It was thus clear that by the turn of the century there was little romance to be found in Southern accounts of Reconstruction, whether fictional, like Dixon's, or semi-fictional, like Mary Boykin Chesnut's *Diary from Dixie* (1905), purportedly a diary of the Civil War years, but later found to have been a retrospective memoir written in the 1880s, more accurately reflecting the bitterness of Reconstruction than the war itself.[36]

After Reconstruction

The two decades on either side of 1900 saw a flowering of literature drawing on the Civil War. In *Tales of Soldiers and Civilians* (1891), Ambrose Bierce, former regimental cartographer to the 9th Indiana Volunteers and participant in some of the war's bloodiest engagements, utilized the terrors of combat to explore the bizarre workings of temporal consciousness under stress. Bierce's story "An Occurrence at Owl Creek Bridge" features a condemned Confederate sympathizer, Peyton Farquhar, who relives his life in great detail in the few seconds it takes for him to reach the end of his hanging rope. Twenty-four-year-old Stephen Crane's *The Red Badge of Courage* (1895) – written by a young man who had never seen combat – convinced many that it was based on battlefield memories, although scholars have argued that it is in fact a naturalistic allegory depicting urban, industrial life as naked warfare.

The early twentieth century was remarkable for the literary appropriation of the Civil War for a variety of political and social objectives. Novelists from the South both interrogated the "Lost Cause" project, as in Ellen Glasgow's *The Battle-ground* (1902), and perpetuated it, as in Mary Johnston's homage to Stonewall Jackson, *The Long Roll* (1911). The early decades of progressive and labor activism saw Vachel Lindsay invoking Lincoln in support of workers' rights in "Abraham Lincoln Walks at Midnight" (1914), while in the sprawling verse epic, *John Brown's Body* (1928), Stephen Vincent Benét constructed the war's outcome as the groundwork for a democratic, industrial future. In direct opposition to Northern-dominated industrialism were the "Nashville Agrarians," led in the 1930s by the literary critics and poets John Crowe Ransom, Donald Davidson, Robert Penn Warren, and Allen Tate, the last of whom in such poems as "Ode to the Confederate Dead" (1926) and "To the Lacedemonians" (1936) depicted the New South as a place of dislocation and misery (inevitably implying a nostalgic fondness for the Old South). For their fellow Southerner, William Faulkner, revisiting the Old South – and the war itself – was a much less nostalgic journey. The first of Faulkner's novels set in the mythical Yoknapatawpha county, *Sartoris* (1929), began the exploration of corrupt Civil War myth-making and turbulent consciousness that was continued in *Absalom, Absalom!* (1936), *The Unvanquished* (1938) – his only novel dealing exclusively with the Civil War era – and *Intruder in the Dust* (1948).

In the years of Franklin Roosevelt's New Deal and the Second World War, Lincoln's wartime crisis again proved useful as a model in Robert E. Sherwood's play *Abe Lincoln in Illinois* (1938) and Carl Sandburg's four-volume biography *Abraham Lincoln: The War Years* (1939). Ben Ames Williams's *House Divided* (1947) and Ross Lockridge's *Raintree County* (1948) redirected national attention from the recent war in Europe back to the domestic front, where black veterans who had fought against fascism abroad faced a new struggle for freedom in the still segregated South. Both novels highlighted Southern destabilization with ominous foreboding, as did Robert Penn Warren's *Band of Angels*

(1955), which depicted the turmoil of a Kentucky plantation belle who discovers that her mother had been a slave – hardly a neutral subject in the first year of mass direct action by African-Americans against Southern segregation. The same year, MacKinlay Kantor focused on Southern guilt in his bleak novel about the infamous Confederate prison camp, *Andersonville* (1955). In the context of civil rights, however, not all fingers pointed to the South. The Boston poet Robert Lowell subsumed racism into a broad catalogue of modern American betrayals in "For the Union Dead" (1960), hearkening back to John Berryman's "Boston Common: A Meditation upon the Hero" (1942), which, like Lowell's poem, bitterly muses on the sacrifice of the young Civil War colonel, Robert Gould Shaw.

The centenary of the Civil War occasioned significant reflection, one out-growth of which was the industry of speculative fiction inaugurated by Kantor's extended essay for *Look* magazine, "If the South Had Won the Civil War" (1960). Largely confined to short military essays and science-fiction tales throughout the 1970s and 1980s, alternative Civil War history has witnessed an explosion since the 1990s, with such titles as Harry Turtledove's *The Guns of the South* (1992), Douglas Lee Gibboney's *Stonewall Jackson at Gettysburg* (1997), and the trilogy by ex-Congressman Newt Gingrich and William R. Forstchen, *Gettysburg* (2003), *Grant Comes East* (2004), and *Never Call Retreat* (2005). These works stand in stark counterpoint to more historically faithful fictionalizations such as Michael Shaara's *The Killer Angels* (1974), his son Jeff Shaara's *Gods and Generals* (1996), and the popular trilogy by John Jakes, *North and South* (1982), *Love and War* (1984), and *Heaven and Hell* (1987). The Civil War has inspired parodic treatments by African-Americans understandably skeptical of the "new birth of freedom" notion conventionally associated with it: these include Ishmael Reed's *Flight to Canada* (1976), two plays by Suzan-Lori Parks, *The America Play* (1990) and *Top Dog / Underdog* (2001), and Alice Randall's novel *The Wind Done Gone* (2001), a controversial rewriting of *Gone with the Wind*. The continued intrusion of the Civil War into modern consciousness is reflected in the fiction of Barry Hannah – notably *Airships* (1978) and *Ray* (1980), in which the Civil War and Vietnam dovetail – and in Allan Gurganus's *Oldest Living Confederate Widow Tells All* (1989). The popularity of Charles Frazier's *Cold Mountain* (1997), his Homeric epic set during the Civil War, indicates that this great American conflict has not yet exhausted its literary capacities.

NOTES

1. "The Civil War in Literature," *Benét's Reader's Encyclopedia of American Literature*, ed. George Perkins *et al.* (Glasgow: HarperCollins, 1992), 192.

2. Shelby Foote in *The Civil War*, dir. Ken Burns (Florentine Films, PBS), broadcast September 23, 1990.
3. Creed of the Children of the Confederacy, United Daughters of the Confederacy. Official homepage: www.hqudc.org/CofC/index.html (accessed January 2009).
4. James Ronald Kennedy and Walter Donald Kennedy, *The South Was Right!* (Gretna, LA: Pelican, 2001), 240.
5. Jennifer C. James, *A Freedom Bought With Blood: African-American Literature from the Civil War to World War Two* (Chapel Hill: University of North Carolina Press, 2007), 36.
6. Joseph Stanley Pennell, *The History of Rome Hanks and Kindred Matters* (New York: Scribner, 1944), 36.
7. Walt Whitman, "The Real War Will Never Get in the Books," *Complete Poetry and Selected Prose* (New York: Library of America, 1982), 778.
8. Ibid., 779.
9. Ibid., 286.
10. Richard Marius (ed.), *The Columbia Book of Civil War Poetry* (New York: Columbia University Press, 1994), xix.
11. Hugh Brogan, *The Penguin History of the United States of America* (London: Penguin, 1990), 319; W. E. B. Du Bois, *John Brown* (New York: Modern Library, 2001), 224–5; J. R. Watson and Timothy Dudley-Smith (eds.), *An Annotated Anthology of Hymns* (Oxford University Press, 2002), 366.
12. Herman Melville, "The Portent," *Battle-Pieces* (Edison, NJ: Castle Books, 2000), 11.
13. Mark Twain, *Life on the Mississippi*, ed. Shelley Fisher Fishkin (Oxford University Press, 1996), 469.
14. Quoted in Annie Adams Fields (ed.), *Life and Letters of Harriet Beecher Stowe* (Boston, MA: Houghton Mifflin, 1898), 269.
15. Richard Gray, "Writing Southern Cultures," *A Companion to the Literature and Culture of the American South*, ed. Richard Gray and Owen Robinson (Oxford: Blackwell, 2004), 3–26: 19.
16. Richard Gray, *Writing the South: Ideas of an American Region* (Baton Rouge: Louisiana State University Press, 1997), 27.
17. William J. Grayson, "The Hireling and the Slave," *Selected poems by William J. Grayson, selected and comp. by Mrs. William H. Armstrong, his daughter* (1907), available at the University of Michigan's "Making of America" Digital Books Project, www.hti.umich.edu/m/moagrp (accessed January 2009).
18. Edmund Wilson, *Patriotic Gore: Studies in the Literature of the American Civil War* (New York: Norton, 1994), 468.
19. Albert Pike, "Dixie," *American Poems, 1625–1892*, ed. Walter C. Bronson (University of Chicago Press, 1912), 498.
20. Julia Ward Howe, "The Battle Hymn of the Republic," *Atlantic Monthly* 9/52 (February 1862), 10.
21. DeAnne Blanton and Lauren Cook, *They Fought Like Demons: Women Soldiers in the American Civil War* (Baton Rouge: Louisiana State University Press, 2002), 5.
22. John Greenleaf Whittier, "Barbara Frietchie," in Marius, *The Columbia Book of Civil War Poetry*, 307–8.
23. "Song of the Banner at Daybreak," Whitman, *Complete Poetry and Selected Prose*, 421.

24. "The Wound-Dresser," Whitman, *Complete Poetry and Selected Prose*, 442–3.
25. Melville, *Battle-Pieces*, 224.
26. Ibid., 260.
27. James, *A Freedom Bought With Blood*, 34.
28. Nina Silber, *The Romance of Reunion: Northerners and the South, 1865–1900* (Chapel Hill: University of North Carolina Press, 1993).
29. William Gilmore Simms, "Preface," *War Poetry of the South* (Whitefish, MT: Kessinger, 2004), 9.
30. Abram Joseph Ryan, *Father Ryan's Poems* (1879), available as an e-text at the University of North Carolina's "Documenting the American South," http://docsouth.unc.edu/southlit/ryan/menu.html (accessed January 2009).
31. Ibid.
32. "When Lilacs Last in the Dooryard Bloom'd" and "O Captain! My Captain!," Whitman, *Complete Poetry and Selected Prose*, 459, 467.
33. Deak Nabors, *Victory of Law: The Fourteenth Amendment, the Civil War, and American Literature, 1852–1867* (Baltimore, MD: Johns Hopkins University Press, 2006), 175.
34. John W. De Forest, *Miss Ravenel's Conversion from Secession to Loyalty* (New York: Penguin, 2000), 519.
35. Thomas Dixon, *The Clansman: An Historical Romance of the Ku Klux Klan* (New York: Doubleday, Page, 1905), 275.
36. C. Vann Woodward and Elisabeth Muhlenfeld (eds.), *The Private Mary Chesnut: The Unpublished Civil War Diaries* (Oxford University Press, 1984).

FURTHER READING

Daniel Aaron, *The Unwritten War: American Writers and the Civil War* (New York: Knopf, 1973).
Jim Cullen, *The Civil War in Popular Culture: A Reusable Past* (Washington, DC: Smithsonian Institution Press, 1995).
Alice Fahs, *The Imagined Civil War: Popular Literature of the North & South, 1861–1865* (Chapel Hill: University of North Carolina Press, 2001).
Will Kaufman, *The Civil War in American Culture* (Edinburgh University Press, 2006).
Elizabeth Young, *Disarming the Nation: Women's Writing and the American Civil War* (University of Chicago Press, 1999).

14

TRUDI TATE

The First World War: British writing

Soldiers and civilians

In May 1917, Virginia Woolf published a review in the *Times Literary Supplement* of *The Old Huntsman*, Siegfried Sassoon's first collection of war poems. Sassoon was to become one of the most famous of the British First World War poets, and Woolf was among the first to recognize the importance of his work. No other poet, she writes, has managed to convey so strongly what is "sordid and horrible" about the war. Many others are writing about the conflict, but Sassoon produces "a new shock of surprise" in his readers. "Yes," writes Woolf, we find ourselves saying, "this is going on; and we are sitting here watching it." She describes the "loathing" and "hatred" at work in Sassoon's poetry (a quality some readers at the time and since have criticized as too obvious) and speculates that it shocks readers into thinking about their role as spectators to the sufferings of war, producing "an uneasy desire to leave our place in the audience." In this, Sassoon's poetry is "realism of the right, of the poetic kind."[1]

Woolf's modest article shrewdly notes two areas that are crucial to an understanding of British writings of the First World War (1914–18). Firstly, it was in literature that readers at the time could learn something of what was really happening ("this is going on"). Secondly, Sassoon, Woolf, and many other writers of the period were troubled by the problem of witnessing. Woolf draws attention to the question of who sees what in war, and how the act of witnessing can make one complicit in events over which one has no control. She also raises the continuing question of how war literature should be judged in aesthetic terms. Is it more important that Sassoon is a soldier, writing out of his own experience, or is it primarily as a poet that he should be read?

Sassoon served in the front lines and was profoundly distressed by his experiences. He was even more troubled by the suffering of others and this informs much of his poetry. He frequently describes ordinary soldiers and their struggle just to survive:

> Disconsolate men who stamp their sodden boots
> And turn dulled, sunken faces to the sky
> Haggard and hopeless.[2]

Despite their apparent despair, the men "cling to life with stubborn hands." But inevitably the war will defeat them:

> O my brave brown companions, when your souls
> Flock silently away, and the eyeless dead
> Shame the wild beast of battle on the ridge,
> Death will stand grieving in that field of war
> Since your unvanquished hardihood is spent.[3]

Striving to express both the depth and the sheer pointlessness of the men's endurance, Sassoon imagines that war itself ("the wild beast of battle") will feel ashamed and even Death will grieve the loss. This despairing concern for fellow soldiers, expressed as a complex of love, mourning, and anger, marks much of Sassoon's poetry, and that of other British trench poets, including Isaac Rosenberg, Ivor Gurney, Edmund Blunden, Richard Aldington, Charles Hamilton Sorley, David Jones, and Herbert Read. Wilfred Owen, too, tries to convey the suffering of the troops, describing the experience from within ("we cursed") and without (the men's feet appear "shod" with their own blood), in one of his best-known poems of the war, "Dulce et Decorum Est" (1917):

> Bent double, like old beggars under sacks,
> Knock-kneed, coughing like hags, we cursed through sludge,
> ...
> Men marched asleep. Many had lost their boots
> But limped on, blood-shod.[4]

Virginia Woolf, on the other hand, was a civilian. Many of her friends and relations served; other friends were conscientious objectors or pacifists (Lytton Strachey, Ottoline Morrell, Duncan Grant, Clive Bell, Aldous Huxley, Sidney and Beatrice Webb, Bertrand Russell). Her husband Leonard Woolf was active in the Labour Party and in movements to promote internationalism and peace after the war. Virginia Woolf herself was very ill in the early part of the war, missing much of the news of 1915.[5] When she recovered, she followed events with dismay. Much of her writing thereafter struggles to bear witness to this terrible period, and to warn against warfare in the future. We see this in different ways in *Jacob's Room* (1922), *Mrs. Dalloway* (1925), *To the Lighthouse* (1927), *A Room of One's Own* (1929), and *The Years* (1937), culminating in her most explicit engagement with the problem of war, *Three Guineas* (1938).

Literature and the press

Woolf's 1917 review of Sassoon marks an important moment in literary history. It signals that modernists such as Woolf were profoundly aware of the sufferings of the First World War and were from the beginning interested in the writings of those who served. Above all, Woolf is aware of the distinction between the role of literature and that of the press during the conflict. She makes this point again in 1918, reviewing Sassoon's next collection of poems, *Counter-Attack*. Here, she praises his capacity to show "the terrible pictures which lie behind the colourless phrases in the newspapers."[6] In contrast to the press coverage of the Crimean War, when the newspapers, for the first and last time, revealed the realities of conflict with considerable accuracy and constituted a reliable source of information, British newspaper reporting of the First War was full of lies, half-truths, and propaganda – alongside much that was true. Very often it was impossible to tell the difference. Official government announcements and army dispatches were no more reliable. It took some time for the shocking reality of the worst of the war experience to be known to British civilians. And that knowledge came, in part, through literature.

This is one reason why the literature of the First World War remains so important, both for historians and for literary critics. Writing of the First World War is an important strand in the complex movements of modernism in the early twentieth century. Though often regarded as a highly aestheticized body of writing – even as "art for art's sake" – much modernist literature had a strong interest in the politics and problems of its day. Alongside the more traditional and realist writers of the period, the modernist, experimental, and avant-garde writers of the early twentieth century attempted to bear witness to the war. The literature tries to tell truths that could not easily be expressed elsewhere and marks a groundbreaking period in the history of war writing.

What, then, is meant by the "literature of the First World War?" Several kinds of writing should be included. The work of the trench poets is most familiar; to this important body of literature can be added combatants' memoirs and fiction; memoirs by nurses and other civilian participants; popular, patriotic, and propagandistic writings; pacifist writings; and civilian reflections upon the war experience. Some of these works can be termed modernist; others are more traditional in form. T. S. Eliot's iconic modernist poem *The Waste Land* (1922) is in part a bitter commentary upon a war that left much of European civilization in ruins. It looks too at the uncertainties created by the peace treaties, and the new borders within Europe, which rendered millions of people homeless or stateless – Eliot's "hooded hordes swarming / Over endless plains."[7]

None of these groups of war writing is discrete. But the categories are helpful as a way of indicating the range of discourses of the First World War. And despite the propaganda and inaccuracies, it is also helpful to read the literature in the context of the press of the day in order to make fullest sense of the issues raised by Woolf and Sassoon. Newspapers such as *The Times*, *Manchester Guardian*, *Daily Mail*, *Daily Mirror*, *Daily Telegraph*, and *Daily Chronicle*, and periodicals such as the *TLS*, *Bookman*, *New Statesman*, *Illustrated London News*, *Land and Water*, *Athenaeum*, *Nation*, and *The British Medical Journal*, can assist understanding of the debates which are taking place, explicitly and implicitly, within the literature – and sharpen perception of how the literature takes up and, especially, refutes the language and sentiments of the press.

Impact and responses

The First World War was much greater in geographical scope and in human cost than any previous war. It is often described as the world's first industrial war – that is, war on an industrial scale using industrial technology.[8] Approximately seventy million people served in the war; more than nine million died. Millions more were mentally or physically injured. The nations involved included, on the Allied side, Britain, France, Russia, Serbia, Australia, Canada, India, New Zealand, and, from 1917 to 1918, the United States; and, fighting as the Central Powers, Germany, the Austro-Hungarian Empire, Turkey, and Bulgaria. Much of the war for British troops took place in Belgium and northern France, but the trenches extended far beyond this, from the Belgian coast to the Swiss Alps, a distance of nearly five hundred miles. At the time it was known as the European War or the Great War, but it was in many respects the first true world war, with fighting occurring in Italy, Russia, Turkey, Egypt, Palestine, Persia, Mesopotamia, Cameroon, German East Africa, the North Sea, and the Falkland Islands.[9] As well as vast international forces of troops, there were large labor corps from China, India, the Belgian Congo, Nigeria, Malta, and Egypt that served Britain in all the major war zones. Mortality rates among these workers were high: more than fifty thousand Chinese and Indian workers died on the Western Front; tens of thousands of African laborers died of disease.[10] The war ended with an Armistice at 11 A.M. on November 11, 1918, a moment that is still commemorated in Britain and the Commonwealth with a two-minute silence and the laying of wreaths at war memorials.

Most British writers of the early twentieth century were affected, one way or another, by the First World War. Owen, Sassoon, Rosenberg, Read, Aldington, Blunden, Robert Graves, Edgell Rickword, Ford Madox Ford,

Wyndham Lewis, and many others served in the armed forces. Winifred Holtby and Vera Brittain both served as nurses in the war; both later became activists in the peace movement. Brittain's *Testament of Youth* (1933) is a powerful account of her nursing experiences, and describes the grief and rage of young people who lose beloved friends and family in a war they come to see as without purpose. E. M. Forster served in the Red Cross in Egypt. Somerset Maugham worked as a volunteer in an ambulance unit and later worked for British Intelligence in the war; his short story collection *Ashenden* (1928) draws upon this experience. Novelist Sylvia Townsend Warner worked in a munitions factory; later she became active in the peace movement. Radclyffe Hall, author of *The Well of Loneliness* (1928), contributed to propaganda work and longed to join the women helping at the front. Rudyard Kipling also assisted with propaganda and played an important role in the memorialization of the war and the work of the Imperial War Graves Commission. Other writers who actively supported the war effort include J. M. Barrie, Hilaire Belloc, Arnold Bennett, John Buchan, John Galsworthy, Ian Hay (author of *The First Hundred Thousand* [1916]), Henry James, May Sinclair, H. G. Wells, and Mrs. Humphry Ward.[11]

A number of writers greeted the outbreak of war with patriotic excitement. Probably the most familiar voice is that of Rupert Brooke, a young man who joined up enthusiastically and encouraged others to do the same. His well-known poem "Peace" (late 1914) celebrates the idea that the war is raising young men from the "sleep" of peace and giving them a chance to prove themselves:

> Now, God be thanked Who has matched us with His hour,
> And caught our youth, and wakened us from sleeping,
> With hand made sure, clear eye, and sharpened power,
> To turn, as swimmers into cleanness leaping,
> Glad from a world grown old and cold and weary.[12]

Where other poets found dirt, suffering, and despair, Brooke imagines the war as clean water, the soldiers swimmers leaping joyfully into its depths. Brooke died of illness in April 1915 on his way to the war, without ever engaging in combat. As many people have commented, his enthusiasm for the war was never to be tested by experience. Other young, idealistic soldiers wrote in praise of the war in the early days of the conflict; many changed their views in the light of their service.

Nonetheless, disillusionment was not universal. While much of the best literature tends to be highly critical of the war and its effects, this is not the only view expressed. There were propagandist writers – mainly civilians – who maintained their enthusiasm throughout the conflict and used their writing to urge others to participate. This kind of propagandist writing can be crude, as in Jessie Pope's doggerel verse, "The Call" (1915):

> Who's for the trench –
> Are you, my laddie?
> Who'll follow the French –
> Will you, my laddie?
> Who's fretting to begin,
> Who's going out to win?
> And who wants to save his skin –
> Do you, my laddie?[13]

Owen originally suggested an ironic dedication of his "Dulce et Decorum Est" to Jessie Pope, bitterly denouncing her propagation of the "old lie" that it is "sweet and decorous" to die for one's country. Pope is an extreme example, and an influential one. But not all of the pro-war writings were so unintelligent, nor did they lack nuance. For example, Kipling and May Sinclair produced some subtle works, and sometimes came to challenge, at least implicitly, their own public support for the war. Even the work of Mrs. Humphry Ward, a dedicated propagandist, is more complex than might be expected. Her war books include *England's Effort* (1916), *Towards the Goal* (1917), *Missing* (1917), *The War and Elizabeth* (1918), and *Fields of Victory* (1919); these raise quiet questions about the conflict, even while maintaining an overtly pro-war attitude.[14]

Writers who were pacifists or opposed the war include Vernon Lee (*Satan the Waster* [1920]), Rose Macaulay (*Non-Combatants and Others* [1916]), Rose Allatini (*Despised and Rejected* [1917] [written under the pseudonym A. T. Fitzroy]), John Rodker, Leonard Woolf, Katherine Mansfield, Bertrand Russell, and George Bernard Shaw. The *Cambridge Magazine*, edited by C. K. Ogden, campaigned vigorously against the war and was much criticized for its pacifism.[15]

Literature and experience

Combatants often express the belief that only those who were present can really understand the enormity of the experience. This is no doubt true, and yet some of the most powerful and enduring works of the First World War draw not simply upon the writers' own experiences but on stories they heard from others. Erich Maria Remarque's *All Quiet on the Western Front* (*Im Westen Nichts Neues*) (1929), for example, is a classic of First World War literature. Some of this book is based upon Remarque's war service in the German Army, but much of it derives from what he heard from other soldiers, and from an earlier war book, *Under Fire (Le Feu)* (1916), by Henri Barbusse, a French socialist and journalist who worked as a stretcher-bearer in the front lines. *Under Fire* was immensely influential at the time. It was quickly translated from French into other languages, was probably the most admired book among British servicemen, and by the end of the war had sold close to 250,000 copies.[16]

While those who served in the front lines argued that their experiences were unique, the writing they produced is concerned to share something of that experience, to explain it to others, to memorialize it. In other words, there is a kind of shared memory of the war, a cultural imagining. Some British memoirs and novels by servicemen appeared shortly after the armistice: A. P. Herbert's *The Secret Battle* (1919); Arthur Jenkin's *A Tank Driver's Experiences* (1922); C. E. Montague's *Disenchantment* (1922). A decade or so later, many more works appeared, including R. H. Mottram's *The Spanish Farm Trilogy* (1924–26), Ford Madox Ford's tetralogy *Parade's End* (1924–28), R. C. Sherriff's play *Journey's End* (1928), Edmund Blunden's *Undertones of War* (1928), Richard Aldington's *Death of a Hero* (1929), Charles Carrington's *A Subaltern's War* (1929), Robert Graves's *Goodbye to All That* (1929), Frederic Manning's *The Middle Parts of Fortune* (1929) (published in expurgated form as *Her Privates We* in 1930), Henry Williamson's *The Patriot's Progress* (1930), Guy Chapman's *A Passionate Prodigality* (1933), V. M. Yeates's air force memoir, *Winged Victory* (1934), David Jones's prose-poem *In Parenthesis* (1937), and Wyndham Lewis's *Blasting and Bombardiering* (1937).

Many women wrote books about the war, based on both their own and others' experiences. Alongside the works of Brittain and Holtby, nursing memoirs include Enid Bagnold's *A Diary without Dates* (1918), Irene Rathbone's *We that Were Young* (1932), and the Anglo-American Mary Borden's *The Forbidden Zone* (1929). Journalist Evadne Price wrote a striking novel about women ambulance drivers at the front, *Not So Quiet: Stepdaughters of War* (1930) (published under the pseudonym Helen Zenna Smith), based upon what she had learned from veterans. May Sinclair, then a well-respected and successful author in her fifties, accompanied an ambulance corps to Belgium in 1914. She published her account of this experience as *A Journal of Impressions in Belgium* in 1915. As Suzanne Raitt points out, Sinclair's war experiences were not edifying: she felt quite useless in the ambulance corps. Three of her beloved nephews served and two were killed. But she maintained an enthusiasm for the conflict and wrote several novels which "explore its attractions," including *Tasker Jevons* (1916), *The Tree of Heaven* (1917), and *The Romantic* (1920).[17]

Sinclair's work sits somewhere between modernism and popular fiction. There are many other writers who had no apparent aspirations to high art or explorations of human complexity, and their work is another element of the literary history of the First World War. As Jane Potter has shown, there was a huge body of romantic, propagandist, and popular fiction, much of it by women – escapist, morale-boosting, sometimes highly implausible, sometimes speaking to the realities of readers' lives (especially civilians) during the war. Writers of such fiction include Ruby Ayres, Olive Dent, Kate Finzi, Marie Belloc Lowndes, and Berta Ruck.[18] Popular fiction supposedly describing military or spy experiences, such as John Buchan's thrillers, W. E. Johns's Biggles books, and Ian Hay's *The First Hundred Thousand*, often promote the "cheery Tommy" view of the war as both a serious call and a great lark. Some popular war books, such as the Bulldog Drummond stories by "Sapper" (H. C. McNeile, an ex-soldier), were popular among veterans after the war.

Other combatant writers express disgust at the lies and fantasies circulating among civilians, cynically promoted, in many cases, to boost recruitment and suppress dissent. How could those involved put the record straight? Soldiers' letters were strictly censored. Often they did not feel able to talk about their experiences when they came home on leave, partly because civilians could be skeptical about their stories, which differed so greatly from the fictions in the press. As Robert Graves remarks in *Goodbye to All That*, when he was sent home in 1916 to recover from his wounds, "England looked strange to us returned soldiers. We could not understand the war-madness that ran wild everywhere ... The civilians talked a foreign language; and it was newspaper language."[19] For Graves, serving the nation paradoxically left him feeling a stranger in his homeland. This was a common view. Britain expected a good deal from the young men and women who served, but seemed to offer little in return. Many veterans found themselves unemployed, impoverished, with little support or recognition. Many were troubled by the long-term effects of war injuries. Thousands were traumatized by the war and suffered long-term mental illnesses, known at the time as "shell shock" or war neurosis.

War neurosis or "shell shock"

Both soldiers and civilians wrote about the terrible effects of war trauma. Wilfred Owen's "Mental Cases" (1918) asks:

> Who are these? Why sit they here in twilight?
> Wherefore rock they, purgatorial shadows,

> Drooping tongues from jaws that slob their relish,
> Baring teeth that leer like skulls' teeth wicked?
> ...
> These are men whose minds the Dead have ravished.

Owen cunningly begins by implying that it is those who see the patients, rather than the patients themselves, who suffer, as if witnessing damage were worse than experiencing it. But his sympathy is entirely with the mentally injured soldiers, who stand as a reproach to an uncaring society. The poem concludes with an image of the traumatized veterans "plucking at each other" and "Snatching after us who smote them, brother / Pawing us who dealt them war and madness."[20]

In similar vein, Ivor Gurney writes:

> There are strange Hells within the minds War made
> Not so often, not so humiliatingly afraid
> As one would have expected.

Gurney suggests the pain and isolation of the "strange Hells" created by war trauma, but, at the same moment, he comments that combatants were not always afraid, nor traumatized, by their terrible experiences. The poem invokes both tremendous resilience and complete collapse. Gurney concludes with a sad and angry account of life for many veterans after the war:

> Where are they now on State-doles, or showing shop patterns
> Or walking town to town sore in borrowed tatters
> Or begged. Some civic routine one never learns.
> The heart burns – but has to keep out of face how heart burns.[21]

Whose "heart burns"? Is the poem speaking in the voice of the neglected veterans or from the point of view of an observer? Why must the justifiable anger implied in "the heart burns" be hidden ("has to keep out of face how heart burns")? Gurney's characteristically elliptical style makes the political point all the more strongly.

Richard Aldington, by contrast, writes angrily and directly about conditions for veterans immediately after the war. His short story "The Case of Lieutenant Hall" (in *Roads to Glory* [1930]) is narrated by a soldier immediately after the armistice. In March 1919, Lt. Hall writes in his diary: "It has been very strange, returning to England, civilian life and ways, after the tremendous physical and moral efforts of the past years." He suffers from nightmares, hallucinating the face of a German soldier he has killed. Peacetime life seems abnormal now:

> All this existence in London seems most unreal. What gave a false appearance of reality to our life in the line was that we were not – at least directly – merely slaves of the economic idea.

Even now, it is difficult for ex-soldiers to get employment. Many of us are in a
rotten state, and quite unfit to perform those actions which would enable us to
"pay our way."

Hall regrets being so eager to come home and wonders if those who died in the
war are actually the lucky ones. He remarks bitterly that civilians make fun of
demobilized soldiers, mocking them for the difficulties in adapting to civilian
life. Aldington's character is clearly traumatized by his war service. The lack
of support or understanding in civilian life makes his condition worse and
eventually he commits suicide.[22]

The trauma of war is as old as war itself, but it was not until the First World
War that it came to be seen as a serious medical problem, and this only after
considerable resistance by military and medical authorities. Traumatized
soldiers were sometimes seen as cowardly or mutinous rather than ill. Some
were shot as cowards or deserters. But the sheer numbers of men suffering
from mental illness induced by their war experiences eventually forced the
authorities to take "shell shock" seriously and to seek medical cures rather
than military punishment. War trauma, then, is an old–new ailment, taking
new forms in the theater of industrial warfare and, it seems, far more prevalent than in previous wars. The precise reason for this is unknown, but it
might be that the experience of the First World War trenches forced soldiers
into extremes of passivity – in effect, waiting to be shelled – at the same time as
the war demanded immense courage, resourcefulness, and action. Threatened
constantly with death or mutilation, frequently witnessing the grotesque
deaths of their friends and companions, men often felt at the mercy of
immense machines that always seemed to be winning.

The problem of trauma continued for many years after the war and is
explored by writers in the 1920s. One of the most notable novels on the
subject is Virginia Woolf's *Mrs. Dalloway* (1925), parts of which present
postwar Britain from the point of view of a war-traumatized veteran,
Septimus Warren Smith. Woolf explores Septimus's experience within the
social and political context of the early 1920s, asking who remembers and
who forgets the sufferings of the war – and who should take responsibility?
Clarissa Dalloway's husband is a Conservative MP, part of a government
which Woolf felt had done badly in the years immediately after the war. Who
pays the price for the bunglings of war and peace? Not the Dalloways and
their circle (which includes the prime minister of the day, an unnamed portrait
of Stanley Baldwin), despite Woolf's often sympathetic representations of
Clarissa. Like many soldier-writers of the day, Woolf here suggests that
combatants were expected to make superhuman sacrifices in the war and
were given little help in coping with life afterwards.

An earlier novel by Rebecca West is one of the first attempts to represent First World War neuroses in fiction. In *The Return of the Soldier* (1918), wealthy officer Chris Baldry is shell-shocked and loses much of his adult memory. This leads to a curious class comedy as he yearns to be with his girlfriend from youth, a girl from a lower social class who is now a dowdy married woman. A doctor proposes an unconventional cure. The soldier should be confronted with an object associated with an earlier trauma – a toy belonging to his son, who died in infancy. One trauma will supposedly mend another. Improbably, this remedy works. Comedy turns to muted tragedy as he returns to his loveless, joyless, middle-class marriage. West's book is compelling, but should not be regarded as an accurate representation of war trauma. Rather, West takes the emerging idea of shell shock to explore other issues, such as memory and class.

For a number of writers, war trauma is the dreadful culmination of a century or more of modern industrialization. The marvelous achievements of science and technology, the immense industrial capacities developed through the nineteenth century, are turned to the specific purpose of destruction. As the narrator in Helen Zenna Smith's *Not So Quiet* complains:

> I see my own father – a gentle creature who would not willingly harm a fly – applaud the latest scientist to invent a mechanical device guaranteed to crush his fellow-beings to pulp in their thousands.[23]

It is important to recover the shock and dismay many people felt at the time. The pinnacle of industrialization was not, as had been hoped at, say, the time of Great Exhibition (1851), peace, prosperity and progress, but the end of civilization, the death and mutilation of immense numbers of people, and the destruction of vast areas of landscape.

Generational hostility

What was all this for, people wondered? And what would become of the young people who served in the war? Smith's narrator in *Not So Quiet* volunteers as an ambulance driver at the front. At twenty-one, she knows nothing of life "but death, fear, blood, and the sentimentality that glorifies these things in the name of patriotism."[24] What sort of future can these women, and the damaged men they look after, expect, and what is expected of them? Smith's expression of resentment can be found in many other literary works of the war, especially those written by men and women sent to serve by an older generation that remained safely at home.

This idea is given its most powerful expression in Wilfred Owen's poem "The Parable of the Old Man and the Young" (1918). Owen begins by retelling the Genesis story of Abraham (Abram) being called upon to sacrifice his only son, Isaac. The father obeys, unprotesting: "So Abram rose, and clave the wood, and went, / And took the fire with him, and a knife." When Isaac wonders "where the lamb, for this burnt-offering?," Owen shifts the story into the present day of the war: "Then Abram bound the youth with belts and straps, / And builded parapets and trenches there, / And stretched forth the knife to slay his son." An angel calls out, as in the biblical story, that the son's life should be spared. But in this version, Abram does not listen: "But the old man would not so, but slew his son, / And half the seed of Europe, one by one."[25] The fathers (and in other works, mothers, too) are held responsible for the war and the suffering of the younger generation. In "Lament" (1920), F. S. Flint writes bluntly:

> The young men of the world
> Are condemned to death.
> They have been called up to die
> For the crime of their fathers.[26]

Curiously, Rudyard Kipling says something similar in his "Epitaphs of the War" (1919). Kipling writes as a father who keenly supported the war. He went to some effort to get his son John accepted into the army. John was killed on his first day of battle. "If any question why we died, / Tell them, because our fathers lied."[27] Kipling never openly changed his views about the rightness of the war. These lines are probably intended as a comment upon Britain's failure to prepare adequately for what he regarded as the necessary war with Germany. But they eerily echo the young writers' resentment of an older generation that took the nation to war, for which the younger generation paid the price. Generational hostility is one of the things most remembered about British literature of the First World War; it continues to speak to young people called to serve in combat and to all those opposed to war. And it is a subject which writers returned to in the late twentieth century – for example, in Pat Barker's *Regeneration* trilogy (1991–95), Sebastian Faulks's *Birdsong* (1994), and Robert Edric's *In Desolate Heaven* (1997).

Writing the landscape

As well as blaming their human parents for the disaster of the war (with considerable historical justification), soldiers' writings also represent the land itself as a kind of mother – as in Ivor Gurney's "Strange Service" or "England the Mother" in his collection *Severn and Somme* (1917) – and the devastated war zones are remembered as a maternal body. The land protects the men, but also threatens to suffocate or drown them in its mud (most powerfully represented in Ford's *Parade's End*). In return for this ambiguous nurturing, the men and their machines attack the land, and one another within it, making their surroundings even more unstable and dangerous. This motif of the maternal land is used in highly complex ways to express the sheer destructive power of the First World War. Isaac Rosenberg's "Dead Man's Dump" (1917) imagines the earth in a frenzy of "savage love" when it is under bombardment:

> Manic earth! howling and flying, your bowel
> Seared by the jagged fire, the iron love,
> The impetuous storm of savage love.
> Dark Earth! dark Heavens! swinging in chemic smoke,
> What dead are born when you kiss each soundless soul
> With lightning and thunder from your mined heart,
> Which man's self dug, and his blind fingers loosed?[28]

Out of the " iron love" and "savage love," a perverse birth – the dead.

Destruction of the land is also used to stand for the death and mutilation of the men who try to shelter within it. Blunden, Gurney, Edward Thomas, and many others drew upon a long tradition of pastoral to try to describe the devastation of the First World War. They mourn the land, and also use it to remember, to bear witness to the often unspeakable effects of the war upon human beings. In Blunden's "The Ancre at Hamel: Afterwards" (1925), the speaker listens to the river Ancre, the site of immense suffering, "grieve and pine":

> As if its rainy tortured blood
> Had swirled into my own,
> When by its battered bank I stood
> And shared its wounded moan.[29]

As the speaker regrets the violence enacted upon the land, the land itself is called upon to mourn.

Conclusion

British literature of the First World War remains immensely powerful, still speaking to readers, and indeed to combatants, in the twenty-first century. It tries to articulate the trauma of industrial warfare, raising questions that are still pertinent. As Gurney asks in his poem "War Books" (c.1925), "What did they expect?":

> What did they expect of our toil and extreme
> Hunger – the perfect drawing of a heart's dream?

> Did they look for a book of wrought art's perfection,
> Who promised no reading, nor praise, nor publication?
> Out of the heart's sickness the spirit wrote
> For delight, or to escape hunger, or of war's worst anger.[30]

What did combatants and civilians expect from the First World War? How did they respond to its excitement (even ecstasy) as well as to its profound sufferings and disappointments? And what did they expect from their war writers? No one knew quite what would come out of the war or the peace that followed, but whatever one expected, the pain and disappointment were profound. The literature tries to express this complex of feelings and to grapple with the fact that, for writers as for other citizens, their faith in civilization had been permanently damaged.

NOTES

1. Virginia Woolf, "Mr. Sassoon's Poems," *Times Literary Supplement* (May 31, 1917); rptd in *The Essays of Virginia Woolf*, ed. Andrew MacNeillie, 4 vols. (London: The Hogarth Press, 1987), II: 120.
2. Siegfried Sassoon, "Prelude: The Troops," *Counter-Attack and Other Poems* (London: William Heinemann, 1918); rptd in Sassoon, *Collected Poems 1908–1956* (London: Faber, 1961), 67.
3. Sassoon, *Collected Poems*, 67.
4. Wilfred Owen, "Dulce et Decorum Est," *The Complete Poems and Fragments*, ed. Jon Stallworthy, 2 vols. (London: Chatto & Windus, The Hogarth Press, Oxford University Press, 1983), I: 140.
5. Hermione Lee, *Virginia Woolf* (London: Chatto & Windus, 1996), ch. 19.
6. Woolf, "Two Soldier-Poets," *Times Literary Supplement* (July 11, 1918); rptd in Woolf, *The Essays of Virginia Woolf*, II: 269–72.
7. T. S. Eliot, "The Waste Land" (ll. 366–8), *Collected Poems 1909–1962* (London: Faber, 1974), 77. See Stan Smith, *The Origins of Modernism* (London: Harvester Wheatsheaf, 1994).
8. Daniel Pick, *War Machine: The Rationalisation of Slaughter in the Modern Age* (New Haven, CT: Yale University Press, 1993).
9. Trevor Wilson, *Myriad Faces of War: Britain and the Great War, 1914–1918* (Cambridge: Polity, 1986); Michael Howard, *The First World War* (Oxford University Press, 2002); John Turner (ed.), *Britain and the First World War* (London: Unwin Hyman, 1988).
10. These figures come from Martin Gilbert, *The Routledge Atlas of the First World War*, 2nd edn. (London: Routledge, 1994), 136.
11. See Peter Buitenhuis, *The Great War of Words: Literature as Propaganda 1914–18 and After* (London: Batsford, 1989).
12. Rupert Brooke, *The Collected Poems* (London: Sidgwick & Jackson, 1989), 312.
13. Jessie Pope, *Jessie Pope's War Poems* (London: Grant Richards, 1915), 38.
14. Helen Small, "Mrs. Humphry Ward and the First Casualty of War," *Women's Fiction of the Great War*, ed. Suzanne Raitt and Trudi Tate (Oxford University Press, 1997), 18–46.

15. Grace Brockington, "Translating Peace," *Publishing in the First World War*, ed. Mary Hammond and Shafquat Towheed (Basingstoke: Palgrave, 2007), 46–58.

16. Samuel Hynes, *A War Imagined: The First World War and English Culture* (London: Bodley Head, 1990), 205; Trudi Tate, *Modernism, History and the First World War* (Manchester University Press, 1998), 69–70.

17. Suzanne Raitt, "'Contagious Ecstasy': May Sinclair's War Journals," Raitt and Tate, *Women's Fiction of the Great War*, 65–84: 66.

18. Jane Potter, *Boys in Khaki, Girls in Print: Women's Literary Responses to the Great War 1914–1918* (Oxford University Press, 2005).

19. Robert Graves, *Goodbye to All That* (Harmondsworth: Penguin, 1988), 188.

20. Owen, *The Complete Poems and Fragments*, I: 169.

21. Ivor Gurney, "Strange Hells," *The Penguin Book of First World War Poetry*, ed. Jon Silkin (London: Penguin, 1979), 114.

22. Richard Aldington, "The Case of Lieutenant Hall" (1930); rptd in Trudi Tate (ed.), *Women, Men and the Great War* (Manchester University Press, 1995), 77–91: 88, 90.

23. Helen Zenna Smith, *Not So Quiet: Stepdaughters of War* (London: Virago, 1988), 165.

24. Ibid.

25. Owen, *The Complete Poems and Fragments*, I: 174.

26. Silkin, *The Penguin Book of First World War Poetry*, 142–3.

27. Rudyard Kipling, "Epitaphs of the War: Common Form," *Rudyard Kipling's Verse: Definitive Edition* (London, Sydney, Auckland, Toronto: Hodder & Stoughton, 1940), 390.

28. Rosenberg, "Dead Man's Dump," Silkin, *The Penguin Book of First World War Poetry*, 206–8. These lines are omitted in the most recent edition of Rosenberg's collected work: *The Poems and Plays of Isaac Rosenberg*, ed. Vivien Noakes (Oxford University Press, 2004), 141.

29. Silkin, *The Penguin Book of First World War Poetry*, 107–8.

30. Ivor Gurney, "War Books," *Best Poems and the Book of Five Makings*, ed. R. K. R. Thornton and George Walter (Manchester: MidNAG, Carcanet, 1995), 83; see R. K. R. Thornton, "'What did they Expect?'," *Ivor Gurney: Poet, Composer*, ed. Kate Kennedy and Trudi Tate (special issue of *Ivor Gurney Society Journal*) (2007), 1–18.

FURTHER READING

Hugh Cecil, *The Flower of Battle: British Fiction Writers of the First World War* (London: Secker & Warburg, 1995).

Debra Rae Cohen, *Remapping the Home Front: Locating Citizenship in British Women's Great War Fiction* (Boston, MA: Northeastern University Press, 2002).

Santanu Das, *Touch and Intimacy in First World War Literature* (Cambridge University Press, 2005).

Paul Fussell, *The Great War and Modern Memory* (Oxford University Press, 1985).

Angela K. Smith, *The Second Battlefield: Women, Modernism and the First World War* (Manchester University Press, 2000).

15

PATRICK QUINN

The First World War: American writing

War and the American tradition

In his 1893 address to the World's Columbian Exposition in Chicago, "The Significance of the Frontier in American History," Frederick Jackson Turner observed that American territorial expansion westwards – the country's "Manifest Destiny" – had ended due to the simple fact of reaching the sea. To avoid stagnation, Turner argued, the country would have to turn to commercial proliferation overseas. The frontiersman spirit embodied in such figures as Andrew Jackson, Daniel Boone, Davy Crockett, and Sam Houston would be translated into economic imperialism. One proponent of this policy was Theodore Roosevelt, President from 1901 to 1909. Famed for his derring-do during the Spanish-American War (1898), Roosevelt asserted the values of the rugged individual in his book *The Strenuous Life* (1899). He would become one of the leading advocates of American entry into the First World War, while the pioneering spirit, recuperated from obsolescence, would form part of its cultural background.

American jingoistic and patriotic literature

When the First World War broke out in Europe in 1914, most Americans were caught off-guard. President Woodrow Wilson, a Democrat, immediately affirmed the United States's neutrality. While most Americans concurred with his stance, many American newspapers characterized the conflict as a clash between the democratic Allies and the autocratic Central Powers. The *New York Tribune*'s dashing war correspondent, Richard Harding Davis (a veteran reporter of the Greco-Turkish and Spanish-American Wars), was sent to the European front and published his observations in *With the Allies* (1914). While claiming objectivity, Davis nevertheless blamed the "German militaristic mind" for the outbreak and stressed that German political ideals were opposed to the democratic ones of France and England (neglecting to

175

mention Tsarist Russia). The book was pro-Allies, but it did not advocate American intervention in this European war.

Using the example of "raped" Belgium and highly charged political rhetoric concerning mankind's responsibilities, Teddy Roosevelt and former US Army Chief of Staff Leonard Wood led a strong lobby supporting American involvement in the war. Supporters of Roosevelt and Wood included Brand Whitlock, US ambassador to Belgium. Whitlock's best-seller *Belgium under the German Occupation* (1919) is filled with stock anti-German generalizations and prejudices. The description of the victorious German troops marching into Brussels on 20 August 1914 is typical of his inflammatory language: "And this was Germany … this dread thing, this monstrous anachronism, modern science yoked to the chariot of autocracy and driven by cruel will of the pagan world."[1]

Throughout the war and even after its conclusion, American writers portrayed Germany as the only nation that wanted and was prepared for war. Even the former muckraker Ida Tarbell's *The Rising of the Tide* (1919) suggested that Germany had been forty years in preparing for the conflict. Her conclusions were likely shaped by Owen Wister's influential *The Pentecost of Calamity* (1915). Wister's novel offers some sympathy with German domestic and social life before the war, but also claims that, since the Franco-Prussian War (1870–71), Germans had accepted Prussian militaristic philosophy and embraced the teachings of Nietzsche, Machiavelli, and Treitschke. The imbibing of these philosophies had resulted in a soulless Teutonic mentality that glorified the state and the Kaiser. This mechanistic blindness was the cause of German atrocities in Belgium.

Among the first American First World War atrocity novels was Robert W. Chambers's *Who Goes There!* (1915), an adventurous spy story with setting and situation borrowed from newspaper reportage. The executed Belgians are all innocent townsmen, while the German officer, von Reiter, is a stereotypical Prussian officer, who shows no mercy. More atrocity tales occur in *My Home in the Field of Honour* (1916), a purportedly biographical chronicling of what the American writer Frances Wilson Huard witnessed during the exodus of refugees from Belgium, and Mildred Aldrich's collection of letters, *A Hilltop on the Marne* (1915). In both works, German barbarity is recounted in almost lovingly sensuous detail, and any claim to objectivity is nonexistent. These images were dredged up repeatedly when America declared war on the Central Powers in April of 1917 – for example, in Gouverneur Morris's *His Daughter* (1918).

A pivotal event influencing the American public's support for war with Germany was the sinking of the *Lusitania* in 1915. No matter that the ship was carrying high explosives and transporting Canadian soldiers to England (both acts in contravention of the Neutrality Act), the initial perception of a German U-boat sinking a defenseless passenger ship prevailed, and countless short stories, plays, poems, and novels were written depicting this action. Joyce Kilmer's poem "The White Ships and the Red," which appeared in the *New York Times* on May 16, gives sympathetic voice to the sinking ship:

> My wound that stains the waters,
> My blood that is like flame,
> Bear witness to a loathly deed,
> A deed without a name.[2]

J. Hartley Manners's play *God of My Faith* (1917) and W. J. Dawson's popular novel *War Eagle* (1918) both emphasized the barbarity of the attack and the consequences for the innocent Americans on board. In Samuel Hopkins Adams's novel *Common Cause* (1919), German-Americans' complacency about the tragedy spawns a fictional outburst that suggests that they are not to be trusted. Indeed, German-Americans are characterized in a great deal of the fiction of the period as the "enemy within." This concept was naturally fertile material for spy novels, in which nefarious agents working as fifth columnists do deeds of destruction to the American war effort. *The Red Signal* (1919) by Grace Livingston Hill Lutz and Alice Brown's *The Black Drop* (1919) both involve red-blooded Americans pluckily foiling direct challenges to American civilization. The finest in this genre is Mary Roberts Rinehart's *Dangerous Days* (1919). Rinehart captures the materialism rife in America in 1916, chronicles the gaiety and selfishness of the period, and frames the work with the story of a German-American cousin's sabotage.

Other novels about German-Americans concern the struggles of an American child of German parentage to overcome the pull of German blood that blinds him or her to the true menacing aspirations of the Central Powers. George Rothwell Brown's adventure novel *My Country* (1917) and Arthur Stanwood Pier's *The Son Decides* (1918) both demonstrate the need for the children of German families to negotiate their heritage and embrace the democratic beliefs entrenched in the American way of life. The most careful, conscientious, and well-documented study of German-Americans' experience during the war is *The Hyphen* (1920) by Lida C. Schem (Margaret Blake), an intricate novel dealing with the problem of mixed blood.

Preparedness

If the threat from German-Americans within the United States was on people's minds, so was the fear of invasion from without. In early 1915, Theodore Roosevelt published a series of newspaper articles under the title

Why America Should Join the Allies. Pleading with President Wilson to upgrade the woefully undermanned and underfunded American military, Roosevelt argued that, if Germany won in Europe, she would immediately invade the United States. The substance of Roosevelt's articles became the foundation for the pro-interventionist platform of "preparedness" on which he would unsuccessfully campaign for the Republican presidential nomination in 1916.

Still, the call for preparedness was strident. After the publication of Roosevelt's *America and the World War* (1915), dozens of works appeared describing what America's fate would be were she not prepared for the German conquest of the world. One of the first was Hudson Maxim's *Defenseless America* (1915). Maxim advanced the thesis that Americans would lose their valuable freedom unless the country's shores were ringed with adequate defenses. This theme was taken up in John Bernard Walker's novel *America Fallen!* (1915). While the plot seems outrageous to the modern audience, with German submarines successfully attacking New York, the Panama Canal, Boston, Norfolk, Charleston, and Pensacola, and holding New York ransom for $5 million, reviewers took it seriously, and the novel fed a frenzy of invasion fear. Cleveland Moffett's *The Conquest of America* (1916) and Thomas Dixon's *The Fall of a Nation* (1916) supplied readers with images of battleships and submarines disgorging millions of German soldiers onto American soil. On a more constructive note, in *The Three Things* (1915), Mary Shipman Andrews suggested that some intellectual snobs might jettison some of their racist tendencies if they served in the military. Her work is a paean for a new world of equal opportunities for all Americans.

War declared

Following the extensive propaganda, many Americans felt relieved when America finally declared war on Germany. Germany had been demonized so successfully that when the Zimmerman telegram[3] was exposed and Germany decided to return to unrestricted submarine warfare, most Americans agreed that a lesson had to be taught. Conveniently, America already had her first literary martyr in place. Alan Seeger had died in 1916 fighting for French civilization against the bloodthirsty Hun. Seeger became the poster-boy for the ennobling virtues of war, and his poems "The Aisne" (1914–15) and "I Have a Rendezvous with Death" (1916) were widely quoted. Seeger's willingness to embrace death for a worthy cause touched many American youths:

> I have a rendezvous with Death
> On some scarred slope of battered hill,

> When Spring comes round again this year
> And the first meadow-flowers appear.[4]

Similar sentiments are found in Joyce Kilmer's "Rouge Bouquet" (1918) and, touched with cynicism, in John Peale Bishop's "In the Dordogne" (1933).

Once the United States entered the war, the cause had to be made worthy of the sacrifice. The propaganda machine found two particularly rich themes to exploit. The first was that this was a war to save democracy; the second was that the conflict would serve as a purging agent for the crass materialism and slackness that had fallen over Americans since the country's founding. In Alice Brown's *Bromley Neighborhood* (1917), the ramifications of war reach an isolated New England community and help to eradicate the pettiness and emptiness of daily existence. Irving Bacheller's *The Prodigal Village* (1920) is set in the winter of 1916–17 and explores with high seriousness how hedonism has corrupted Bingville. Thanks to the war, individuals live cleaner and less materialistic lives.

In *The Builders* (1919), Ellen Glasgow also reaffirms the war as a cleansing agency. The novel propagates the view that a finer, more equitable society will emerge from the crucible of war, that the United States has an opportunity to snatch the spiritual initiative from the corrupt Europeans and impose American values and leadership over the civilized world. Theodore Roosevelt's friend Edith Wharton attempted in her novels *The Marne* (1918) and *A Son at the Front* (1923) to persuade Americans that French civilization resembled their own and was therefore worth saving. Wharton uses a blood transfusion metaphor extensively in *The Marne*: the American Republic pours forth from the reservoirs of the New World her willing and courageous troops "to replenish the wasted veins of the old."[5]

As US losses accelerated, American fiction, almost exclusively written by noncombatants, began to echo the idealistic propaganda that had sustained the American war effort from the day war was declared. *The American* (1919) by Mary Dillon offers a credible example of how serving the American cause would help immigrants achieve full fellowship with their "real" American counterparts.

Postwar reaction and antiwar literature

By the middle of 1919, even an ailing President Wilson had to admit that these idealistic visions of a finer and better democratic world were not about to materialize. The United States had failed to ratify the Versailles Treaty, and Wilson's Fourteen Points, a blueprint for European peace, were largely ignored. Now there appeared American literature that suggested that the war had not lived up to politicians' promises. Ironically, much of the sham and illusion of the American war experience had already been foreseen in Randolph Bourne's celebrated essay "The War and the Intellectuals" (1917). For Bourne, and subsequently for most American authors writing about the conflict, the blame for America's joining of hostilities belonged to those intellectuals who had not argued for a strict neutrality policy, but who had foisted their class prejudices on the masses, promising that the American entry was free from any taint of self-seeking. Bourne believed the claim that the war was being fought to support democracy instead of the greedy interests of big business and industry along the eastern seaboard to be a class-ridden lie.

Upton Sinclair's much maligned novel *Jimmie Higgins* (1919) closely mirrors Bourne's analysis. Jimmie, a devoted socialist who eventually volunteers, serves, and is wounded while being transported to Europe, is portrayed as a victim of capitalist dogma. Tortured by the American Army because they believe he is disseminating communist propaganda, he eventually goes mad. Two novels similar in tone and theme were written by a volunteer ambulance driver who joined the American Expeditionary Forces just as the war was ending. John Dos Passos's *One Man's Initiation: 1917* (1920) and *Three Soldiers* (1921) are early examples of fiction reflecting growing disillusionment with the patriotic vision of the war effort and beginning to construct the myth of "the Lost Generation." *One Man's Initiation* is a series of impressionistic sketches chronicling ambulance driver Martin Howe's increasing disenchantment. Advocating pacifism, Dos Passos is sexually explicit and liberal in his use of profanity. *Three Soldiers* is a vitriolic attack on the military machine that encourages three honest men to enlist and then proceeds to ruin them with senseless disciplinary restrictions. The overriding theme is the wastage of human potential; by the conclusion of the novel, all three soldiers are either under arrest or crazy.

Unsurprisingly, Dos Passos would favorably review e.e. cummings's account of his detention in a Normandy prison camp for writing letters home about the poor morale of the French troops in 1917.[6] Cummings was a volunteer with the Norton-Harjes ambulance corps, and his novel *The Enormous Room* (1922) is a fictionalized account of that detention camp experience. This experimental novel jettisons the veneer of realism and replaces it with a disjunctive use of language that accurately reflects the prisoners' hysteria and fear. In "my sweet old etcetera" (1926), cummings turns his scorn onto his self-righteous family who pushed him into uniform to show their support for the American cause. As a result, the soldier-speaker finds himself up to his knees in French mud, dreaming of his girl and her

"Etcetera."[7] The sheer frustration and despair felt by these writers is summed up by Ezra Pound, a noncombatant, in "Hugh Selwyn Mauberley" (1920):

> There died a myriad,
> And of the best, among them,
> For an old bitch gone in the teeth,
> For a botched civilization.[8]

A year after *The Enormous Room*, Thomas Boyd's action-packed *Through the Wheat* (1923) appeared, an early chronicle of personal battlefield experience. Boyd had served with the Marine Corps in the front lines, and his novel concludes with an incident in France when the Fourth Brigade was ordered forward into enfilading machine-gun fire through endless fields of wheat. In the tradition of Stendhal's depiction of Waterloo in *The Charterhouse of Parma* (1839), the story focuses on the odyssey of an individual soldier in a particular battle. Private Hicks is a rifleman who is not at all sure why he is in this war or why he should go through the wheat fields into what appears to be suicide, but he does it nonetheless. The novel foregrounds the young, inexperienced Hicks as he is initiated into horrendous deaths, festering wounds, fetid odors, rats and lice, and terrible hunger.

Another naturalistic novel based on personal experience is Laurence Stallings's *Plumes* (1924). A captain in the Marine Corps, Stallings lost a leg at Belleau Wood. The novel is set mostly in Washington, where Richard Plume attempts to understand and protest the cultural forces that set the war in motion and cost him his leg. His reflections on his heritage make him realize that war has always been a part of his family's experience: his grandfather had fought under General Andrew Jackson and his father under General Robert E. Lee. Richard himself left his pregnant wife in order to find glory for himself and his country. However, he has come back shattered and will face comparative poverty due to his government's neglect of veterans. The novel condemns the War Department's indifference to the soldiers who have been wounded by their experiences in body and soul. It is clearly didactic in its antiwar sentiment, but also demands that writers cease romanticizing conflict. Stallings's call for realism can also be observed in a play he co-wrote with Maxwell Anderson. *What Price Glory* (1924) depicts the brutality of battle and the animal nature of man that lurks just beneath the veneer of civilized behavior.

A rich crop of First World War novels appeared in the United States during 1926. One which caused quite a stir was Elliot White Springs's *War Birds: Diary of an Unknown Aviator*. It was probably the most popular novel about the war in the air, and the plot, setting, and characters were appropriated in films such as *Wings* (1927) and *Dawn Patrol* (1930). One reason for its popularity was the description of the dissipated life pilots led as they faced death almost daily on their missions. True to the spirit of the times, Springs details the heavy drinking and loose sex available to the modern "knights of the air." But he also exposes the combat fatigue that prematurely aged the young airman and the violence of death at 5,000 feet in the air.

Another novel of 1926 which tried to capture the harrowing nature of war at its most violent was Hervey Allen's *Toward the Flame*. The reader is once again back with the infantry, this time for six weeks with the Twenty-Eighth Pennsylvania Division as they tramp, bivouac, and fight in the summer of 1918. Allen's fictional memoir of his division's march inland from the French coast to the insignificant village of Fismette, where a disastrous battle is fought, is a moving tribute to the men of the Twenty-Eighth Pennsylvania, who had no training in open warfare and died for little reason.

Though he joined first the Canadian and then the Royal Air Force, William Faulkner never saw active duty in the war, but he experienced its reverberations in the rural South. *Soldiers' Pay* (1926) deals with the aftermath of the armistice and the difficulties American soldiers had in adjusting to civilian life after the horrors of the Western Front. Donald Mahon, a severely wounded fighter pilot, is the focus of the novel. His family believes he has been killed in action, but somehow he survives with little memory of his prewar life in Charleston, Georgia. The novel tracks his slow degradation through the spring and summer of 1919. Not only is he slowly dying physically, but he is an embarrassment to his family and his fiancée, Cecily Saunders, who cannot bear to look at his facial scars. Eventually, she will marry a noncombatant, leaving the moribund Donald to marry Margaret Powers, who feels guilty about wanting to leave her former husband before she was informed of his death on the battlefield. She becomes his "soldier's pay." In this novel and in *Sartoris* (1929), Faulkner traces the mental and emotional condition of returning veterans – their nervousness, their craving for heightened sensations to relieve their memories, and their stinging awareness of the futility of their sacrifice.

Weak vision rendered Ernest Hemingway unable to join the American Expeditionary Forces, but he volunteered in the spring of 1918 to drive an ambulance for the American Red Cross in Northern Italy. In July, he was injured by an Austrian trench mortar shell and hospitalized in Milan, where he fell in love with an American nurse, Agnes von Kurowsky, who became the model for Catherine Barkley in his 1929 novel *A Farewell to Arms*. This semi-autobiographical tale tells the story of Frederic Henry, an American ambulance driver wounded on the Italian front, and his love affair with his nurse Catherine as he recuperates. Once healed, he returns to the front, where he is caught up in the chaos of the Caporetto retreat and nearly shot as a spy. With difficulty, he returns to his lover, finding Catherine pregnant with their child. The only hope of escape from the Italian authorities is to row stealthily into Switzerland by nightfall. Upon successful arrival, they steal a few idyllic days before Catherine dies giving birth to a stillborn baby. For Henry, as for all the "Lost Generation," the existential realization dawns that the only way to survive in the modern godless world is to be faithless and cynical.

One of the most effective antiwar works of the 1930s was written by one of the most decorated Marines in the history of the Corps. William March published *Company K* (1933) as a denunciation of the bravery myths that continued to cling to memoirs and stories about the First World War. *Company K* is a series of 113 brief sketches, each of which bears the name of a member of the company. The unsentimental sketches are told in the first person and demonstrate repeatedly that war is not glamorous, that it is an economic boon for business back home, and that it is the most horrific phenomenon man has ever created. The work is preoccupied with the unmitigated violence and ugly, obscene deaths that war generates. Death can happen by gunshot, gas, grenade, bayonet, machine gun, bombs, or high explosive. Soldiers commit suicide and murder prisoners in cold blood.

But the United States's preoccupation in the 1930s was the Depression and its consequences: American experience of the 1914–18 conflict was largely assimilated. Though some works appearing in the decade did refer to the First World War – for example, Charles Yale Harrison's *Generals Die in Bed* (1930) and Dalton Trumbo's horrific *Johnny Got His Gun* (1939) – by now this was an antiwar literature which looked forward as much as back.

NOTES

1. Brand Whitlock, *Belgium Under German Occupation: A Personal Narrative by Brand Whitlock* (London: William Heinemann, 1919), 81.
2. Joyce Kilmer, *Main Street and Other Poems* (New York: George H. Doran, 1917), 74.
3. A telegram from the German Foreign Minister instructing the German ambassador in Mexico to propose an alliance against the United States.
4. Alan Seeger, *Poems* (London: Constable, 1917), 144.
5. Edith Wharton, *The Marne* (New York: Appleton, 1918), 17.
6. John Dos Passos, "Off the Shoals," *The Dial* 73 (July 1922), 97–102.
7. e. e. cummings, *Complete Poems 1910–1962*, ed. George J. Firmage, 2 vols. (London, Toronto, Sydney, New York: Granada, 1973), I: 275.
8. Ezra Pound, *Selected Poems 1908–1959* (London: Faber, 1975), 101.

FURTHER READING

Peter Buitenhuis, *The Great War of Words: British, American, and Canadian Propaganda and Fiction, 1914–1933* (Vancouver: University of British Columbia Press, 1987).

Charles A. Fenton, "A Literary Fracture of World War I," *American Quarterly* 12.2 (1) (Summer 1960), 119–32.

Charles V. Genthe, *American War Narratives, 1917–1918* (New York: D. Lewis, 1969).

Meirion Harries and Susie Harries, *The Last Days of Innocence: America at War, 1917–1918* (New York: Vantage, 1997).

David M. Kennedy, *Over Here: The First World War and American Society* (Oxford University Press, 1980).

David Lundberg, "The American Literature of War: The Civil War, World War I, and World War II," *American Quarterly* 36.3 (1984), 373–88.

Patrick Quinn, *The Conning of America: The Great War and American Popular Literature* (Atlanta, GA: Rodopi, 2001).

Jeffrey Walsh, *American War Literature, 1914 to Vietnam* (London and Basingstoke: Macmillan, 1982).

16

VALENTINE CUNNINGHAM

The Spanish Civil War

All wars capture the imagination, get aestheticized, inspire literature. But none more so than the Spanish Civil War (July 18, 1936 to April 1, 1939). This short-lived conflict was almost instantly read, across the globe from Santiago de Chile to Moscow, as the ultimate battleground for democracy, freedom, modernity, and art against reaction, oppression, censorship, old power, and repressive (especially religious, Roman Catholic) tradition. Spain was the apogee of what W. H. Auden, England's foremost young poet, had labeled "this hour of crisis and dismay."[1] Spain was, as Auden put it in "Spain," the most famous English poem to appear about the war, where "the menacing shapes of our fever / Are precise and alive."[2]

Worldwide fascism was the essence of the "crisis." The Left had long been preaching the need for writers to take up history's challenge, commit their whole being – time, energy, bodies, as well as their art – to resisting fascism by "going over" wholeheartedly to the side of "the people." The military rising of General Franco against Spain's republican government, amply assisted by his Italian and German allies, brought that demand to a head.[3] If the Right wasn't stopped in Spain, where would fascism's push end? Very many intellectuals, writers and other artists responded to the challenge.

Of course the Spanish Civil War was not the Poets' War it was sometimes billed as. Most of its participants – including the majority of the 40,000–60,000 international volunteers, most of whom were with the communist-organized International Brigades – were not intellectuals or writers or artists. But the war certainly involved – and divided – the literary and cultural worlds as no war before it. Writers and artists took sides:[4] one hundred and twenty-seven authors declared themselves FOR the republican government in the 1937 *Left Review* survey organized by Nancy Cunard, Louis Aragon, Heinrich Mann, Pablo Neruda, Auden and Stephen Spender, published as *Authors Take Sides on the Spanish War*. They included Mulk Raj Anand, Auden, George Barker, Samuel Beckett, Cecil Day Lewis, Havelock Ellis, Ford Madox Ford, David Gascoyne, Geoffrey Grigson, Aldous Huxley,

John and Rosamond Lehmann, Rose Macaulay, Hugh MacDiarmid, Louis MacNeice, Charles Madge, Arthur Calder-Marshall, Sean O'Casey, Llewellyn Powys, V. S. Pritchett, Herbert Read, Edgell Rickword, Spender, Rex Warner, Sylvia Townsend Warner, and Leonard Woolf. The survey unearthed only a handful of Franco supporters, most notably Arthur Machen, Edmund Blunden, and Evelyn Waugh, whose convert-Catholic proclivities had him supporting the English Catholic upper classes' organization of backing for what they saw as Franco's Christian crusade against socialism and atheism. Even if certain other known Francoists had appeared – like Roy Campbell, the egregious, right-wing, homophobic, pseudo-tough-guy author-to-be of the posturing *Flowering Rifle: A Poem from the Battlefield of Spain* (1939) (a field on which he never actually fought) – the Franco party would still be tiny.

Genuine neutrals, such as H. G. Wells and Charles Morgan, were also scarce. Sean O'Faolain, T. S. Eliot, and Ezra Pound were included as "Neutral?" – though O'Faolain's contemptuous insistence on artistic individuality, Pound's rant about Spain as "an emotional luxury to a gang of sap-headed dilettantes," and Eliot's remaining "isolated" though "naturally sympathetic," all merit more than that question mark. George Orwell's own rant about the "bloody rot" of the survey got edited out. Some writers, like Graham Greene, chose not to reply at all. This genuinely split man, a socialist and a Catholic, reserved fire until a December 10, 1937 *Spectator* article, "Alfred Tennyson Intervenes," in which he dwelt ironically on the dangerous folly of Tennyson and his fellow Cambridge Apostles aiding Spanish exiles against the Bourbon oppressor back in 1830. But still the English picture was clear – not much Francoism, few neutrals, lots of republican enthusiasm. And this proportion was true of the whole cultural world. The clutch of French right-wing Catholic novelists supporting Franco – François Mauriac, Pierre Drieu La Rochelle, and Robert Brasillach – is characteristically small, as well as uncharacteristically rather good.

Culture was plainly on the Republic's side. The host of writers who toured republican Spain in July 1937 as the Second Congress of the International Association of Writers, organized by the great Chilean poet Pablo Neruda, indicate just how much.[5] This crowd of intellectual supporters included Spender, Rickword, Claud Cockburn, Valentine Ackland, and Sylvia Townsend Warner from Britain; Malraux, André Chamson, Julien Benda, and René Blech from France; the exiled Germans Ludwig Renn and Erich Weinert; Octavio Paz and his wife Elena Garro from Mexico; the Russians Ilya Ehrenburg, Alexei Tolstoy, and Mikhail Koltsov; and of course the distinguished Spanish poets Antonio Machado, Miguel Hernández, and Manuel Altolaguirre. "Hard lines Azana!" Roy Campbell jeered at the

Republic's president in a poem published in the first number of Oswald Mosley's fascist *British Union Quarterly*: "The Sodomites are on your side, / The cowards and the cranks."[6] But actually the pro-republicans were some of the very best, as well as some of the most promising, of the world's writers and artists: participants in what quickly became the Spanish War of words and images, a contention of poems, novels, photographs, films, music, and painting, they produced often momentous works.

Siding with the Republic often meant direct action. The Irish republican writers Thomas O'Brien, Alec Digges, and Seán Ó hEidirsceoil went over to fight. So did the London communist Miles Tomalin, "poet of the International Brigade," (he edited the English version of the International Brigade paper *Volunteer for Liberty*). Irish poet Ewart Milne drove an ambulance all through to the end of the war. Spender joined the Communist Party in a blaze of publicity and went over seeking radio propaganda work in Valencia, translated Spanish poems, wrote a fine series of poems and elegies, and edited with John Lehmann the influential *Poems for Spain* (1939). Orwell fought with the Independent Labour Party-associated anti-Stalinist Partido Obrero de Unificación Marxista (POUM) militia, was badly wounded by a bullet in the throat, got caught up in the notorious 1937 May Days in Barcelona when the communists tried to wipe out their POUM opponents, was on the run in Barcelona evading Stalinist hit men, and produced a whole chain of "beans-spilling" articles and the best of the many documentary-autobiographical accounts of the war, *Homage to Catalonia* (1938). Auden went out intending to drive an ambulance ("I shall probably be a bloody bad soldier"),[7] did some propaganda work in Valencia, came home speedily, shocked by Barcelona's churches burned out by republicans, and wrote "Spain," which, more than any other Spanish War text, captures the dark side of the "struggle" to which the volunteers it celebrates had traveled so sacrificially. Ernest Hemingway certainly visited the trenches; was photographed at least handling weapons; wrote and spoke the sound track for the important propaganda-documentary film *The Spanish Earth*, made with Joris Ivens and John Dos Passos; wrote a set of tough-guy short-story-like articles for the North American Newspaper Agency, the play *The Fifth Column* (1938), and the novel *For Whom the Bell Tolls* (1940) about an American International Brigader on a suicidal bridge-blowing mission.[8]

For his part, André Malraux, famous French flyer and novelist, became colonel of the small republican air force; flew many combat missions; and speedily produced his epic novel about the fight on the ground and in the air, *L'Espoir* (1937) (translated as *Days of Hope* and *Man's Hope*) – which he immediately turned into a propaganda-documentary film in Barcelona in 1938. Laurie Lee, itinerant Gloucestershire musician, fought with the

International Brigaders, and was pressed into serving with the Stalinist hit men – dark truths about which he divulged very belatedly, to the great vexation of communist veterans, in his third autobiographical volume, *A Moment of War* (1991).[9] Clive Branson, communist painter and poet, was captured to spend eight months in a Franco prison camp, where he wrote a wonderfully pathetic series of prisoner poems, published posthumously in 1980 to take their rightful place in modern incarceration literature.[10] Claude Simon, a young French communist, fought only briefly, but with telling effect on his long career as a war-obsessed novelist, the Spanish conflict infiltrating *Le Palace* (1962) and his (late) military-horror bricolage fiction *Le Jardin des plantes* (1997), as well as *Les Géorgiques* (1981), the great and greatly perverse novel rewriting and rebuking Orwell's *Homage to Catalonia* from the standard communist perspective.

The German writer Ludwig Renn commanded the German Thälmann Battalion in the successful early defense of Madrid and became chief of staff of the XIth International Brigade. Gustav Regler, another exiled German, became political commissar of the XIIth International Brigade, producing in 1940 his great fact-fiction about the defense of Madrid, *The Great Crusade*. The Russian Mikhail Koltsov, "Stalin's Man in Spain," managed also to produce the communist-enthusing 1938 memoir, *Diary of the Spanish War*. The period in Spain of the young religious leftist French schoolteacher Simone Weil was short-lived and disappointing – she joined Durutti's Anarchist Flying Column, had her gun and fighter's overalls confiscated, was confined to the cookhouse, and was horribly burned by hot cooking oil; she was horrified too by republicans torturing and killing Francoists. She was deeply moved by the leading French Catholic novelist Georges Bernanos's *Les Grands Cimetières sous la lune* (*A Diary of My Times*) (1938), stunning record of the Nationalist terror he had witnessed on Mallorca, where he lived, and which turned this rightist into that rare period cross-breed, a Catholic republican. Her Spanish knowledge profoundly marked Weil's later career as Christian mystic.[11]

Inevitably, some of these active writers and artists were killed in action. The first Briton to be killed in the war was the young socialist artist Felicia Browne, who was in Barcelona when the Right rose up, wangled her way into a republican militia, and was shot while trying to blow up a train.[12] The violinist George Green was killed at the end of September 1938 in the disastrous Battle of the Ebro.[13] Around New Year 1937, the just-graduated Cambridge communist John Cornford was mowed down on the Cordoba front (leaving a handful of compelling political lyrics, including "Heart of the heartless world / Dear heart, the thought of you," addressed to his communist girlfriend Margot Heinemann, one of the most moving soldierly love poems in the English language).[14] Early in 1937, Ralph Fox, biographer, translator, novelist, *Daily Worker* columnist, founder editor of the left-wing cultural journal *Left Review*, was machine-gunned dead at Lopera; Christopher St. John Sprigg, writer of aeronautical books and thrillers, who had driven an ambulance down to Spain, leaving behind with his publisher Britain's first extended work of Marxist literary criticism, *Illusion and Reality*, to be published posthumously under his *nom de plume* of Christopher Caudwell, was killed on the chaotic first day of the Battle of the Jarama; and Charles Donnelly, IRA activist from Tyrone, author of a group of poems on Irish selfhood and modern violence, was shot dead on the Jarama front. In June 1937, the Hungarian novelist Mate Zalka, known as General Lukács, commandant of the XIIth International Brigade, was killed by a shell while supervising the republican attack on Huesca. In mid-July of that year, Julian Bell, nephew of Virginia Woolf, a young socialist poet with two volumes of verse under his belt, was fatally wounded during the unsuccessful Brunete offensive.

Death came for writers, from start to finish, because they put themselves in the firing line. The war began with perhaps the most momentous of writer's deaths – the assassination by nationalist militiamen on the night of August 18–19, 1937 of Spain's most important poet and playwright, the surrealist modernist Federico García Lorca – with extra bullets in the buttocks because he was homosexual.[15] "Federico fell dead / – blood on his face, lead in his bowels," as Antonio Machado put it in his outraged memorial poem about this "Crime in Granada" – the event which pushed Neruda into the heart of the republican cause, just as it pushed the cause into his heart – *España en el corazón* as his November 1938 collection of Spain poems declared it. The poetic war culminated with the deaths of Machado in exile in the south of France and Hernández in a Franco jail. Reminders of the deadly kinship between this war and writers was proven not least in the war's most world-disconcerting event – the destruction – just days after Malraux's *L'Espoir* came out in March 1937, with its adulation of fighting flyers – of Guernica by bombs. This worst act of war terrorism to date became the most written about and photographed event of modern warfare up until then. It was indeed the first act of modern total war: the destruction of a whole town from the air by the latest German bombing and fighter planes; the killing and injuring of hundred and hundreds of civilians, the old, women, and children included. The triumph of fascist militarism, it was a complete technical success according to its mastermind – none other than the First World War German air-ace, Lieutenant-Colonel Wolfram von Richthofen, Hitler's favourite air chief-to-be, cousin of Manfred von Richthofen, the German air-ace known as the Red Baron, who was a cousin of Frieda von Richthofen, who was Mrs. D. H. Lawrence.

Here was the total warmonger as appalling practitioner of the visionary apocalyptic bloodlusts of his English cousin-by-marriage.

Total war: the shock of the militarily new, and in Spain. Here were the very
latest military technics, and they ran in parallel with the latest technics of
communication and art, of text-making. The latest art of war was not to be
outdone by the latest arts of war. Malraux obviously thinks the point of
L'Espoir will be the more effective as a movie; Hemingway and Dos Passos
will write their newspaper articles and books, but meanwhile they're rushing
to get *The Spanish Earth* into the world's picture houses. Auden keeps
exploiting the written word, but it's the Valencia radio station he heads for,
and the fetching republican poster-art which really catches his eye:

> Altogether a great time for the poster artists and there are some very good
> ones ... in photomontage a bombed baby lies couchant upon a field of
> aeroplanes.[16]

In photomontage. This war was indeed, as Claud Cockburn dubbed it, a
photogenic one. Photographs dominate the texts of Spanish reportage, such as
G. L. Steer's foundational *The Tree of Gernika* (1938) and Arthur Koestler's
L'Espagne ensanglantée (1937) (forerunner of his *Spanish Testament* [1937]) –
photographic images precisely like the one on the Valencia poster Auden
describes, which kept on getting, parasitically, into Spanish writing. George
Barker's "Elegy on Spain" (1940), dedicated "to the photograph of a child
killed in an air raid on Barcelona," is clearly an ekphrasis of that same photo.[17]
This photo was, probably, one of that group of atrocity photos issued by the
republican government which prompted the appalled Spanish War meditations
in Virginia Woolf's pacifistic *Three Guineas* (1938).[18] It is arresting how many
poems describe that or similar photos – Spender's "The Bombed Happiness"
(1939), Herbert Read's "Bombing Casualties in Spain" (1939), F. L. Lucas's
"Proud Motherhood (Madrid, AD 1937)" (1939). Notable, too, is how far the
ekphrastic urge of Spanish writing extends – Claude Simon describing in *Les
Géorgiques* a well-known photograph of volunteers entrained for Spain;
Anthony Powell describing the film *The Spanish Earth* for readers of *Night
and Day* magazine (August 19, 1937); Bernard Gutteridge describing it in his
poem "Spanish Earth" (1939); Graham Greene reviewing newsreels about
Spain (*Spectator*, September 29, 1939); the heaps of contending words from
the likes of art critics Antony Blunt and Herbert Read about the most momentous pictorial works emerging from the war when they were exhibited in
London on their world tour, namely Picasso's vast montage of anguish and
pain, *Guernica* (1937), and its accompanying preparatory etchings, *Sueña y
Mentira de Franco* (etchings themselves accompanied by an ekphrastic poem
by Picasso – here was ekphrasis piled upon ekphrasis).[19]

So, dramatically new kinds of writing, apt to the newnesses of this conflict? Margot Heinemann evidently thought so. Her poem for the dead John Cornford urges that we "Grieve in a New Way for New Losses" (1937). Poetic grief, in this new kind of war – especially new, she thinks, in its socialist, unbourgeois aspects – is, then, to be different from the old kind, as to form and content? Only up to a point. Most striking is how much the new wine of this new totalizing revolutionary conflict arrives in the oldest of generic bottles, namely as texts of witness-bearing, testimony, autobiography, report, and elegy.

In terms of physical bulk, the I-narrating texts of witness dominate. How they pour out, and almost overnight, the memories, diaries, testifyings: Frank Pitcairn's *Reporter in Spain* (1936), John Sommerfield's *Volunteer in Spain* (1937), Esmond Romilly's *Boadilla* (1937), Koestler's *Spanish Testament* (1937), Cecil Gerahty's *The Road to Madrid* (1937), Orwell's *Homage to Catalonia* (1938), Dos Passos's *Journeys Between Wars* (1938), Jef Last's *The Spanish Tragedy* (1939), all meeting the immediate 1930s market for travel writing, reportage, document. Later arrivals were Spender's *World Within World* (1951), Regler's *The Owl of Minerva* (1959), Jason Gurney's *Crusade in Spain* (1974), T. A. R. Hyndman (Spender's friend, the "Jimmy Younger" of *World Within World*) in Philip Toynbee's collection *The Distant Drum: Reflections on the Spanish Civil War* (1976), Lee's *A Moment of War*, and so on.

Their collective boast is Franz Borkenau's: *The Spanish Cockpit* (1937) is characteristically subtitled *An Eye-Witness Account of the Political and Social Conflicts of the Spanish Civil War*. "I have seen – I've seen with my own eyes," Bernanos insists in *A Diary of My Times*. Photographic evidence afforces the verbal testimony – like those photographs of bomb ruins and German shell-cases in *The Tree of Gernika*. Hemingway's journalism and *The Spanish Earth* flaunt his being-thereness, as does his novel – and Malraux's: the novel as hard news. Poetry like MacNeice's *Autumn Journal* (1939) has the same air of reportage. "And the day before we left / We saw the mob in flower in Algeciras / Outside a toothless door, a church bereft / of its images and its aura," sounds like his January 20, 1939 *Spectator* report of the last days of Barcelona.[20]

It is telling that so many writers went to Spain to act as news correspondents – Ernst Toller, Martha Gellhorn, Antoine de St. Exupéry, Jay Allen, Steer, Hemingway, Dos Passos, Orwell, Jef Last – and that so much of the best reporting texts came from them.[21] It is no surprise that their books incorporate material that appeared earlier in newspapers, as in *The Tree of Gernika* and Koestler's *Spanish Testament*, nor that their narratives feature so much the behavior of journalists. From their perspective, Spain was a kind of journalists' war. Much of *Homage to Catalonia* is devoted to contesting journalistic untruths: the *Daily Mail's* poster "REDS CRUCIFY NUNS"; manufactured Stalinist "shit" about the POUM from Ralph Bates (distinguished novelist of peasant Spain and a commissar in the International Brigade) and in John Langdon Davies's *News Chronicle* stories about POUM troops firing first in May 1937, when "I and many others saw" the POUM being shot at first.[22]

What was at stake was a distorting politicization of language that would lead straight to the Newspeak of *Nineteen Eighty-Four*; what Koestler labeled the Grammar of Fiction: the persuading of people, in Swift's formula, to say the thing which is not – the trauma of Koestler's great post-Spain novel *Darkness at Noon* (1940). A pit of lies it was, apparently, rather easy to get political partisans to fall into, putting party advantage before truth-telling. Koestler himself fell into it. His *Spanish Testament* is contaminated from the start with its opening talk of his being a liberal journalist and arranging with the *News Chronicle* to gain entry to Seville. In fact, he was a communist agent and propagandist in the pay of Willi Münzenberg, the official Comintern organizer. He wasn't alone – for instance, the reports of "Frank Pitcairn" for the *Daily Worker* and his *Reporter in Spain* were really from the pen of Claud Cockburn, loud mouthpiece of the Comintern.

Per contra, despite all of the persistent communist efforts to undermine his reliability, Orwell's narrative does stack up. Spectacularly so, in fact, as Claude Simon's underminings of Orwell's veracity in *Les Géorgiques* and in his notorious interview in *The Review of Contemporary Fiction* (*Homage* is "faked from the very first sentence"; Orwell can't have met the Italian soldier and joined the POUM in the Lenin Barracks because they didn't exist)[23] all crumbled in the face of the Barcelona photographer Agustí Centelles's pictures being unearthed (literally) and showing Orwell right there in the Caserne Lenin with his POUM comrades. The "ring of truth" resounding through Orwell's writing – that massively authenticating trademark capacity of his to be candid about his own side's faults and failings – keeps getting vindicated. Propagandists whose propagandizings make them stand loose to the truth – on the Left but much more so on the Right (think Roy Campbell, for a start) – lack this capability of not flinching from dark sayings about one's own people: that unflinching acknowledgment of Auden's of the Left's "conscious acceptance of guilt in the necessary murder" in "Spain" (political murder, mind, not just killing);[24] or Hemingway's unexcelled early narrative in *For Whom the Bell Tolls* of republicans forcing local fascists over the cliffs; or Orwell's blunt admission that "The only apparent alternatives are to smash dwelling houses to powder, blow out human entrails and burn holes in children with lumps of thermite, or to be enslaved by people who are more ready to do these things than you are yourself."[25]

In such reports tragedy segues into that other (and ancient) Spanish mode, namely elegy. Elegy, the melancholy mode of absence and loss, celebrating death – of persons, friends, loved ones, comrades, and also of hopes, dreams, faith. Elegy intrudes everywhere, swamping the poems, the memorializing pages, and more and more so as the war continues and the death toll mounts: the writing of death – which negates presence, creates absences, tears holes. "He is Dead and Gone, Lady," as Donagh McDonagh's elegy for Charles Donnelly puts it, in the words of Ophelia's lament for her dead father.[26] "Where is Ralph Fox of Yorkshire?"; "Where is John Cornford of Cambridge?"; "Where is Syd Aylmer of Stoke Newington?":[27] Jack Lindsay's "Requiem Mass: For the Englishmen Fallen in the International Brigade" (1938) is a litany for the missing of the war – poem as war memorial, listing the names of the absent in a (vain) attempt to grant them some continuing presence. "Grieve in a new way?" This sounds remarkably like the old way. The bereft poet is as pierced, as punctured with grief as any widowed relict of the tradition.

These Spanish wartime elegies are especially mindful of the ruinous holes made in bodies and things by weaponry – the holes made by thermite in those Orwellian children; the bullet holes in the body of assassinated Lorca; everywhere the holes made by bullet and shrapnel in soldiers' spoiled bodies. "I will sing thy fleshless bones / thy eyeless holes" – that's Machado in "The Crime Took Place in Granada" (1938).[28] Elegy gives us too the punctures of the city, massively holed by the destructive technics of the new total war – "the meccano framework" of the bombed city in Steer's memorable metaphor about Guernica's burned-out buildings.[29] The bombed city as meccano: the photographs from Guernica and other bombed Spanish cities are dementing emblems of all the puncturings and holings of Spanish hopes and desires.

Naturally enough there were many attempts to sound some sort of positive note in the teeth of the pervading sense of ruin and loss that marks the best of the Spanish survivors' and onlookers' texts. "We excavate our story, give a twist / To former endings in deliberate metre, / Whose subtle beat our fathers could not count," insists Roy Fuller's staunch elegy for his communist friend Maurice Stott, "Poem (For M. S., Killed in Spain)" (1938).[30] The poem declares that this friend, who in a real sense took stay-at-home Fuller's political hopes and dreams with him to Spain (he's "noblest" of the Blackpool socialist friends in Fuller's memoir Vamp till Ready [1982]), died as "the hero." In a dream, the poet even sees "my friend rising from the tomb."[31] So the republican dream can be thought of as living on, even though M. S. is emphatically dead, along with his dreams, and the poet's – but living on only in elegy's peculiar way. The leaves of summer, in Randall Jarrell's "A Poem for Someone Killed in Spain" (1942), "are passionate / With the songs of the world where no one dies."[32] And poetry, especially this elegiac poetry of melancholy loss, does indeed survive. It is the essence of the elegiac text to live on after its subject. That it can manage its own surviving, but not its subject's, is its irony – the marked irony of the Spanish texts of memory. They live on, they sing on; but their living noise mocks the silence of their subjects.

Spain endures in the living heart of the survivor and in his poem, his *Himno a las glorias del pueblo*, as the subtitle of Neruda's *España en el corazón* has it. Spain lives on in those voices of the London Cooperative Chorus at the London Festival of Music for the People (April 5, 1939), joined in the words of Auden and Randall Swingler in Benjamin Britten's Opus 14, "Ballad of Heroes," composed for the returning remnants of the British section of the International Brigades. "Honour, honour them all ... they die to make men just / And worthy of the earth," they sang, Swingler's lines echoing Tennyson's great heroic "Ode on the Death of the Duke of Wellington" (1852), and penetrated with recall of Christ's positive, redemptive piercings on the cross.[33] But still these positive notes were inerasably penetrated by elegy's perennial and inevitable sense of permanent losses, losses signified in the defeated remnant the music and those words were for – physically broken men, limbless many of them, veterans pierced, too, with grief for absent comrades. That marred and tattered remnant was a substantive manifesto, a set of terrible metonyms, of the downbeat end of their great cause – signifiers in the flesh of that elegiac note of loss, degradation, and ruin which is the final note of so much Spanish writing.

In the unforgettable final, elegiac words of England's most potent Spanish poem, the one by Auden himself, the survivor of this great historical cause was "left alone," defeated, bereft of comrades, allies, former hopes; and

> History to the defeated
> May say Alas but cannot help nor pardon.[34]

NOTES

1. W. H. Auden, "August for the People," *The English Auden. Poems, Essays and Dramatic Writings 1927–1939*, ed. Edward Mendelson (London: Faber, 1977), 157.
2. Valentine Cunningham (ed.), *The Penguin Book of Spanish Civil War Verse* (Harmondsworth: Penguin, 1980; rev. edn. 1996), 99. Auden revised the original poem, "Spain," as "Spain 1937."
3. See Antony Beevor, *The Spanish Civil War* (London: Orbis, 1982); Paul Preston, *A Concise History of the Spanish Civil War* (London: Fontana, 1996).
4. See Valentine Cunningham, *British Writers of the Thirties* (Oxford University Press, 1988), 418–61; Robert Stradling, *History and Legend: Writing the International Brigades* (Cardiff: University of Wales Press, 2003).

5. See Niall Binns, *La Llamada de España: escritores extranjeros en la Guerra Civil* (Barcelona: Montesinos, 2004).
6. Roy Campbell, "Hard Lines, Azana!," *The British Union Quarterly* 1.1 (January–April 1937), 104.
7. Auden, Letter to E. R. Dodds (December 8, 1936) (Bodleian MS Eng. lett. c. 464), 8.
8. See William White (ed.), *By-Line: Ernest Hemingway: Selected Articles and Dispatches of Four Decades* (London: Collins, 1968).
9. See Richard Baxell, *Laurie Lee in the International Brigade: Writer or Fighter?* Third Len Crome Memorial Lecture (March 6, 2004) (London: International Brigade Memorial Trust, 2004).
10. Cunningham, *The Penguin Book of Spanish Civil War Verse*, 211–20.
11. Valentine Cunningham (ed.), *Spanish Front. Writers on the Civil War* (Oxford University Press, 1986), 253–7.
12. Tom Buchanan, "The Lost Art of Felicia Browne," *History Workshop Journal* 54 (2002), 180–201.
13. See Nan Green, "Death on the Ebro," Cunningham, *Spanish Front*, 235–42.
14. Cunningham, *The Penguin Book of Spanish Civil War Verse*, 110.
15. See Ian Gibson, *The Assassination of Federico García Lorca* (London: W. H. Allen, 1979).
16. Auden, "Impressions of Valencia," *New Statesman & Nation* 13 (January 30, 1937), 159.
17. Cunningham, *The Penguin Book of Spanish Civil War Verse*, 157.
18. Cunningham, *Spanish Front*, 223–6.
19. Cunningham, *Spanish Front*, 191–3, 208–11, 212–13, 211–12, 213–20.
20. Cunningham, *The Penguin Book of Spanish Civil War Verse*, 456.
21. See *Corresponsales en la guerra de España 1936–1939* (Madrid: Instituto Cervantes, 2006), catalogue of an exhibition about the Spanish War correspondents at the Instituto Cervantes, Madrid.
22. George Orwell, *Homage to Catalonia*, *The Complete Works of George Orwell*, ed. Peter Davison, 20 vols. (London: Secker & Warburg, 1986–98), VI: 208, 238.
23. Anthony Cheal Pugh, "Interview with Claude Simon: Autobiography, The Novel, Politics," *The Review of Contemporary Fiction* 5.1 (1984), 9.
24. Cunningham, *The Penguin Book of Spanish Civil War Verse*, 100.
25. Orwell, "Terror in Spain," *Time and Tide* (February 5, 1938), 177.
26. Cunningham, *The Penguin Book of Spanish Civil War Verse*, 175.
27. Ibid., 175.
28. Ibid., 205.
29. Cunningham, *Spanish Front*, 137. "Meccano" is the name of a British toy model construction kit, the pieces of which are perforated at half-inch intervals.
30. Cunningham, *The Penguin Book of Spanish Civil War Verse*, 190.
31. Ibid., 190, 191.
32. Cunningham, *Spanish Front*, 343.
33. Boris Ford (ed.), *Benjamin Britten's Poets: The Poetry He Set to Music* (Manchester: Carcanet, 1996), 67–70.
34. Cunningham, *The Penguin Book of Spanish Civil War Verse*, 99.

FURTHER READING

Valentine Cunningham, *British Writers of the Thirties* (Oxford University Press, 1988).

H. Gustav Klaus (ed.), *Strong Words Brave Deeds: The Poetry, Life and Times of Thomas O'Brien, Volunteer in the Spanish Civil War* (Dublin: O'Brien, 1994).

Alberto Lázaro (ed.), *The Road from George Orwell: His Achievement and Legacy* (Bern: Peter Lang, 2001).

Peter Preston, *Doves of War: Four Women of Spain* (London: HarperCollins, 2002).

Robert Stradling, *History and Legend: Writing the International Brigades* (Cardiff: University of Wales Press, 2003).

17

MARK RAWLINSON

The Second World War: British writing

Unlike the First World War, Britain's Second World War did not have, nor has it acquired, a hegemonic setting. Vera Brittain and Stephen Spender both thought that the no-man's-land of their war, its "background," was the bombed city, an equation that is fulfilled in the extraordinary air-raid climax to James Hanley's novel *No Directions* (1943). All three writers were civilians (Spender volunteered in the Auxiliary Fire Service). That their writing from wartime London has moral and historical authority says a good deal about the heterogeneity of the literary record of the Second World War, and the variety of possibilities for reading it. This is thrown into relief by comparisons with the writing of the First World War, which is still appraised largely in terms of the values and experience of the combatant.

It was claimed that the literature of the Second World War would only repeat that of the First World War (Keith Douglas, in "Desert Flowers," a poem paying homage to Isaac Rosenberg); that it would only be "created after war is over" (Douglas again); and even that the war "will have no literature" (a character in Elizabeth Bowen's 1941 story "Sunday Afternoon").[1] Robert Graves thought it unlikely poets would "write horrifically about it," given broad assent to the struggle against Nazi Germany.[2] Later it would become a convention that writing of the Second World War was inferior to that of the First, an act both of forgetfulness, as Alun Munton has pointed out, and of presumption about what war writing should be like.[3] Wartime skepticism about war literature points to another qualification. This literature is still being written sixty years on, and its contents and forms are still being determined: Ian McEwan's *Atonement* (2001) rewrites narratives of the retreat from Dunkirk published in the early 1940s (such as *Return via Dunkirk* by "Gun Buster" [1940]); Tom Paulin's *The Invasion Handbook* (2002) revises, among other things, Richard Hillary's wartime memoir of the Battle of Britain (*The Last Enemy* [1942]) and Henry Williamson's postwar novel sequence about the route from Versailles to the Nuremberg Trials. The most controversial dimension of this retrospective is the literature of the

Holocaust (once a literature by survivors, now a literature reproducing a Western "post-memory"), which is conceived in such exceptional terms that it is rarely considered in relation to the literature of the war (this is not unrelated to the fact that for the vast majority in Britain, as in the United States, genocide – a postwar neologism – occurred *cognitively* after the war).

A case can be made, then, for preferring literature *about* rather than *of* the Second World War as an organizing concept for purposes of survey (as is the case with the literary testament to the First World War). Franco Moretti has taken 1939–45 to be exemplary of the *lack* of correlation between the significance of a historical event and its "pertinence" to explaining literary forms: the Second World War "does not seem to have much usefulness for literary periodization or interpretation: this does not, obviously, make it a secondary episode or one without enormous explanatory power in other areas."[4] Yet the field of literary writing *about* 1939–45 raises another challenging set of questions about the formal dimension of troping one event in another, so central have stories of the war been to Western cultures during an era of Cold War, welfarism, post- and neo-imperialism, and, latterly, the declaration of another world war, the "war on terror." But it seems equally likely that, confining our attention to wartime's duration, the variety of that literature will elude us if we seek some essential ethico-political reflection of a necessary but horrible war.

The factors which had the greatest force in multiplying the occasions, forms, and themes of Second World War writing were geographical, technological, and demographic. The war's theaters were numerous (and truly global); its machinery allowed the destruction of life and matériel to be undertaken at ever greater distances – across five continents, throughout the troposphere, and under the oceans – and whole populations were directly conscripted to the war efforts of nation states. Britain's war was imperial in its resources, techno-managerial in its strategies, and progressively gender-indifferent in its manpower requirements, though McEwan's play about Bletchley Park and Alan Turing, *The Imitation Game* (1981), repudiated the egalitarian implications later grafted onto this fact (in contrast to Robert Harris's 1995 novel *Enigma*). The massings and dispersals of the early 1940s meant many people had different war stories to tell, at the same time as they inhabited reiterable legends (both witnessed in the continuing readability of non-celebrity diaries, such as those produced for Mass Observation).[5]

Two trends can be discerned in surveys of wartime literary culture. One is concerned with how the war impacted on the careers of writers with established reputations, for instance T. S. Eliot, Virginia Woolf, Henry Green, Elizabeth Bowen, Evelyn Waugh, Dylan Thomas, George Orwell, J. B. Priestley.[6]

The other attends to the writing that, in a sense, required the war as its occasion, a literature that is at once more ephemeral, but also more topical; a literature without historical perspective but which may incarnate the grain of history, or how the times presented themselves then. Literary history in this less canonical mode is unavoidably bound up with literary myth-making. The first attempt at a debunking cultural history of wartime was Angus Calder's *The People's War* (1969). Born in 1942, Calder could be more dispassionate than his readers, who read the book as evidence for the populist legend it set out to correct.[7] Accounts of the artistic culture of wartime London ("Fitzrovia"), of the expatriate Cairo of Olivia Manning's *Levant Trilogy*, or of the soldier poets – whether the dead (Sidney Keyes, Alun Lewis, Keith Douglas, Hamish Henderson) or the surviving (Roy Fuller, Vernon Scannell, Geoffrey Matthews) – burnish icons of the glamor and austerity of a "good war."[8] In a similar vein of nostalgic investment, wartime miscellanies and journals (most notably the 1940 creation of *Horizon* by Cyril Connolly, and the revitalization of John Lehmann's editorial career with *Penguin New Writing*) have been read in terms of a culture of fragments that reflects the conditions of the emergency. It is claimed that the pressures of wartime denied writers the long view, but a historicizing culture, just like wartime propaganda, nevertheless discovers centers of value in the parochial, those islands of Britishness cut off in the midst of global conflict, whether these be the temporarily isolated districts of the bombed city or rural fastnesses.

There is no doubt that, as with First World War writing, a substantial part of our interest is in the historical emergency that the literature documents. Readers are drawn to the heroism, the dereliction, and the sociability of fighting legitimized by states, before they attend to the formal implications of, say, the short story as a mode of reportage. In this sense, wars are well served by anthologies of literature, which are emblems of the public, popular character of war in the era that ended in 1945. Of necessity, this chapter shares something of the form of an anthology, pretending to subdue the undisciplined crowdedness of the scene to orderly ranks and divisions.

"Less said the better": the war in the air[9]

British literature of the Second World War made no rhetorical or political fuss about being a war literature. It is as if there were just nothing else than the war (unless you could bury yourself in Trollope and other distractingly lengthy fictions) and, after the spring of 1940, relatively few questions about the war's necessity, if not its conduct. The cognitive divisions – soldier/civilian, masculine/feminine, overseas/Home Front – that shaped the adversarial character of the most plangent First World War verse were being eroded by technology (everyone was a potential target), by the economic costs of the arms race, and by both official and unofficial calls to imperial and domestic unity. "Business as Usual," or "taking it," a quite unexpected reaction from the point of view of defense experts to the totalization of war, had their literary equivalents in a studied laconicism (the public face of the denials and silences which mark the representation of traumatic experience).

The stiff upper lip, a verbal reservation or continence, is significantly associated with military aviators, both those whom Richard Hillary depicted as latter-day duelists, knights of the air, in his popular and influential memoir *The Last Enemy*, and the aircrews of Bomber Command. John Pudney, employed as a writer by the Air Ministry, was one laureate of the laconic. His reputation crystallized around the attribution of his poem "For Johnny" to Michael Redgrave's Flight Lieutenant Archdale in Anthony Asquith's film *The Way to the Stars* (1945). The indomitable widow Toddy embodies the poem's counsel against melancholy, with its concomitant infantilization of the pilot: "Do not despair / For Johnny-head-in-air."[10] In the Terence Rattigan play adapted in this film, *Flare Path* (1942), "Johnny" is what everyone calls the Polish pilot Prince Skriczevinsky, whose name is otherwise too much of a mouthful. Where the film urged procreation as a higher duty than the emotional restraint of the doomed airman, Rattigan's marital drama was resolved by the leading lady's belated preference for her pilot husband over her actor lover. Husband Teddy may play an unsophisticated part (imitating a flight manual cartoon called P. O. Prune), but film-star Peter just isn't reading from the same script as everyone else:

> It's the war, you see. I don't understand it … democracy – freedom – rights of man – and all that – I can talk quite glibly about them, but they don't mean anything, not to me.[11]

The "five gallon words" have changed since Hemingway's repudiation of the language of *gloire* in *A Farewell to Arms* (1929),[12] but speaking up for these unimpeachably good ideals can be an empty gesture even for those committed to them. This is because of the bodies burned and broken up in substantiating abstractions. H. E. Bates, writing for the Air Ministry as "Flying-Officer X," turned out short stories in which airmen refuse to dress up their heroic deeds in heroic terms; the official writer here acts as secretary to the few and shoots a line in their stead, using his own version of understatement to glorify their amateur but warrior-like enterprise.

The literary discovery of the war in the air was undoubtedly Roald Dahl. Dahl's break as a writer for children came when Walt Disney took up his story "Gremlins" in 1942 (since "gremlins" were part of RAF slang – devils responsible for equipment malfunction – there were irresolvable rights problems which halted production). Dahl's stories of the war in North Africa, where he was shot down in 1940, are arguably some of the most effective solutions to a problem which presented itself to writers from Keith Douglas, taking the measure of men burned in tanks in Libya, to William Sansom, recording the falling of buildings in bombed London – how to describe the core of war, the heart of the violent moment? "A Piece of Cake" (1945) (yet more understatement or euphemism) registers in slow motion the relays between body and brain as an airman is burned in his crashed plane; "Death of an Old Man" (1945) is even more daring in its breaching of documentary conventions, shifting between first- and third-person perspectives as the frightened pilot turns into a metalized, airborne warrior – getting shot down takes "perhaps as long as it would take you to light a cigarette" – and then relaxes into a dispassionate state of death.[13]

Street fighting: urban war

The dark twin of the airman duelist was the bomber pilot, lead protagonist of the strategic bombing campaign waged in imitation and defiance of the Luftwaffe's bombing of Britain into legendary solidarity. The power of this latter myth, and of aesthetic appropriations of the ruined city (the realization of a romantic urban picturesque), should not occlude the literary representation of human suffering at home, an outstanding example of which is Dan Billany's narrative of the provincial bombing in *The Trap* (published posthumously in 1950). Adam Piette has memorably demonstrated how Philip Larkin's Coventry poem "I Remember, I Remember" (written in 1954) – "'You look as if you wish the place in Hell,' / My friend said" – is haunted by the adolescent wish that was actualized by the November 14, 1940 "Coventration" raid.[14] For Brian Moore's Belfast ARP volunteer Gavin Burke, war produced "a shameful secret excitement, a vision of the grown-ups' world in ruin."[15] In Larkin's wartime novel, *Jill* (1946), it is the fact that Oxbridge might soon lie in ruins, and hence that scholarship exams should not be deferred, that initially frees the hero from his working-class home. He returns in expectation of its destruction when "Huddlesford" is raided, only to find home undamaged and his dependence on family complete.[16] Like a British Dresden, Coventry remains a counter-image to humanist political myths of the bombing as a force for national unity (a source of the welfarist consensus) and as a strategic-economic rationalization of offensiveness against Germany.

The metropolis underwent a radical reordering, in both spatial and causal terms, with the Blitz and the V-weapon campaigns late in the war. Writers seized on this with differing motives. In Graham Greene's *Ministry of Fear*

(1943) and *The End of the Affair* (1951), the indiscriminacy of the weapon which falls from the air produces miraculous confusion, out of which can be generated, respectively, a fifth-column thriller and a metaphysical love story. Henry Green's *Caught* (1943) is less about fighting fires (which prove to evade the hero's powers of recall and relay) than the sensuous and sexual disorientation of the blackout (*Loving* [1945] explored the equally disorienting libidinous effects of living with the lights blazing in a fairy-tale neutral Ireland). Elizabeth Bowen, who monitored opinion in the Irish drawing rooms of the Dominion for the British Government, turned the altered streets of London into an arena both Gothic ("The Demon Lover") and romantic ("Mysterious Kôr") (both in *The Demon Lover* [1945]). The compulsion and seductions of ideology and of the unnerving dissolution of boundaries (wrecked buildings stand for porous selves and for the ineluctable proximity of the dead) are revealed in what has become a newly liminal place: the capital city at war is both rear area and battlefield, as far from and as near to war as you can get.

Less familiar, but equally significant in their use of a fractured, or reoriented, environment, are the novels of Nigel Balchin, who, like Henry Green, worked in manufacturing (as an industrial psychologist) and, like another author of unorthodox blitz-fiction, Nevil Shute, was a professional writer on aviation. *The Small Back Room* (1943) is a narrative about willpower, in the setting of wartime scientific bureaucracy and the emergency created by a cunning booby trap. *Darkness Falls from the Air* (1942) is a still droller account of the war industry, represented here as the capture of the war effort by civil servants often working against the needs of the military. The novel's startlingly modern *ménage à trois* pits a posturing and verbose "artistic" boyfriend against the cynical, laconic husband who is the first-person narrator and vehicle of an understated resentment of all manner of phoniness.

Home front versus second front

The early months of the war, when little happened in the West, were known as the phoney war. Later, while the Luftwaffe and Kriegsmarine attacked British cities and Allied convoys, it could seem that the army was largely confined to barracks. It belatedly joined the continental war against the Wehrmacht, till then shouldered by the Soviet Army, in the opening of a *second* front (in fact, there was plenty of fighting in the Mediterranean and "forgotten" armies fought in Italy and in the Pacific). The home front, with its bomb damage, blackout, queues, evacuees, civil defense, and Home Guard voluntarism dominates the writing of the period, and scenes of combat take second place. In contrast with a minority discourse of combatant protest that has shaped public history of the First World War, Second World War Britain fostered, through print but also radio and screen documentary, a middle-to-highbrow culture of reconstruction, a commentary on the dangers, privations, and collective heroism of the present that was directed to the future. Its concerns were with planning a new social order that would look to the flourishing of all members of what Orwell conceived as a national family (in "The Lion and the Unicorn" [1941]). The strains on the whole population produced by economic direction – measures regulating both production and consumption – were represented positively as means of leveling social distinctions and as coming together in shared emergency, and until the 1980s it just seemed obvious, both to Left and Right, that the Welfare State was what Britons fought for (what they accomplished for themselves in beating Hitler).

Writing from the army appears by contrast domestic and marginal (as, perhaps less surprisingly, is the genre of prisoner-of-war writing, which became a staple of the 1950s' boom in paperback war stories). The soldier is a figure excluded from the great struggles and social experiments of the times, arrested in service bureaucracy and strategic limbo. Julian MacLaren-Ross, later notorious as a Fitzrovian dandy, wrote stories based on the life in the ranks from which he ultimately deserted. Circulating in periodicals like the illustrated, sexually suggestive *Lilliput* (edited by Stefan Lorent, a Hitler emigré), and gathered in *The Stuff to Give the Troops* (1944), they turned the enlisted man's struggles to interpret inscrutable regulations (a sarcastic, non-metaphysical English *Catch-22*) into a demotic version of Josef K's predicament. This vision was less sinister than Rex Warner's Kafkaesque fable of indigenous fascism, *The Aerodrome* (1940), or than Jocelyn Brooke's manifold memories and fantasies about soldiers turned into fiction and memoir in the later 1940s, notably in *The Image of a Drawn Sword* (1948). MacLaren-Ross also depicted a land under military occupation, only in his case the occupiers were the regimented mass of unoccupied, barracks-bound soldiery.

Alun Lewis's homage to Edward Thomas's great poems of military solitude was written in the first person plural, as if to underline the democratic character of the war's aggregations of individuals (though taking a commission would change all that for Lewis):

> All day it has rained, and we on the edge of the moors
> Have sprawled in our bell-tents, moody and dull as boors,
> ...
> And we stretched out, unbuttoning our braces,
> Smoking a Woodbine, darning dirty socks,
> Reading the Sunday papers – I saw a fox.[17]

This was a "poem in khaki" rather than a war poem. Soldiering was drill and waiting. Henry Reed famously adumbrated "The Lessons of War" (1942–45) by syncopating citations from weapons drill (anticipating the techniques of James Fenton); Sidney Keyes delineated "Two Offices of a Sentry" (1942). By contrast, Keith Douglas, unable to stand more delay, ran away from giving camouflage instruction to join in the El Alamein offensive. His poems, and a memoir *Alamein to Zem Zem* (1946), focus the grotesque traces and the hidden surprises of the mobile battlefield from neither a strategic, clarifying altitude, nor from the comradely – we'd now say "embedded" – perspective of the platoon (as in Norman Mailer's *The Naked and the Dead* [1948]). Instead, Douglas portrayed the military "as a body would look to a germ riding in its bloodstream."[18] There are echoes here of Isaac Rosenberg's louse- and rat-level vision; Douglas pares away his own humanist assumptions to mirror the burned and eaten corpses he seeks out as readily as battlefield loot: "the wild dog finding meat in a hole / is a philosopher."[19]

The literary combat novel would largely wait until the end of the war and had to compete with the accounts of war correspondents like Alan Moorehead. *From the City, From the Plough* (1948), a narrative by the Jewish novelist Alexander Baron of the invasion of Europe, exemplifies a brand of serious, non-glamorizing war fiction that appeared at the end of the 1940s. This moment lasted as long as the problem of Germany remained structurally central in the transition from peace to Cold War, and until the publishing boom in military memoirs and heroic narratives of the 1950s. The invasion and occupation of Germany presented writers with moral and political dilemmas, as well as with the drama of service and combat. Jack Aistrop, John Prebble (historian), Colin MacInnes (novelist of 1950s' youth culture), John Bayley (critic), and Kingsley Amis would all produce nuanced fictional accounts of English servicemen abroad, negotiating a way between the victor's swank and lust for loot, and the need to acknowledge the terrors of the different wartime experienced by liberated European and occupied Axis populations.[20]

J. B. Priestley, Churchill's rival on the radio as a diviner of the political meaning of the war effort (see his *Postscripts* [1940]), and an emblem of a non-deferent, reformist wartime spirit, maintained a steady production of topical fiction. *Black-out in Gretley: A Story of – and for – Wartime* (1940) anticipates the contemporary historical-police-procedural with its realization that a writer could use genre-fiction conventions to occupy an imaginative space that opened up between the denial of war and war's disordering of domestic routine: "most of the time we really dodge the stupendous terrifying reality of it, and merely try to come to terms with its various inconveniences and restrictions."[21] *Daylight on Saturday* (1943), an industrial novel, commemorates "a mountain of a job" (aircraft building, at peak production) and anticipates the critical idealism about postwar class relations made explicit in the demobilization narrative, *Three Men in New Suits* (1945). In that latter-day symposium, the guarantee of social change is to be sought within: "Nothing's happened to them inside. They haven't changed. They haven't learned anything – except how to make bigger and bigger bombs and hate like hell."[22] Priestley's celebrity and historical prominence should not suggest his politics were universal. Among his rivals in turning contemporary history into narrative entertainment and edification were the First World War correspondent Philip Gibbs and, notably, the occultist Dennis Wheatley, whose penchant for war planning, veiled in the fantastic and in antistatism, was less threatening to the establishment than Priestley's. Lord Haw-Haw's broadcasts would not be stopped until Hamburg was occupied in 1945; Priestley's "Postscripts" didn't continue after 1940.

The enemy

In the postwar era, the enemy has been redefined in numerous contexts, from the trials of major war criminals, through varieties of sexualized exploitation of Nazi regalia, to the rehabilitation and rearmament of the Bundesrepublik within NATO. After the election victory of Labour in 1945 and until the dropping of the weapon that would define the postwar world, it was the Japanese. The Holocaust, which made a greater public impact after the Jerusalem Eichmann trial in 1961 than during the Nuremberg hearings of 1945, provided further impetus to "understanding" the banality and the incomparable enormity of Hitler's Germany. Wartime Britons knew, or rather constructed, a different German and a different Germany, inoculated by their own liberalism (and their anti-semitism) from conceiving of just what was going on in occupied Europe even as they fought to resist Nazi expansion.[23] Hitler was a comic as well as a rapacious figure in contemporary literature, graced by the BBC with a courtesy title (Herr Hitler) even as he was popularly portrayed as insane.[24] The narrator of Geoffrey Household's wonderfully Buchanish *Rogue Male* (1939) is on the run after being caught on German soil with a telescopic sight. It is a freelance job: "No government – least of all ours – encourages assassination."[25] Nor does Household name the Führer as the target. And while the war was fought remotely (air-to-ground; submerged vessel-to-surface; by Allied armies overseas), the enemy occupied a realm of virtuality. There was none of the proximity that permitted the formation, in 1914–18 France, of iconic accommodations between nationally differentiated cannon fodder such as the Christmas Truce of 1914.

Encounters with enemy servicemen are rarely discoveries of mutual humanity (Wilfred Owen) or mutual depravity (Erich Maria Remarque, James Hanley) in British Second World War writing; they more likely involve the humbling of a chillingly or ludicrously regimented member of the *Herrenvolk* or master race.

The Nazi of wartime literature is not, however, the *Star Wars* Stormtrooper of postwar culture, when the reality of superpower hostility, if not the concept of totalitarianism, encouraged a linkage between the ruthlessness of the KGB and the record of the SS (the glamorization of Nazi elites is another matter). Graham Greene's story "The Lieutenant Died Last" (1940) belongs to the genre of counterfactual or alternative history. The *mise-en-scène* evokes the history of invasion scare fiction, from the Napoleonic to the Wellsian, but with an ironic edge: the village of Potter is an island within an island, buried away in Metroland, but in no way an unlikely place to hear low-flying airplanes or see uniforms. Greene questioned the tale's plausibility when explaining its absence from his 1972 *Collected Stories*. His act of suppression was in part due to the difference between his Nazis and the stock figures of postwar popular culture. Greene's Nazis fire "humanely, at his legs,"[26] when stopping Young Blewitt from foiling their sabotage plans. By contrast, Alberto Cavalcanti's film treatment, *Went the Day Well?* (1942), makes the German invaders, transplanted to rural southern England, "great bullying brute[s]."[27] The signal difference between story and film is the dispersal of the role of resistance fighter from the poacher Bill Purves (Greene's Boer War veteran) to the whole village of Bramley End and the creation of a Fifth columnist in the shape of the local Squire. Both changes reflected the modernizing populism found, for example, in the anonymous anti-appeasement polemic *Guilty Men* (1940) and the rhetorical construct of "the People's War."

While many contributed to visions of national unity, few writers imagined what life in wartime Europe was like. H. E. Bates's *Fair Stood the Wind for France* (1942) resembles Powell and Pressburger's film *One of Our Aircraft is Missing* (1942), as a story focused on airmen escaping Europe. Storm Jameson's *The Fort* (1941) and *The Power House* (1944) by the pacifist poet Alex Comfort fictionalize the fall of France, rare cross-channel complements to the literature of defeat and Vichy being composed in France. Unlike Comfort, who was vilified for his pacifism by Orwell, Jameson saw a choice between "two guilts," as she later put it. In *Then We Shall Hear Singing* (1942), she produced a fable of resistance to tyranny, a tyranny that is tellingly imagined non-corporeally as a technical intervention – "some quite simple interference with the brain ... turning men and women of an occupied country into obedient docile animals."[28] For all its bloodlessness, Jameson's connection between power and memory anticipates both Orwell's epoch-defining totalitarian dystopias and our own turn-of-the-century cultural politics of identity and memory.

The communist John Prebble, later famous for his military histories of the Highland Clearances, wrote *Where the Sea Breaks* (1944) while getting into trouble campaigning for a second front. It is unusual in employing psychological realism to emplot a Nazi occupation of British soil (a Scottish island) and hence is more directly comparable to *Went the Day Well?* or *49th Parallel* than to a fantastic fiction of the Channel Tunnel (Graham Seton's 1941 *The V Plan*). The clenched, cold indifference of the Nazi officer (a party member and Condor Legion veteran, who amuses himself with memories of strafing Polish cavalry) is dramatized in his shooting of a collie dog: he is the antithesis of Orwell's Englishman, who hates war and militarism, and whose country's civil defense measures, Orwell alleged, included "Animals' ARP Centres, with miniature stretchers for cats."[29] The islanders ultimately confront this pilot with the apparent flaw in the logic of liquidation: "you must kill us all if you want to be really triumphant, until there is no one else in the world but yourselves, and that you canna do."[30] Edward Upward's "New Order" similarly imagined the limits to tyranny in the obdurate facts of "human nature": "The invaders can march no further," cannot kill or subdue everyone.[31] It is this faith, tested to destruction in *The Last Man in Europe* (the publishers, Warburg, changed the title to *Nineteen Eighty-Four*), but triumphant with the aid of the American economy in 1945, which Auschwitz calls into question.

"Young England"

Evelyn Waugh's *Brideshead Revisited* (1945) is "a souvenir of the Second World War" because of the manner of its regret over the coming "age of Hooper," named after Charles Ryder's "commercial" subaltern. Just as Churchill's anxieties about a world without war were encapsulated in the electoral gibe about Labour's need for a Gestapo, so Waugh identifies Hooper with Nazi eugenics and diagnoses postwar Britain as fascist.[32] Orwell would be scarified by the Left for a similar collapsing of differentials in *Nineteen Eighty-Four* (1949), another text about the rebirth of Britain as a socialist society, and one which, like *Brideshead*, critiques the postwar world by asserting its militarist character.

Wartime writing was much taken up with the implications of inhabiting a militarized world and is divided between individualist chaffing against disciplinary structures that compromise liberal ideals on the one hand, and texts that seek to translate the achievements of the regimented collective into the promises of peace on the other. While the former mode has a legacy in the mockery of military institutions by writers like Spike Milligan and Brian Aldiss, it is the latter which has come down to us bearing historical authenticity, despite its proximity to the themes and symbols of wartime and welfarist state propaganda. Where the characteristic narrative of First World War literature is an ironic tale of disillusion, its Second World War counterpart, like Waugh's Hooper, "had no illusions about the Army."[33]

Nicholas Monsarrat's *H. M. Corvette* (1942) demonstrates the formation of this apparently unromantic view of war as everyday work and an investment in a common future, a view that has subsequently been romanticized in many genres of historical fiction and film, not least because of its remoteness from the universes of Nazi-occupied Europe. Monsarrat's first-person narrative was revised and expanded into the influential third-person novel *The Cruel Sea* (1951), filmed by Charles Frend in 1953 with Jack Hawkins. It is a story about induction into naval traditions, marine technologies and environments, and the duties of the convoy escort, and it is told in an ironic style pitched at undercutting its own efforts to relay reports of war over gulfs of language, experience, ontology. The writing produces oppositions that shape our apprehension of war – the domestic (the universe of the vessel) versus the elemental; dispassion in doing one's duty versus idealism. It is the sea that is cruel; the thought that war is cruel threatens to undermine duty. Erikson's depth-charge run kills merchant marine survivors (as a side effect), just as Monsarrat's writing alludes to "the brief horrors of the war" (why brief?) as "the other side of the medal."[34] For war is "the plain *success* of comradeship," and camaraderie is not a badge of exclusion (as it is in the poems of Owen), but a metaphor for social cooperation, service, generosity: "with a few blind spots, the war has produced evidence of all these things, in abundance."[35]

"This is not war"[36]

Alan Moorehead, knowing he was "still too close to the scene," tried to alert readers to some of these blind spots in the summer of 1945. Writing about the recent liberation of Belsen, the Australian war correspondent cautioned against blinkered perceptions, such as a short-term, shocked attention to the camps on the part of Allied populations which is merely "a justification for their fight," or the "downright childishness of saying that all Germans are natural black-hearted fiends capable of murdering and torturing and starving people at the drop of a hat."[37] Like Owen before him, Moorehead imagines a future of "mental indifference" (in both cases contradicted by a politics of remembrance and an extraordinary cultural appetite for history as remembering), and he does so in part because "This is not war" – it doesn't fit cultural and social paradigms of conflict.

Wartime culture made sense of present desperation or privation by the way it dealt with discipline. Nazi discipline was suspect: humorless and cruel, the warrior German was at once arrogant overman and regimented automaton, bent on inflicting his own domination on the world (a malign imperialism). The discipline of the citizen-warrior, whether in uniform or out of it, was quite different; it involved consent to the rational direction of individual effort in a collective enterprise which would grow into a new domestic (not world) order. The classics could be conscripted to provide mythic vehicles for these new styles of national and class ideology, as in the cinematic appropriation of Shakespeare and Chaucer in Olivier's *Henry V* and Powell and Pressburger's more internationalist *A Canterbury Tale* (both 1944). This national self-image remains potent, and its literature resonant; it is not canonical, but much of it remains in print, not least because its documentary and ideological content is recognizably reproduced in contemporary fiction and cinema. Both historiography and literature have challenged the blind spots in the home front, people's war stories of Britain's Second World War, but these are regularly reinvented on TV and in contemporary genre fiction (popular "street at war" saga-fictions that have supplanted to some degree the *Battle Picture Library* of the 1970s). If the First World War is, in Ted Hughes's memorable phrase, Britain's "national ghost," the Second World War represents the nation's best self.[38] The literary record of this time is alternately laconic about the horrors of war and loquacious about the potential for turning swords into plowshares. Its propriety and its complacency went hand in hand, and anticipated in this the crises of historical identity which have emerged in the one postwar Europe state where the memory of war might have been expected to be unproblematic.

NOTES

1. Keith Douglas, *The Complete Poems of Keith Douglas*, ed. Desmond Graham (Oxford University Press, 1978), 102; Keith Douglas, *A Prose Miscellany*, ed. Desmond Graham (Manchester: Carcanet, 1985), 120; Elizabeth Bowen, *The Collected Stories* (Harmondsworth: Penguin, 1980), 618.
2. Robert Graves, "The Poets of World War Two" (1942), *The Common Asphodel* (London: Hamish Hamilton, 1949), 311.
3. Alun Munton, *English Fiction of the Second World War* (London: Faber, 1989), 4.
4. Franco Moretti, *Signs Taken for Wonders: Essays in the Sociology of Literary Forms*, rev. edn. (London: Verso, 1997), 20.
5. Begun in 1937, the Mass Observation project recruited volunteers from the British public to record their views and experiences in diaries and questionnaires.

6. See, for instance, Sebastian Knowles, *A Purgatorial Flame: Seven British Writers in the Second World War* (Philadelphia: University of Pennsylvania Press, 1990); Gill Plain, *Women's Fiction of the Second World War: Gender, Power and Resistance* (Edinburgh University Press, 1996).
7. Angus Calder, *The People's War* (London: Cape, 1969).
8. Robert Hewison, *Under Siege: Literary Life in London, 1939–1945* (London: Weidenfeld & Nicolson, 1977); Artemis Cooper, *Cairo in the War* (London: Hamish Hamilton, 1989); Olivia Manning, "Poets in Exile," *Horizon* 10.58 (October 1944), 270–9.
9. John Pudney, *Beyond This Disregard* (London: John Lane, 1943), 12. Johnny-head-in-air was the creation of Heinrich Hoffmann (1809–94), creator of Struwwelpeter.
10. Ian Hamilton, ed., *The Poetry of War 1939–45* (London: Alun Ross, 1965), 114.
11. Terence Rattigan, *The Collected Plays*, 4 vols. (London: Hamish Hamilton, 1953), I: 126.
12. The phrase is spoken by Raymond Massey in Michael Powell and Emeric Pressburger's film *49th Parallel* (1941).
13. Roald Dahl, *Over to You: Ten Stories of Flyers and Flying* (Harmondsworth: Penguin, 1973), 19.
14. Philip Larkin, *Collected Poems*, ed. Anthony Thwaite (London: Faber, 1988), 83; Adam Piette, "Childhood Wiped Out: Larkin, his Father and the Bombing of Coventry," paper given at the Institute of English Studies, University of London Conference, "Larkin and the 40s," July 16–17, 1999.
15. Brian Moore, *The Emperor of Ice-Cream* (London: Deutsch, 1966), 7.
16. Philip Larkin, *Jill* (London: Faber, 1946), 214.
17. Alun Lewis, "All day it has rained …," *Raiders' Dawn and Other Poems* (London: George, Allen and Unwin, 1942), 15–16.
18. Keith Douglas, *Alamein to Zem Zem* (London: Editions Poetry London, 1946), 9.
19. "Dead Men," Douglas, *The Complete Poems*, 96.
20. Aistrop, *The Lights Are Low* (1946); Prebble, *Edge of Darkness* (1948); MacInnes, *To the Victor the Spoils* (1950); Bayley, *In Another Country* (1955); Amis, "My Enemy's Enemy" (1955).
21. J. B. Priestley, *Black-out in Gretley* (London: Heinemann, 1942), 10.
22. J. B. Priestley, *Three Men in New Suits* (London: The Book Club, 1945), 104.
23. See Tony Kushner, *The Holocaust and the Liberal Imagination* (Oxford: Blackwell, 1994).
24. For Hitler in wartime fiction, see Tristram Hooley, *Visions of a New Jerusalem: Predictive Fiction in the Second World War*, unpublished PhD thesis, University of Leicester, 2002.
25. Geoffrey Household, *Rogue Male* (London: Michael Joseph, 1964), 7.
26. Graham Greene, *The Last Word and Other Stories* (London: Penguin, 1991), 52.
27. *Went the Day Well?*, dir. Alberto Cavalcanti (Warner, 1942).
28. Storm Jameson, *Journey from the North*, 2 vols. (London: Virago, 1984), I: 96, 94.
29. George Orwell, *The Complete Works of George Orwell*, ed. Peter Davison, 20 vols. (London: Secker & Warburg, 1986–98), XVI: 202.
30. John Prebble, *Where the Sea Breaks* (London: Secker & Warburg, 1944), 116.
31. Edward Upward, "New Order," *Penguin New Writing* 14 (September 1942), 9.

32. Evelyn Waugh, *Brideshead Revisited* (London: Chapman & Hall, 1945), 8.
33. Ibid., 11.
34. Nicholas Monsarrat, *Three Corvettes* (London: Cassell Military, 2000), 25.
35. Ibid., 193.
36. Alan Moorehead, "Glimpses of Germany: II-Belsen," *Horizon* 12.67 (July 1945), 31.
37. Ibid., 34–5.
38. Ted Hughes, *Winter Pollen: Occasional Prose*, ed. William Scammell (London: Faber, 1994), 70.

FURTHER READING

Jenny Hartley, *Millions Like Us: British Women's Fiction of the Second World War* (London: Virago, 1997).
Alan Munton, *English Fiction of the Second World War* (London: Faber, 1989).
Adam Piette, *Imagination at War* (London: Papermac, 1995).
Mark Rawlinson, *British Writing of the Second World War* (Oxford: Clarendon, 2000).
Victoria Stewart, *Narratives of Memory: British Fiction of the Forties* (Basingstoke: Palgrave Macmillan, 2006).

18

WALTER HÖLBLING

The Second World War: American writing

Stories of war display essential cultural concepts, expectations, and self-images more prominently than other kinds of literature. In the extreme situation of war, society demands that its (mostly young) citizens risk their lives for the common good. So conflict becomes the occasion for questioning the validity of those individual and collective values and concepts of self and other in whose name one might die prematurely – especially at moments when victory is uncertain. Thus, the literature of war brings forth models of a nation's (or a people's) "storifying of experience": acts of "literary sense-making"[1] (or the lack of it) performed in response to particular historical situations – situations that, effectively, require the suspension of norms crucial in peaceful societies and sanctify the use of collective violence.

American experiences of the Second World War provided ample scope – and need – for storifying. The Japanese attack on Pearl Harbor on December 7, 1941 created a massive consensus in the USA about the moral and political necessity of fighting the Japanese military hegemony in Asia and its fascist European allies. The ensuing conflict saw US armed forces deployed all over the globe – on land, on sea, and in the air – for nearly four years. According to estimates,[2] about fifty million people died from 1939 to 1945 in combat, through bombing, in prisoner-of-war (POW) and concentration camps, or through famine and disease induced by the conflict. American troops not only faced a multitude of different theaters of operation and types of military action, they also had to learn to live with the awesome destructive power unleashed by the first US nuclear bombs, with the horror they found when liberating Nazi death camps, with prolonged POW experience, and with their new role as members of an occupation force responsible for re-educating, administering, and reconstructing a number of morally, socially, and economically devastated countries. Following the experience of the First World War, attitudes towards conflict itself were more pragmatic and provided much less ground for the disillusionment of great romantic expectations; war was seen as an unpleasant obligation rather than an opportunity for

individual heroism or male initiation rituals. Military strategy had also changed significantly: the high command as well as the troops had learned to
employ high-tech weaponry efficiently in more mobile battle structures. In the
Second World War, infantry soldiers rarely died in prolonged trench warfare.
Even battles with high casualty rates, like the retaking of the Pacific islands or
the D-Day landings in Normandy, were accepted because they resulted in
concrete military victories. Last but not least, in 1945 the USA emerged from
the war as the victorious and dominant military power, unchallenged until the
1950s. Such were the military and cultural conditions in relation to which
"acts of literary sense-making" had to be attempted.

Most authors chose the form of the novel to tell their stories, and there are
(depending on the inclusiveness of the definition) between 1,500 and 2,200
American Second World War novels, the majority published between 1945
and 1958. There is also an abundant body of poetry, several significant plays
that reflect quite varied understandings of "the good war" (as the Second
World War came to be known), and memoirs, personal narratives, letters,
and diaries too copious to be cited individually here.

Fiction

The rich literary legacy of the First World War proved adaptable to the
experience of the next generation of authors who, sooner than they had
expected after the "war to end all wars," were living through one of their
own. As Malcolm Cowley, somewhat tongue-in-cheek, puts it in his postwar
assessment:

> One might say that a great many novels of the Second World War are based on
> Dos Passos for structure, since they have collective heroes in the Dos Passos
> fashion, and since he invented a series of structural devices for dealing with such
> heroes in unified works of fiction. At the same time, they are based on Scott
> Fitzgerald for mood, on Steinbeck for humor, and on Hemingway for action
> and dialogue.[3]

In fact, the major points of criticism of American novels about the Second
World War up to the 1960s were that they were neither formally nor thema-
tically innovative, nor did they have the wide and powerful effects on their
audience that many novels about the previous war had achieved. There is
some truth to this charge, as the first generation of Second World War authors
did not feel an immediate need to look for new and adequate forms of literary
discourse. It should be remembered, though, that the innovative writers of
the First World War, like cummings, Dos Passos, Faulkner, Fitzgerald, and
Hemingway, were a minority among *their* contemporaries, and that the

first generation of Second World War writers widely adopted and developed the styles and narrative techniques of their immediate predecessors. Yet the new war also spawned new literary modes: novels such as William Eastlake's *Castle Keep* (1965), John Hawkes's *The Cannibal* (1949), Joseph Heller's *Catch-22* (1961), Kurt Vonnegut's *Mother Night* (1961) and *Slaughterhouse-Five* (1969), and Thomas Pynchon's *Gravity's Rainbow* (1973) pioneered different forms of *postmodern* discourse, not only in war literature but in American literature in general. It is this marked difference in literary discourses that signals the distinction between the two major schools of American fiction about the Second World War – the mimetic mode and the postmodern mode.

Fiction: the mimetic mode

The more traditional authors, such as John Horne Burns and Leon Uris, present the war as an extraordinary event which can be placed in its time–space continuum in history and acquires meaning in the framework of ameliorative evolutionary concepts as one more step in the progress of civilization. The mode is generally mimetic, employing conventional literary structures: the focus is on telling a "story" whose chronology more or less corresponds to the historical sequence of events. Characters conform to the tradition of psychological realism that encourages readers to identify with protagonists, and the connection of events by means of chronological narrative and plot structure suggests that the sense-making of the fictional "story" is more or less identical with what took place. At the end, readers have a sense of closure and the feeling that the things that happen in this fictional world can be explained and understood. Primary subject matter includes descriptions of battle scenes and the fate of a military unit and its individual members, while themes cover comradeship, courage, cowardice, endurance, the experience of death and danger, as well as the often problematic relations between officers and the lower ranks.

"Combat novels" are the most numerous in the mimetic mode; they focus on concrete missions that are rendered in detail and without much concern for a wider political or ideological context. Only a few of them rise above the level of what John Keegan once called the "Zap-Blatt-Banzai-Gott im Himmel-Bayonet in the Guts" adventure story.[4] A notable exception is Harry Brown's *A Walk in the Sun* (1944), the tersely told story of a company's mission in southern Italy. Brown reveals the existentialist underpinnings of Hemingway's factual style and also convincingly illustrates the effects of what has been called "combat numbness" – the prolonged exposure to the violence of war – on the soldiers. The main character, Corporal Tyne, sets the tone for his GIs' attitude towards war when he reflects, as he and his men are about to storm an ominously harmless-looking farmhouse, "What they were about to do was merely a job … It was the war. It was the job. It was *their* job. Get it done and then relax, that was the thing to do."[5] Compared to Brown's plain style, later novels often show more action, suspense, and patriotic fervor, as, for example, Leon Uris's *Battle Cry* (1953), a very realistically written tale from the Pacific Theater of Operations about the battles of Guadalcanal and Tarawa, employing the army-as-microcosm device to signal the "unity in diversity" of the American melting pot. Glenn Sire's *The Deathmakers* (1960) and James Jones's *The Thin Red Line* (1962) are other works replete with action and suspense. James Dickey, who served in the US Army's night squadrons during the war, published *Alnilam* in 1987, which explores the secrets and codes of the "higher military," and *To the White Sea* in 1993, which presents the fight for survival of an American Air Force gunner shot down during a bombing raid over Tokyo. William Chamberlain's two collections of skillfully crafted short stories about the Second World War and Korea (*Combat Stories of World War II and Korea* [1962], *More Combat Stories of World War II and Korea* [1964]) likewise feature a large variety of attitudes in characters trying to cope with military, logistic, and psychological challenges in their course of duty.

Another identifiable group of authors writing in the mimetic mode expand their vision beyond the immediate horizon of combat, problematizing the role of the military as a hierarchic structure within a democracy and the potential danger for civil society if its power runs unchecked. Dos Passos's techniques of the collectivist novel are often deployed in this genre. These novels tend to be critical of the excessively authoritarian behavior of the military command. Such works include "classics" like Norman Mailer's *The Naked and the Dead* (1948), James Jones's *From Here To Eternity* (1951), James Gould Cozzens's *Guard of Honor* (1948), and Herman Wouk's *The Caine Mutiny* (1951).

A related group of authors provides an even stronger critical focus that clearly points to their roots in the progressive and socially oriented movements of the American 1930s. Their novels are examples of what Frederick J. Hoffman called "ideological melodrama"; they often feature a liberal "intellectual who must mature, the external menace or bogey, the signs of inner corruption that resembles the enemy."[6] These novels include Irwin Shaw's best-selling *The Young Lions* (1948), Stefan Heym's muckraking *The Crusaders* (1948), Anton Myrer's *The Big War* (1957), John Hersey's chilling "factional" account *Hiroshima* (1946), and his psychopathological case study *The War Lover* (1959). These authors often filter their views of individuals, (military) society, and the war through evolutionary models of

Freudian or Marxist origin and present Nazism and fascism as a regression to lower forms of cultural as well as personal individual development.

In view of the broad consensus during the war and the general climate of the following Cold War years, which was not very congenial to critical voices or texts, it is a clear sign of intellectual sincerity and vitality that American literature brought forth a remarkable number of novels with these critical perspectives. Hersey, Heym, Mailer, and Shaw are foremost among those who, while supporting the goals of the Second World War, pointed to its potentially dangerous effects on the victors. However, no matter how severe their critiques, these authors never attempted to discard basic American values. Rather, they warned of abuses of power and of corruption within the USA, early critics of what at the end of the Eisenhower years became known as the "military-industrial complex."

The fact that the war brought Americans into contact with a multitude of different cultures also yielded a rich literary harvest; a good number of novels explicitly or implicitly compare their home country with other cultures, not always completely in favor of the American way of life. In *The Gallery* (1947), finished shortly before he died near Naples, John Horne Burns portrays the suffering of Italian civilians with great sensitivity and sympathy, as do John Hersey in *A Bell for Adano* (1944) and Alfred Hayes in *The Girl on the Via Flaminea* (1949). James Michener's *Tales of the South Pacific* (1947) counteract prevailing negative attitudes towards Asians with tales of love and humaneness.

The noncombatant auxiliary's experience features in Thomas Heggen's *Mister Roberts* (1946), an instant success upon publication, which provides a behind-the-lines view of the Pacific Campaign. Mr. Roberts, First Lieutenant and Cargo Officer of the USS *Reluctant*, which carries supplies between the tiny islands of Tedium, Apathy, and Ennui, is a born leader who meets life's and the war's challenges with laconic humor. The highly successful dramatic version (1948) diminishes the tragic elements and highlights the farcical aspects of the novel, as does the film version, starring Henry Fonda as Mr. Roberts and Jack Lemmon as Ensign Pulver.

American women had widespread experience of service in noncombatant units or as journalists during the Second World War. Novels based on these experiences by American women writers include Cathleen Coyle's *To Hold Against Famine* (1942), Grace Livingston Hill Lutz's *Time of the Singing of Birds* (1944), Martha Gellhorn's *The Wine of Astonishment* (1948), Susan Cooper's *Dawn of Fear* (1970), and Janet Hickman's *The Stones* (1976). Kay Boyle, who lived in Austria, England, and France from 1922 to 1941, very perceptively catches the rise of Nazism in Austria in her story "The White Horses of Vienna" (1935), and in "Defeat" (1941) portrays the collapse of

France in 1940. Her novels *Primer for Combat* (1942), *Avalanche* (1944), and *A Frenchman Must Die* (1946) are penetrating stories of life in France under the German occupation. A more recent text is Marge Piercy's *Gone to Soldiers* (1987), which creates a kaleidoscope of women's manifold roles in the European and the Pacific Theaters, as well as on the home front.

In view of the fact that segregation in the American military was legally abolished as late as 1948, it is no surprise that African-American writing about the war reflects the highly ambivalent and complex situation of US citizens who are risking their lives for rights and freedoms which they themselves are denied in the military as well as in the civil world of their home country: W. E. B. Du Bois's "double consciousness" applied with a vengeance. Chester Himes's *If He Hollers, Let Him Go* (1945) presents one aspect of this dilemma: after Robert Jones, a foreman at a Californian war plant, ends his relationship with a white woman, she accuses him of rape. The jury is aware of what really happened, yet cannot acquit him. Instead, he is offered two options – jail or the military. By contrast, John O. Killens in *And Then We Heard the Thunder* (1963) takes the reader right into the reality of the African-American experience in the US armed forces. A racial war between black and white soldiers stationed in Australia leads to bloodshed and death, leaving both parties ashamed and sobered at the end – an impressively realistic presentation of the grave problems that white supremacist attitudes in the military created among the troops. William Gardner Smith's *Last of the Conquerors* (1948) is set in postwar Berlin and adds one more level of intricacy to the racist attitudes of white US Army personnel and military police: the occupied Germans treat African-Americans as equals – yet these same Germans were "The Enemy" and the perpetrators of the Holocaust.

Native Americans also wrote about their experience in a conflict they were fighting on behalf of a nation that still discriminated against them and deprived them of their rights. In Navarre Scott Momaday's *House Made of Dawn* (1968), the first critically as well as commercially successful novel by a Native American, the young protagonist, Abel, returns from armed service in July 1945 to his grandfather's farm in New Mexico. The fact that he gets off the bus drunk and falls into his grandfather's arms signals from the very beginning that his experience in the white world of war has unsettled the young man; we do not learn much about his recent past, except that he was considered rather reckless by his fellow soldiers. He is clearly disoriented and lost between the Native American and the white world. It takes Abel years and the help of several mentor characters to reconnect to his original culture and to regain his identity. Tayo, the protagonist of Leslie Marmon Silko's novel *Ceremony* (1977), is even more severely affected by his service in the

Pacific Theater. Not only does he feel a certain kinship with his Asian enemies, he also suffers from guilty feelings about the death of his cousin on the Bataan Death March and feels responsible for a drought back home on the reservation since, on the Death March, he cursed the rain. Again, it takes several years and many a real and mythic healer-figure to cure him of his guilt and reintegrate him into his native culture.

Fiction: the postmodern mode

The second major form of discourse in American novels about the Second World War is the postmodern. Most of the works in this style were written under the shadow of the escalating Vietnam conflict and they present quite different (fictional) realities from those in the mimetic mode. Most importantly, "war" in these novels is no longer a concrete historical event limited in space and time, but becomes a complex metaphor for our contemporary industrialized society in which traditional distinctions between "peace" and "conflict" are rapidly losing their validity. War threatens to become a way of life, dominated by the business interests of global military-industrial corporations. As Joseph Heller puts it succinctly in *Catch-22*, "Business boomed on every battlefront."[7] Accordingly, in novels such as John Hawkes's *The Cannibal*, Joseph Heller's *Catch-22*, Kurt Vonnegut's *Slaughterhouse-Five*, and Thomas Pynchon's *Gravity's Rainbow*, war is ubiquitous and ever-present. Peace exists, if at all, only temporarily, in the shape of ideal contrasting spaces to the fictional world of war – Sweden in *Catch-22*, Tralfamadore in *Slaughterhouse-Five* – and inevitably turns out to be but a figment of the narrator's or protagonist's wishful thinking. The protagonist in Thomas Pynchon's *Gravity's Rainbow*, Tyrone Slothrop, suffers from what might be called "identity diffusion" (a recurring phenomenon in Pynchon's characters), as he disperses himself between different identities in diverse cities. The novel's final image of a V2-rocket suspended over a bizarre crowd of movie-goers appears as a pertinent metaphor of the new threat in the form of long-distance destruction that originated in the Second World War and dominated the Cold War era. Less diffuse but even more complex is the character of Vonnegut's Howard W. Campbell, Jr., in *Mother Night*. An American who moved to Germany after the First World War, Campbell becomes a successful playwright and also works as a Nazi propaganda speaker, sending coded messages to the Allies during broadcasts. After his return to the USA, he is hijacked by the Israeli Secret Service who think he is a real Nazi, put in a prison cell next to Adolf Eichmann, and in the end commits suicide in order to avoid interrogation by the pending tribunal and, perhaps to an even greater extent, his own self-questioning. All Billy Pilgrim, protagonist of Vonnegut's *Slaughterhouse-Five* and probably the most passive character ever created in American fiction, can do is reenact traumatic memories from his war experience as a German POW and ear-witness of the firebombing of Dresden. Unable to forget these memories, he cannot find any meaning in them either. In a seriously playful postmodern mode, Vonnegut offers the reader two popular conventions – pyschopathology and science fiction – to explain Billy's strange narrative, yet neither model ultimately succeeds. One of the novel's key lines, "There is nothing intelligent to say about a massacre,"[8] also indicates that making sense of the horrors of war, explaining events in order to provide a sense of understanding and closure in cause-and-effect-oriented chronological language, has become impossible. In a different vein, William Eastlake's *Castle Keep* is a more surreal postmodern text set in France, intermingling realist with highly symbolist images in a satirical story about war, art, and culture.

Overall, these postmodern novels not only challenge traditional realistic storytelling and logical sense-making, but also display an almost eerie anticipatory vision: they no longer conceive war as an exceptional historical situation that has a cut-off date after which everybody returns to "normal." Rather, war and peace are a matter of location, that is, geographically situated rather than defined by a historical timeline. This reflects the real situation in the Vietnam War, where one of the most difficult feats for the GIs to handle was the quick transition from "Nam" to "The Real World" via jetliner. Indeed, our current situation at the beginning of the twenty-first century is that "war" and "terror" can be localized permanently (and simultaneously) in various parts of the globe.

Poetry

Many more American poets wrote about the Second World War than about the First, though there is little of the heroic idealist rhetoric and personal drama of Alan Seeger or Joyce Kilmer. In poetry (unlike fiction), the modernist aesthetics that flowered between the wars are continued and developed. The new style is mostly nonchalant, cool, sometimes laconic, with a preference for brevity and minimalism, often reminiscent of the complex compactness of imagism and occasionally of e. e. cummings's linguistic experiments. A good example is Randall Jarrell's five-line "The Death of the Ball Turret Gunner" (1945):

> From my mother's sleep I fell into the State,
> And I hunched in its belly till my wet fur froze.
> Six miles from earth, loosed from its dream of life,

> I woke to black flak and the nightmare fighters.
> When I died they washed me out of the turret with a hose.[9]

cummings himself, in his cranky, individualist way, also contributed some critical poems, speaking out against the racism at home and the glorification of the war as "noble" in "ygUDuh" (1944), "why must itself up every of a park" (1950), "neither awake" (1950), "where's Jack Was" (1950), and "I'm" (1950). To the wholesale destruction of Hiroshima and Nagasaki he responded with a sonnet – "whose are these (wraith a clinging with a wraith)" (1950) – suggesting that militarism and scientific imagination have succeeded in making chaos absolute. Serious ethical questioning, though rare, is revealed in Richard Eberhart's "The Fury of Aerial Bombardment" (1945):

> Was man made stupid to see his own stupidity?
> Is God by definition indifferent, beyond us all?
> Is the eternal truth man's fighting soul
> Wherein the Beast ravens in its own avidity?[10]

The poem ends, not with meaningful answers to these questions, but with a list of names of fallen soldiers. Likewise, the poems of Phyllis McGinley and William Meredith explore the ethical and religious aspects of the war. Karl Shapiro served in the Pacific Theater and provides the most diverse insights among American poets in his collections about his conflict experience, *Person, Place and Thing* (1942), *V-Letter and Other Poems* (1944), *Trial of a Poet* (1947), and *The Bourgeois Poet* (1964). His verse is highly polished yet unsentimental about the war and soldiering, the tone is often one of irony, combined with matter-of-fact understatement. This quality also characterizes much of the work of Richard Wilbur, Kenneth Patchen, Louis Simpson, James Dickey, Lincoln Kirstein, Howard Nemerov, and John Ciardi. This does not prevent these poets from creating powerful images that bring the horror of war home to the readers. Louis Simpson's "Carentan O Carentan" (1949), about a devastating ambush in a pastoral French landscape, envisions in archetypal imagery an innocent soldier's first encounter with death:

> There is a whistling in the leaves
> And it is not the wind,
> The twigs are falling from the knives
> That cut men to the ground.[11]

James Dickey also writes some of his finest poems on war experiences: "The Jewel" (1960), "The Performance" (1960), and "The Firebombing" (1965), about the haunting memories of bomber pilots; "Between Two Prisoners" (1962), about the beheading of an American prisoner by a Japanese guard; and "Drinking from a Helmet" (1964), about a young GI's growing awareness of death. John Ciardi's collection *Other Skies* (1947) traces the poet's development and maturation from the beginning of the war (Ciardi served as a B-29 gunner) until his return to civil life. Notable pieces are "Poem for My 29th Birthday" and "Autobiography of a Comedian." A distinct voice against the rise of fascism, but also against America's entry into the war, was that of Robinson Jeffers, whose collection *The Double Axe and Other Poems* (1948) includes outspoken antiwar poems like "Ink-sack," "The Eye," "Historical Choice," and "The Inhumanist," all of which caused serious irritation among his audience and contributed to his fall from grace with the American public after the war. Richard Wilbur, former United States Poet Laureate, was less drastic in his verse: his *The Beautiful Changes and Other Poems* (1947) includes several poems dealing directly with war experience – for example, "Tywater," about random death on the high-tech battlefield; "Mined Country," a rather prophetic piece about land mines; and a strongly emotional poem, "On the Eyes of an SS Officer."

Among African-American poets, Langston Hughes, like many politically active intellectuals, followed events in Europe from the Spanish Civil War onwards; his early poems about the Second World War, "Jim Crow's Last Stand" (1943) and "Will V-Day Be Me-Day Too?" (1944), voice his hope that the fight against fascism and its supremacist ideology will also help to abolish racism in the USA. His later verse – for example, "Mother in Wartime," "War," "Official Notice," and "Total War"[12] – show considerably less optimism about the war's positive effect on these domestic issues. Another perspective on the same problem is provided by Gwendolyn Brooks's series of war sonnets, "Gay Chaps at the Bar" (from *A Street in Bronzeville* [1945]), inspired by the V-letters of black soldiers who worry about how they will be received when they return home. With her Japanese-American heritage, Mitsuye Yamada gives the reader access to another variant of American racism in wartime; in 1942, she and her family were sent to the Minidoka War Relocation Center, Idaho, an internment camp. Her experience there and her eventual repatriation into American culture are the themes of her collections *Camp Notes* (1976) and *Desert Run* (1988).

A notable exception to the dominant American poetic discourse about the Second World War should not go unmentioned. In 1945, Peter Bowman published a book-length, free-verse narrative titled *Beach Red*, which was a Book-of-the-Month Club selection in December 1945 and was made into a movie in 1967. For the narrated time of one hour, we experience the invasion of a Japanese island through the mind of one US soldier; beyond the mere rendition of vivid battle scenes, the reader also learns what that soldier's generation is thinking about the war and its legacy.

Drama

American playwrights responded to the Second World War in sizeable numbers, yet, perhaps because of the numerous movies about the war, their work has received only moderate critical attention. Lillian Hellman's *Watch on the Rhine* (1941) successfully alerted Americans to the dangers of fascism and her *The Searching Wind* (1944) portrayed the failure of naïve liberalism, but the plays' merits today are considered to be political rather than dramatic. Similarly, the plays of Maxwell Anderson – *Candle in the Wind* (1941), *The Eve of St. Mark* (1942), *Storm Operation* (1944), and *Truckline Café* (1946) – though quite successful when they came out, remain very much products of the war years. Far less successful was Harry Brown's *A Sound of Hunting* (produced 1945, published 1946). Of the great American dramatists, Arthur Miller uses the war as a significant if not central structural element in his first successful play, *All My Sons* (1947), setting off business interests against humanist ethics in a tragic family drama about an American factory-owner who knowingly delivers a batch of faulty airplane engines, causing the death of twenty-one pilots, including his elder son. In three of his later plays, *After the Fall* (1964), *Incident at Vichy* (1964), and *Playing for Time* (1980), Miller explores the themes of complicity, guilt, resistance, and moral responsibility under the Nazi regime and in the concentration camps. One of the most important contemporary African-American playwrights, Charles Fuller, received the 1982 Pulitzer Prize for Drama for his 1981 work *A Soldier's Play*, which is set on an army base in Louisiana during the Second World War. As in African-American fiction, the central themes include racism, power, and the convoluted relationships between blacks and whites. Probably one of the most influential comedies about the war was Donald Bevan and Edmund Trzcinski's *Stalag 17* (1951), based on the authors' experience in an Austrian POW camp; it was also made into a successful motion picture by Billy Wilder in 1953 and became the prototype of many other war comedies. A different kind of comedy is William Styron's *In the Clap Shack* (1973). In this dark, scathing satire about the incompetent medical system of the US Navy during the war, a young Southern sailor is wrongly suspected to have contracted syphilis.

The Holocaust

Interwoven with the military events of the Second World War is the Holocaust or *Shoah*, the Nazis' systematic attempt to exterminate Jewish life and culture, as well as members of other ethnicities they considered inferior, including Roma, Sinti, and Slavs. Many Jewish survivors settled in the USA, and the body of American writing about their and/or their family members' experience in the death camps, during their escape and in the aftermath, is huge and continues to grow, currently being added to by the second and third generations of descendents. Eli Wiesel, recipient of the 1986 Nobel Peace Prize, survived the *Shoah*, came to the USA in 1955 and became an American citizen. *Un di velt hot geshvign* (*And the World Kept Silent*) (1956), his 900-page book originally written in Yiddish about his experiences, was published in three separate volumes in English: *Night* (1960), *Dawn* (1961), and *Day* (1962) (previously titled *The Accident*). Altogether, Wiesel has written over forty books of fiction and nonfiction about the Holocaust. One of the most significant texts from the second generation is Art Spiegelman's comic-book novel *Maus*, originally published as a strip in an underground comic from 1972 to 1977. The narrative is based on Spiegelman's father Vladek's memories of life in Poland under the Nazi occupation. All characters are presented as anthropomorphic animals: the Jews are depicted as mice (hence the name Maus), the Germans as cats. Parallel to the tale of Vladek's survival runs the story of his son Art, who tries to understand his father's appalling experiences.

More or less explicitly, the Holocaust experience is present in the works of most Jewish-American authors published after 1945: Hannah Arendt, Saul Bellow, Raymond Federman, Bernard Malamud, Cynthia Ozick, Philip Roth, and Wendy Wasserstein. An outstanding Holocaust novel by a non-Jewish writer about a non-Jewish victim is William Styron's *Sophie's Choice* (1979), made into a highly praised film in 1982. Set in Brooklyn, in 1947, it is the tale of Stingo, an aspiring Southern writer who becomes involved with the lives of his neighbors, Sophie, a Polish-Catholic survivor of Nazi concentration camps, and her ingenious but crazy Jewish-American lover Nathan, whose mental instability prevented him from serving in the war. The complex narrative juxtaposes flashbacks of Sophie's traumatic experience with Stingo's memories of growing up in the South; one of the parallels that caused a controversy upon publication of the novel is between the worst abuses of the American South (both its slave-owning past and the lynchings of the book's present) and Nazi anti-semitism. When Stingo discovers that both Sophie and Nathan have committed suicide in their room by way of sodium cyanide, he is devastated, yet the last sentence in the novel suggests a shred of optimism: "This was not judgment day, only morning. Morning: excellent and fair."[13] A new generation of Jewish-American writers – among them Jonathan Safran Foer, Nathan Englander, Allegra Goodman, Thane Rosenbaum – is now tackling the phenomenon of "post-memory" of the Holocaust.

Conclusion

American writing about the Second World War reveals an impressive diversity of themes as well as discourses in all literary genres, traditional and experimental. The search for words which adequately present the war experience yields the most innovative results in the novels of the postmodernist writers, since they permit their readers – sometimes even force them – actively to participate in their characters' attempts to make sense, more or less successfully, of events. The later texts of the 1960s and 1970s in particular include major works of the American postmodernist movement and set new standards for depicting historical events in a globalized context. Novelists writing in the traditional mimetic mode create characters with whom readers can identify, and often convincingly recreate "how it really was" – insofar as this is possible. The richness and power of poetic expression are likewise remarkable and, as in fiction, often serve as inspiration for poetic styles from the 1960s to the 1980s. American authors successfully rise to the challenge of sharing the experience of the most massive and chronic global war to date with their readers.

NOTES

1. Philip Beidler, *American Literature and the Experience of Vietnam* (Athens: University of Georgia Press, 1982), 138, 198.
2. For example, Martin Gilbert, *The Second World War. A Complete History* (London: Phoenix, 1989), 1.
3. Malcolm Cowley, *The Literary Situation* (New York: Vintage, 1969), 41.
4. John Keegan, *The Face of Battle* (New York: Viking, 1976), 31.
5. Harry Brown, *A Walk in the Sun* (New York: Knopf, 1944), 57.
6. Frederick J. Hoffman, *The Mortal No: Death and Modern Imagination* (New Jersey: Princeton University Press, 1964), *passim*.
7. Joseph Heller, *Catch-22* (New York: Dell, 1973), 259.
8. Kurt Vonnegut, *Slaughterhouse-Five* (New York: Dell, 1982), 8.
9. Randall Jarrell, "The Death of the Ball Turret Gunner," *The Complete Poems* (New York: Farrar, Straus & Giroux, 1969, 1996), 144.
10. Richard Eberhart, "The Fury of Aerial Bombardment," *Collected Poems, 1930–1986* (Oxford University Press, 1987), 90.
11. Louis Simpson, "Carentan O Carentan," *The Arrivistes* (New York: Fine Editions, 1949), 24.
12. Langston Hughes, *The Collected Poems of Langston Hughes*, ed. Arnold Rampersad and David Roessel (New York: Knopf, 1995), 588, 599, 558, 577.
13. William Styron, *Sophie's Choice* (New York: Random House, 1979), 515.

FURTHER READING

Marty Bloomberg, *The Jewish Holocaust: An Annotated Guide to Books in English* (San Bernadino, CA: Borgo Press, 1995).

Paul Fussell, *Wartime: Understanding and Behavior in the Second World War* (Oxford University Press, 1989).

Jennifer C. James, *A Freedom Bought with Blood. African American War Literature from the Civil War to World War II* (Chapel Hill: University of North Carolina Press, 2007).

Michael Lee Lanning, *The African-American Soldier: From Crispus Attucks to Colin Powell* (Secaucus, NJ: Carol, 1997).

Biancamaria Pisapia, Ugo Rubeo, and Anna Scacchi (eds.), *Red Badges of Courage. Wars and Conflicts in American Culture* (Rome: Bulzoni, 1998).

Maggie Rivas-Rodriguez (ed.), *Mexican Americans and World War II* (Austin: University of Texas Press, 2005).

Albert Wertheim, *Staging the War: American Drama and World War II* (Bloomington: Indiana University Press, 2004).

19

JEFFREY WALSH

American writing of the wars in Korea and Vietnam

Korea as a rehearsal for Vietnam

Although different in important respects, the wars in Korea (1950–53) and Vietnam (1965–73) had much in common. Both were Cold-War conflicts conceived as limited, non-nuclear wars to halt the spread of communism, and both resulted in heavy losses: in Korea, some 36,000 US troops died; in Vietnam, 58,000. Other parallels extend beyond these statistics: before the wars began, both Korea and Vietnam, through international agreement, had been partitioned into a communist north and a US client-based south, making both countries potentially combustible. The outcome of the two conflicts was the opposite of what America and its allies intended: at the time of writing (2008), North Korea remains a nuclear-armed communist state ruled by a despot, and the Socialist Republic of Vietnam continues to be a united communist nation whose relations with the USA were normalized only in 1995.

In both wars, the USA was taught a traumatic lesson in the new realities of warfare as its advanced technology proved insufficient to achieve victory in either the cold, mountainous terrain of Korea or the paddy fields and jungles of Vietnam. US military theorists remained fixated on conventional war as fought on the battlefields of Europe, and its politicians too often ignored low troop morale and motivation. In these two remote Asian wars, the American public, after an initial period of enthusiasm, soon grew disillusioned, and US soldiers found it increasingly difficult to believe in the causes they were supposedly fighting for. This was partly because the US puppet regimes were increasingly corrupt and led by unpopular leaders. Neither war measured up to the morally justifiable fight to defeat fascism and genocide in the Second World War.

However, it is the differences between the wars in Korea and Vietnam that are especially relevant to literary output. Korea, although ostensibly fought under the auspices of the United Nations, is often referred to as a forgotten war that generated only a small fraction of the literature and cinema inspired by Vietnam; it was less visibly projected than the later war and occurred before the advent of television into American homes. Soldiers in Vietnam were better educated than those in Korea, better culturally equipped to be writers, and also received superior medical treatment. The writers who fought in Vietnam, mostly as nineteen-year-olds, grew up as part of a 1960s' generation familiar with a counterculture of rebellion that supplied glamorous slogans and images. Korea could never be a rock-and-roll war like Vietnam, which was associated with box-office cinema, antiwar songs, the Civil Rights movement, West Coast rock, pop-art posters, political protest theater, and artistic photography. Korea appeared inherently uncharismatic, a sterile conflict involving attrition and bloody stalemate, with few clear-cut victories, endless wrangling over prisoners-of-war, and a singularly futile ending. Poor timing also contributed to the dearth of high quality literature emanating from Korea; the conflict followed on too quickly after the Second World War, and the market was saturated with best-sellers written by such notable authors as Norman Mailer, James Gould Cozzens, and James Jones.

Korean War fiction

Korean War fiction may be studied in categories such as Marine novels (for example, Pat Frank's *Hold Back the Night* [1952] or Ernest Frankel's *Band of Brothers* [1958]); Army fiction (such as Thomas Anderson's *Your Own Beloved Sons* [1956] or Curt Anders's *The Price of Courage* [1957]); POW stories (for example, Francis Pollini's *Night* [1960] or Charles B. Flood's *More Lives than One* [1967]); and works concerning the suffering of the Korean people (such as Chaim Potok's *I Am The Clay* [1992]).[1] Another analytical approach is to explore how the dominant form of realism is subverted by such satirical or formally experimental novels as Melvin B. Voorhees's *Show Me A Hero* (1954), Edward H. Franklin's *It's Cold in Pongo-Ni* (1965), and Richard Hooker's *M*A*S*H* (1968). Taken collectively, such works and others constitute a cognitive map of the Korean War and show how Korea anticipated Vietnam in the use of napalm, helicopters, troop rotation, and ideological confusion, especially the mistaken belief that superior firepower would achieve victory.

Of the critically acclaimed novels, William Styron's *The Long March* (1952) and James Salter's *The Hunters* (1956) are most aesthetically coherent. Set in the months leading up to the Korean conflict, *The Long March* chronicles a 36-mile march, foregrounding a clash between a reservist and his commanding officer. The novella acts as a metaphor for the Korean War and comments upon Cold-War military posturing. Salter's *The Hunters*, written in taut and understated prose, explores the ethos of "the kill" in aerial combat, contrasting the ideal virtues of leadership, integrity, pride, and grace under pressure, with the more compromised and pragmatic conduct evident in self-promotion, machismo, and taking a utilitarian approach at the expense of others.

The diversity of Korean War fiction is represented in three novels by well-known writers: James Michener's jingoistic action novella, *The Bridges at Toko-Ri* (1953), Richard Condon's political thriller, *The Manchurian Candidate* (1959), and Stephen Becker's historically wide-ranging *Dog Tags* (1973), which extends from the Second World War to a POW camp in Korea and then to the Vietnam era. Ideologically, the three novels are strikingly different: Michener celebrates the fact that naval pilots and aircraft-carrier personnel fight an unpopular war to support American civilization; Condon's virtuoso pastiche attacks McCarthyism by portraying brainwashing techniques to demonstrate the corruption of US political elites; and Becker's *Dog Tags* constructs a charismatic, meditative character whose spirituality and humanitarianism transcend the POW genre's central theme of dehumanization.

Korean War poetry

Until 1997, Korean War poems were extremely difficult to locate. In that year, the poet W. D. Ehrhart produced for the journal *War, Literature, and the Arts* an invaluable critical anthology: *I Remember: Soldier-Poets of the Korean War* (1997). Later, Ehrhart collaborated with Philip K. Jason in *Retrieving Bones: Stories and Poems of the Korean War* (1999), which also included a selection of short fiction together with critical material. The work of the six poets anthologized, William Childress, Rolando Hinojosa, James Magner, Jr., Reg Saner, William Wantling, and Keith Wilson, comprises a unique poetic record, their collective mood one of elegy.[2]

Such a tone, evoking a mixture of loss and regret, characterizes the work of William Childress.[3] Childress's poetry is difficult to study as it often conflates Korea and Vietnam. Indeed, his later works, such as "The Long March" explicitly connect the two conflicts.[4] The landscape often informs the sparse imagery of his poems, as in "Soldier's Leave" or "Letter Home," in which the soldier's lamenting voice aptly compares the tragic Korean children to "broken stalks," their faces "petals all torn."[5] Resignation yields to anger in "The Soldiers," where the paddies "heavily seeded / with napalm mines, can grow red flowers / at a touch, with a blossom that kills."[6] One way of approaching Childress's work is by noting variation of narrative voice – for example, observing how the helplessness of the first-person singular narrator of the

Korean poem, "Shellshock," spoken by a survivor with post-traumatic stress disorder,[7] is subsumed into the tone of a harsher, pacifist first-person plural narrator who, in the Vietnam era, attacks generals and politicians for their cowardice and self-seeking. Childress moves elegantly between free verse and formal regularity, making subtle use of vowel coloring, assonance, half-rhyme, and fire-dominated imagery.

Although he wrote only eight poems about Korea,[8] William Wantling is its most naturally gifted poet. He served in the Marine Corps, and became addicted to heroin, which is alluded to in his poem "Pusan Liberty" as a response to "the absurdity of War and State." In Wantling's prison poem "Poetry," he describes the inadequacy of poetic language to express the reality of bloody murder, perhaps an oblique commentary on his own war poems. Wantling, who died at forty-one from drug addiction, was haunted by guilt for what he perceived as the war crimes he had committed. His confessional poetry, raw, urgent, built on intricate syntax and convoluted sentence structure, seems at times like a *mea culpa*. In "Without Laying Claim," he admits to a war atrocity; in "The Korean" he watches an undeserved execution; in "Korea 1953," the collective voice acknowledges the soldiers' descent into "a pack of maddened dogs." "Sure" and "The Day the Dam Burst" question the possibility of a belief in pacifism.[9]

At issue in all war poetry, and especially in the case of Korea, "a distant war which was no war,"[10] is the space the war occupies in postwar consciousness. For Rolando Hinojosa, a prolific Spanish-American poet, it provided a copious source of somewhat prosaic narrative. In the hard-edged maritime poems of Keith Wilson, a naval officer, episodes of combat yield postwar, in *Graves Registry* (1992), to powerful memories of death and destruction, which should act as a warning to America. James Magner, Jr.,[11] who spent five years in a Roman Catholic monastery after being discharged, incorporated his Korean experience into a didactic Christian vision, except for three or four haunting poems, such as "The Man Without a Face," "Zero Minus One Minute," and the poignantly elegiac "Repository."[12] For Reg Saner, who tried to avoid confrontation with Korea and later Vietnam, memories surfaced in disguised form within familiar images of hunting, school-days, or driving. Only in his magnificent prose-poem "Flag Memoir" does the monumental reality of his experiences break through.[13]

Vietnam: America's shame and the search for literary expression

It is often suggested that America lost its self-esteem in Vietnam because of an inability to reconcile myths of national virtue with the history of the conflict. The war was frequently portrayed in literary discourse as uniquely resistant to meaning and necessitating a radically different kind of "sense making." Such mystification is unwarranted when set against the political realities of US involvement in Indochina. America's leaders did not stumble innocently into a quagmire; they pursued policies designed to undermine communism and export the values of democratic capitalism. In so doing, they underestimated the support for national unity latent throughout Vietnam after centuries of foreign occupation. The United States's defeat was also caused by an under-valuing of the resolve of the North Vietnamese army and the National Liberation Front (Viet Cong), and a related failure to develop a popular alternative government in South Vietnam. After the Tet Offensive by the North Vietnamese in 1968, American public opinion turned irrevocably against the war. The disturbance to the national psyche was more serious than any trauma evident from Korea, and was reflected in contradictory narrative patterns of literary output.

Vietnam: fiction

Philip D. Beidler and Thomas Myers have demonstrated how the American war novel evolved from the traditional model of realism inherited from James Jones and James Gould Cozzens into a more experimental discourse antici-pating postmodernism, poststructuralism, and metafiction, the territory of Heller, Vonnegut, and Pynchon.[14] The search for verisimilitude and mimetic authenticity is evident in such works as David Halberstam's *One Very Hot Day* (1967), which addresses the part played by South Korean allies; William Pelfrey's *The Big V* (1972); Josiah Bunting's *The Lionheads* (1972); and Winston Groom's *Better Times Than These* (1978). The most outstanding of such novels are James Webb's *Fields of Fire* (1978) and John del Vecchio's *The 13th Valley* (1982). Both Webb and del Vecchio empathize with the common soldier, and both have also produced ambitious trilogies of novels portraying the continuing impact of Vietnam upon the United States. Their work may usefully be compared with later realist texts such as Jack Fuller's bleak *Fragments* (1984) or Richard Currey's elegant *Fatal Light* (1988). Such comparisons reveal the potential of realism, which lies not in its epic sweep or prophecy, but in detail of a particularized, historical kind.[15]

Nevertheless, traditional realism, often supplemented by maps, glossaries, and other factual information, yields in the work of the most celebrated Vietnam War novelists, Robert Olen Butler, Larry Heinemann, Tim O'Brien, and Gustav Hasford, to innovatory formal procedures and different conventions. Robert Olen Butler's accomplished trilogy, *The Alleys of Eden* (1981), *Sun Dogs* (1982), and *On Distant Ground* (1985), addresses the concept of atonement for America's actions towards the Vietnamese. *The*

Alleys of Eden, which narrates how an alienated deserter returns with his mistress to America, suggests how closely Vietnam and the USA are psychologically linked. Butler manages something rarely achieved – a profound sense of historical awareness arising from its characters' sense of guilt and shame. Vietnam is thus presented as a Vietnamese rather than – as often portrayed – an American tragedy. This is reinforced by the fact that Butler, a student of Vietnamese language and culture, produces a convincing rendition of Vietnamese people and their speech.

Compared with Butler's close-knit cycle, Larry Heinemann's powerful war novels, *Close Quarters* (1977) and *Paco's Story* (1986), are disconnected works. *Close Quarters*, narrated by Philip Dosier, member of an armored vehicle company, focuses on the experiences of a single platoon. At its heart are passages of hallucinogenic intensity that enact the horrors of modern warfare such as the desecration of bodies by high-tech weapons. The novel affirms few virtues, concentrating instead upon the existential obscenity of war and the way in which soldiers live in a separate domain, often acting instinctively out of vengeance and malice. *Close Quarters* and novels in similar vein, such as Gustav Hasford's *The Short-Timers* (1979) and *The Phantom Blooper* (1990), although fictional works, comment obliquely upon US atrocities such as the notorious massacre at My Lai in 1968. Both Heinemann's *Close Quarters* and Hasford's *The Phantom Blooper* are stylistically varied, drawing upon imagery (for example, of corpses, sexual humiliation, and environmental degradation), dialogue, colloquial slang, and graphic, ultra-realistic detail. The effect of this energetic and angry language is to create a hermetically sealed environment that is claustrophobic, and emphasizes the inhuman behavior of some individuals.

Any charge of distancing history cannot be leveled against *Paco's Story*, a narrative told by the ghosts of soldiers who died when all the members of Paco Sullivan's company – except himself – were wiped out. Heinemann's portrayal of the shadowy veteran, who received multiple wounds and is still severely disabled, omits to inform the reader of Paco's private life; his mutilated body is more significant as a sign of the war's legacy. Although there is frequent use of analepsis (flashback) to recall the circumstances of the battle, it is equally important that Paco's present life is explored. As the novel's first few sentences in "Foreword" suggest, *Paco's Story* is not a conventional war story, but a more wide-ranging and inclusive tale which depicts the lives of drifters, vagrants, hobos, and other neglected street folk of America. It has thus a blue-collar feel, a rootedness that avoids the solipsistic, self-absorbed genre of writing that sometimes reifies Vietnam.

Tim O'Brien, author of a personal memoir, *If I Die in a Combat Zone* (1973), and of several Vietnam-themed novels, *Going After Cacciato* (1978),

The Things They Carried (1990), *In the Lake of the Woods* (1994), *Tomcat in Love* (1998), and *July, July* (2002), is one of Vietnam War fiction's most distinguished writers. *Going After Cacciato* and *The Things They Carried*, in particular, have been influential in offering a different template for addressing the war, one that breaks with realism while not entirely supplanting it. *Going After Cacciato* is an interrogative text, asking more questions of the reader than it answers. A large part of the narrative centers on the pursuit of Cacciato (the name means "hunted"), who deserts in the first chapter. Cacciato is trailed through exotic Eastern and Middle Eastern countries all the way to Paris – or is he? The hunt might be entirely a fantasy. Two other strands of narrative are juxtaposed against this picaresque, episodic tale – realist passages situated in the historical Vietnam War, and short chapters of meditation and interpretation called "Observation Post." The result of such interweaving of themes is an original and profound novel, which explores the conflict in relation to such problematical matters as the nature of reality and our ways of understanding social and individual responsibility.

Continuing the concerns treated in *Going After Cacciato*, *The Things They Carried* develops the theme of fictionality. Situated within the parameters of postmodernism, its overriding theme is storytelling, its method self-analytical, its nature metafictive, its mood commemorative. Its collage-like arrangement of stories, some confessedly untrue, others autobiographical, a few endorsed as authentic or real, collectively questions the traditional identity and conventions of the novel form. The reader is unsure of the collection's provenance, of its formal status, of its connection, if any, with more orthodox war fictions.

O'Brien – like earlier novelists such as Norman Mailer in *Why Are We In Vietnam?* (1967) and William Eastlake in *The Bamboo Bed* (1969), and later writers such as Stephen Wright in *Meditations in Green* (1983) – is an urbane writer whose formal experiments construct war as multifaceted, fragmentary, kaleidoscopic, absurd, and surreal in character. A critique of this experimentation might argue that such a mode of representation signifies that the conflict is not only decentered but indeed meaningless or, at least, impenetrable – a kind of "ghost story country," as Michael Herr called Vietnam.[16] One intriguing way of combining the technically avant-garde with the lucidly political is evident in Robert Stone's *Dog Soldiers* (1974). Stone's novel, initially set in Vietnam, is an angry condemnation of America's involvement in the war and its destructive foreign policy. Its account of heroin smuggling, gratuitous violence, and moral devastation assumes a symbolic and nightmarish quality.

Vietnam: the "nonfictional novel"

Compared with other prose genres, the creative demands of novelistic fiction to invent and imagine stories inhibit the direct expression of authorial opinion. This can be unhelpfully restrictive, especially when a conflict – as in the case of Vietnam – is unusually susceptible to contestation, revision, and reinterpretation. A remedy – and the genre with which Vietnam is particularly associated – is the hybrid factual/fictional (or "factional") account. The best of such writing is related to the New Journalism of the 1960s, as exemplified by Norman Mailer's *The Armies of the Night* (1968). This experimental "nonfictional novel" narrates an antiwar march on the Pentagon, and attempts to write, as the subtitle has it, "history as a novel; the novel as history." Mailer's iconoclastic book, in which he includes himself as protagonist, acted as a paradigm for others, especially for the journalist Michael Herr in *Dispatches* (1977). Herr's series of free-standing meditations offers a critique of conventional war reporting, substituting instead an imagistic prose that communicates radical insights and draws upon the oppositional values and language of the counterculture.

Personal war journals have long been a persuasive form of witness, since their authors' combat experience authenticates them as credible texts both ideologically and epistemologically. *Dispatches* stands out aesthetically and linguistically from those conventional war journals that narrate a predictable spiritual odyssey of initiation that debunks traditional myths of patriotism and ends in the veteran's disillusionment. Herr's individualistic "illumination rounds"[17] – reports which were initially intended for readers of magazines – do not conform to this common format, and *Dispatches* does glamorize war somewhat through its iconography of music and rebellion. Many of the justly acclaimed war memoirs, such as Ron Kovic's *Born on the Fourth of July* (1976), Philip Caputo's *A Rumor of War* (1977), Robert Mason's *Chickenhawk* (1983), and W. D. Ehrhart's *Vietnam–Perkasie* (1983), rarely mystify war, and this lends their work historical seriousness. They also demonstrate affinity with Mailer's idea of generic crossover from fact to fiction – the radical concept of the nonfictional novel.

Vietnam: women's prose

The area of women's writing and the feminine point of view have generally been neglected in scholarly studies of Vietnam War literature, and there is a substantial archive to be recovered.[18] Certain Vietnam novels by women try to extrapolate meaning from seemingly pointless events. In Bobbie Ann Mason's *In Country* (1985), the young heroine poignantly seeks to understand her father's war experience and death, a situation paralleled in Jayne Anne Phillips's *Machine Dreams* (1984), in which a young woman tries to discover the truth about her dead brother. Joan Didion's *Democracy* (1984) and Susan Fromberg Schaeffer's *Buffalo Afternoon* (1989), about a male veteran, explore related themes. In these novels, the war's repercussions are filtered through a generational and gendered consciousness, where truth is hard to find for daughters, sisters, other female characters, and women readers.

Several works by women journalists also attempt to clarify the historical realities of a highly mediated, male-dominated conflict. Frances FitzGerald's *Fire in the Lake* (1972) addresses the gulf between Vietnamese and Americans; Gloria Emerson's *Winners and Losers* (1976) and Myra MacPherson's *Long Time Passing* (1984) present a collective portrait of the "Vietnam Generation." Most significant of these ideological critiques of the war are three radical books by Mary McCarthy: *Vietnam* (1967), *Hanoi* (1968), and *Medina* (1972), which criticize US cultural imperialism. Personal journals and women's oral history create a less overtly politicized perspective on the war than McCarthy's, yet raise equally wide internationalist and humanitarian concerns. Among such works are Lynda Van Devanter's *Home Before Morning: The Story of an Army Nurse in Vietnam* (1983); Le Ly Hayslip's *When Heaven and Earth Changed Places* (1989) and *Child of War* (1993); Wendy Wilder Larsen and Tran Thi Nga's *Shallow Graves: Two Women and Vietnam* (1986); and Kathryn Marshall's *In The Combat Zone* (1987).[19]

Vietnam: African-American prose

Ethnicity and race, like gender, are key ideological factors in evaluating Vietnam War literature. Black Americans, either enlistees or career soldiers, originally supported the war; however, after 1966, new conscription legislation, due to growing manpower shortages, resulted in a disproportionate and unfair drafting of black soldiers, together with Chicano and poor working-class draftees. Consequently, black conscripts associated more actively with the Civil Rights movement, especially after the assassination of Martin Luther King, and opposed the conflict as a "White Man's War." US atrocities and bombing after the Tet Offensive in 1968 also contributed to black soldiers showing sympathy for Vietnamese troops and civilians. These issues are addressed in such works as Wallace Terry's oral history *Bloods* (1984), Clyde Taylor's anthology *Vietnam and Black America* (1973), Robert W. Mullen's *Blacks and Vietnam* (1981), Stanley Goff's *Brothers, Black Soldiers in the Nam* (1982), and George Davis's *Coming Home* (1972). The main form of black opposition to the war was through music, although two novels, Ben Cunningham's *Green Eyes* (1976) and John A. Williams's *Captain Blackman* (1972), broadly address the issues.

Vietnam: drama

America's defeat in Vietnam had more to do with Russian and Chinese logistical and financial support for the North Vietnamese than with the antiwar movement that inspired Vietnam-related theater. In analyzing the role of drama in depicting the conflict, J. W. Fenn and Nora M. Alter both locate plays in wider contexts: Fenn in the evolution of American theater; Alter in American and European political drama and in television.[20] In Vietnam drama, performance date and mode of audience engagement are crucial data. Plays such as Megan Terry's *Viet Rock* (1966), Joseph Heller's *We Bombed in New Haven* (1967), and Tuli Kupferberg's *Fuck Nam* (1967), are sometimes criticized for their extreme and distracting performance techniques. The dramatist David Rabe also shows the influence of absurdism, surrealism, and the theater of cruelty in his cycle of plays, *The Basic Training of Pavlo Hummel* (1969), *Sticks and Bones* (1972), *The Orphan* (1975), and *Streamers* (1977). Other significant plays are Arthur Kopit's frontier-based *Indians* (1968) and Amlin Gray's *How I Got That Story* (1981), a critique of New Journalism.

Vietnam: poetry

An understanding of Vietnam War poetry is assisted by some seminal works. James F. Mersmann's *Out of the Vietnam Vortex* (1974) addresses the antiwar verse of Allen Ginsberg, Denise Levertov, Robert Bly, and Robert Duncan. Two early anthologies, *Winning Hearts and Minds* (1972), edited by Larry Rottmann, Jan Barry, and Basil T. Paquet, and *Demilitarized Zones* (1976), edited by Jan Barry and W. D. Ehrhart, set the chronology. Ehrhart later edited two other anthologies, *Carrying the Darkness* (1985) and *Unaccustomed Mercy* (1989). The scope and richness of Vietnam War poetry, perhaps the outstanding genre for representing the conflict, is best apprehended by reading the four poets examined in the last part of this chapter (John Balaban, W. D. Ehrhart, Walter McDonald, and Bruce Weigl) and by also considering the work of other notable poets, such as D. F. Brown, Michael Casey, David Huddle, Bryan Alec Floyd, Yusef Komunyakaa, Basil T. Paquet, D. C. Berry, and Gerald McCarthy.

John Balaban's poetry, principally *After Our War* (1974), *Blue Mountain* (1982), and *Words for My Daughter* (1991), places the Vietnam War in the contexts of oriental, classical, and western European culture. A collector and translator of Vietnamese folk poetry, Balaban produces work that is learned, spiritual, and built upon close observation. A conscientious objector who carried out children's relief work in Vietnam, his focus is understandably upon the situation of Vietnamese civilians rather than American soldiers. His poetry, free from ethnocentrism, expresses sympathy for Vietnamese custom and tradition, an approach that lends his work historical impartiality and bridges the gulf in understanding between occupier and occupied. His best poems, such as "Mau Than" (1974), "The Dragonfish" (1974), "After Our War" (1974), and "Newsdate" (1982), together with his prose output like the memoir *Remembering Heaven's Face* (1991), bring a studied repose and transfiguration of the ordinary to harrowing conflict situations.

W. D. Ehrhart has written some of the most celebrated poems addressing Vietnam – works such as "A Relative Thing" (1975), "Letter" (1978), "A Confirmation" (1978), "The Blizzard of Sixty Six" (1984), "The Distance We Travel" (1993), and "Beautiful Wreckage" (1999). More than any other poet, he has engaged with the human repercussions of the war, producing a succession of volumes, including *A Generation of Peace* (1975), *To Those Who Have Gone Home Tired* (1984), *The Distance We Travel* (1993), and *Beautiful Wreckage* (1999). His Vietnam War poems blend into a critique of his country's other military interventions abroad, and they demonstrate political courage as well as perseverance. Ehrhart's poems are usually unsentimental, written in sparse free verse, displaying a precision of utterance and a rhetorical skill that conceals their artistry. His later works, which subtly employ voice, tone, and rhythm to enhance the cadences of common speech, demonstrate respect towards the Vietnamese, as in the formally exquisite "The Lotus Cutters of Ho Tay" (1993).

Walter McDonald, an air force officer and trained pilot, drew upon his service in Vietnam to write some of the war's most enduring poems, such as "For Kelly Missing in Action" (1973), "The Retired Pilot to Himself" (1974), "Caliban in Blue" (1976), "Night at Cam Ranh Bay" (1976), "The Winter Before the War" (1979), "Storm Warning" (1987), "Once You've Been To War" (1988), "The Food Pickers of Saigon" (1988), "After the Noise of Saigon" (1988), and "Out of the Stone They Come" (1995). These poems are principally found in five collections: *Caliban in Blue* (1976), *The Flying Dutchman* (1987), *After the Noise of Saigon* (1988), *Night Landings* (1989), and *Counting Survivors* (1995). McDonald's work emphasizes the act of remembrance, creating recurrent iconic figures – the airman risking danger and causing havoc; helpless Vietnamese victims; the postwar veteran. His poems, rhetorically bold and resonant, evoke devastation and, later, adaptation and recovery, expressed through a stoical Texas landscape.

Bruce Weigl's poetry is aesthetically distinctive in its use of narrative and visionary patterns to encapsulate the evolving history of the Vietnam conflict.[21] This artistic, surreal quality is registered in experimental poems such as "Monkey" (1979) and the well-known "Song of Napalm" (1985). Many of his poems – for example, "Temple Near Quang Tri, Not on the Map" (1985), "Surrounding Blues on the Way Down" (1985), "Girl at the Chu Lai Laundry" (1985), and "Burning Shit at An Khe" (1985) – are impressionistic vignettes. In his later work, the war becomes a ghostly presence in American life. Weigl's principal war volumes are *Executioner* (1976), *Like a Sack Full of Old Quarrels* (1976), *A Romance* (1979), *The Monkey Wars* (1984), and *Song of Napalm* (1988). A scholar of Vietnam War literature, Weigl has also collaborated with Thanh T. Nguyen on a collection of poems written by North Vietnamese soldiers, *Poems from Captured Documents* (1994).

Conclusion

Literary output from the Korean War is modest compared with that generated by the Vietnam conflict. In literature, as in life, Vietnam still exerts a post-traumatic stress effect, reminding Americans of a failed military enterprise and warning of the dangers of ill thought-out foreign policy. For most writers who fought in Korea or Vietnam, the memory of hundreds of thousands of Korean, Chinese, and Vietnamese deaths remains on their conscience. For readers, literature of the Korean and Vietnam Wars offers prescient comment on America's subsequent military engagements, such as her lengthening involvement in Iraq and Afghanistan.

NOTES

1. See Arne Axelsson, *Restrained Response: American Novels of the Cold War and Korea, 1945–1962* (New York: Greenwood, 1990), 59–110.
2. Quotations from the poems by Childress, Hinojosa, Magner, Saner, Wantling, and Wilson are all from W. D. Ehrhart and Philip K. Jason (eds.), *Retrieving Bones: Stories and Poems of the Korean War* (New Brunswick, NJ: Rutgers University Press, 1999).
3. The poems by William Childress all appear in William Childress, *Burning the Years and Lobo: Poems 1962–1975* (East Saint Louis, IL: Essai Seay, 1986).
4. Ehrhart and Jason, *Retrieving Bones*, 167.
5. Ibid., 161, 162, 162.
6. Ibid., 163.
7. Ibid., 164.
8. "The Korean," "Without Laying Claim," "Korea 1953," and "Sure," William Wantling, *The Source* (El Cerrito, CA: Dustbooks, 1966); "Pusan Liberty," "The Day the Dam Burst," and "The Awakening," Wantling, *The Awakening*, ed.

Edward Lucie-Smith (London: Turret, 1967); "Poetry," Wantling, *San Quentin's Stranger* (Dunedin, New Zealand: Caveman, 1973).

9. Ehrhart and Jason, *Retrieving Bones*, 189, 187, 187, 186–7, 187, 190, 191.
10. Childress, *Burning the Years*, 164.
11. "The Man Without a Face" is from James Magner, Jr., *Toiler of the Sea* (1965); "Zero Minus One Minute" is from Magner, *Although There Is Night* (1968); "Repository" is from Magner, *Rose of My Flowering Night* (1985) (all published Francestown, NH: Golden Quill).
12. Ehrhart and Jason, *Retrieving Bones*, 178, 179, 180–1.
13. Reg Saner, "Flag Memoir," *Ontario Review* 34 (Spring/Summer, 1991).
14. Philip D. Beidler, *Re-Writing America: Vietnam Authors in Their Generation* (Athens: University of Georgia Press, 1991), 9–103; Thomas Myers, *Walking Point: American Narratives of Vietnam* (Oxford University Press, 1988), 169–85.
15. See Philip H. Melling, *Vietnam in American Literature* (Boston: Twayne,1990), 112–24.
16. Michael Herr, *Dispatches* (London: Pan, 1978), 8.
17. "Illumination Rounds" is the title of a major section of *Dispatches*, ibid., 137–52.
18. See Susan Jeffords, *The Remasculinization of America: Gender and the Vietnam War* (Bloomington: Indiana University Press, 1989), xi–xv.
19. Alf Louvre and Jeffrey Walsh (eds.), *Tell Me Lies About Vietnam: Cultural Battles for the Meaning of the War* (Milton Keynes: Open University Press, 1988), 14–23.
20. J. W. Fenn, *Levitating the Pentagon: Evolutions in the American Theatre of the Vietnam War Era* (Newark: University of Delaware Press, 1992), 23–65; Nora M. Alter, *Vietnam Protest Theatre: The Television War on Stage* (Bloomington: Indiana University Press, 1996), 1–23.
21. Bruce Weigl's *The Monkey Wars* (Athens: University of Georgia Press, 1985) offers a representative introduction to his work.

FURTHER READING

Philip D. Beidler, *Re-Writing America: Vietnam Authors in Their Generation* (Athens: University of Georgia Press, 1991).

Vicente F. Gotera, *Radical Visions: Poetry by Vietnam Veterans* (Athens: University of Georgia Press, 1994).

Philip K. Jason, *Acts and Shadows: The Vietnam War in American Literary Culture* (Lanham, MD: Rowman and Littlefield, 2000).

John Carlos Rowe and Rick Berg (eds.), *The Vietnam War and American Culture* (New York: Columbia University Press, 1991).

20

DAVID PASCOE

The Cold War and the "war on terror"

Desktop secrets

At the climax of John le Carré's *Absolute Friends* (2004), the finest fictional evocation of the deep genealogical links between the Cold War and the ongoing "war on terror," the novel's hero, Ted Mundy, is discovered alone on the premises of his bankrupt language school in Heidelberg. Mundy, a former British Council employee who has drifted into intelligence jobs organized by his "absolute friend," Sasha, a Stasi double agent, sets about cracking open boxes of what he supposes is a consignment of countercultural textbooks sent to him by a mysterious benefactor, Dimitri, for the purpose of establishing a "Counter-University" in the ancient German city. He is disconcerted instead to discover handbooks of terrorism techniques, reams of inflammatory literature, and further within, rows of hand grenades and what he assumes are timers for home-made bombs. His bewilderment is interrupted by the chatter of automatic gunfire, and the view, as he peers from his window, of Sasha's slain body in the courtyard. Moments later, as Mundy attempts an inexpert escape, clinging to a window ledge, he too is torn apart by heavy caliber bullets fired by a "masked languid" counterterrorist officer. Within a matter of moments, what will come to be known as the Siege of Heidelberg is over.[1]

There then emerges a counternarrative: an account posted on "a not-for-profit website pledged to transparency in politics" by one "ARNOLD," who claims to be a recently resigned, long-serving field operative of British Intelligence. His blog maintains that the siege was a piece of theater created by a "shadowy former operative of the CIA" on behalf of a neoconservative junta now running Washington politics, and that, while Mundy "may have looked like an ex-British council deadbeat," he was, in fact, "an unsung hero of the Cold War [who had] supplied the Western Alliance with priceless intelligence on the Communist threat." However, in the United Kingdom, in response to these allegations, "a well-placed and reliable senior official with access to the highest levels of government [is] reported as saying that some people these days [are] getting a bit too George Orwell for their own health."[2]

It is appropriate that Orwell should be invoked so cynically as a source of paranoia – of an awareness of conspiracy – in the last pages of le Carré's fiction, for to be "George Orwell" is to be almost uncannily aware of the nature of the Cold War and its future repercussions. From the perspective of another century, it is clear that the conflict had begun the moment the heat radiated by the atomic explosions in western Japan in August 1945 began to dissipate. By October of that year, Orwell was sketching out "the kind of world-view, the kind of beliefs, and the social structure that would probably prevail in a state which was at once unconquerable and in a permanent state of 'cold war' with its neighbours" – a cultural conflict which would imply "an end to large-scale war at the cost of prolonging indefinitely a 'peace that is no peace'."[3] Two years later, with the now capitalized Cold War well under-way, sanctioned by Churchill's observation that an Iron Curtain had des-cended, the proclamation of Truman Doctrine, and the implementation of the Marshall Plan, Orwell suggested that the fear inspired by the atom bomb would lead to the worst possibility of all: "the division of the world into two or three vast superstates, unable to conquer one another and unable to be overthrown by any internal rebellion."[4] Hence, the central geographical conceit of Nineteen Eighty-Four (1949), possibly the first novel of the Cold War, sees the world divided up into the land masses of Eurasia, Eastasia, and Oceania, each constantly at war with the others – a projection of the Yalta conference at which Churchill, Roosevelt, and Stalin carved up the postwar world into "spheres of influence." Within each state, overseen by the surveil-lance technologies personified in Big Brother, Orwell predicted that "the necessary psychological atmosphere would be kept up by complete severance from the outer world."[5]

The Cold War largely depended upon "severance" to maintain the balance of power – the execution of a strategic containment framed, simply enough, by the global awareness that an act of preemption would bring on mutually assured destruction – a mad stability necessitating the kind of securely closed worlds that Orwell described. On the front line were not the fabulously complex weapons systems nestling in their silos in the wheatlands of the Midwest or beneath the steppes of central Asia; or held fast in a nuclear submarine just under the waves of the North Atlantic; or strapped in the belly of a B-52 or a Backfire bomber crossing the Arctic Circle. On the front line, amounting to the poor bloody infantry of the Cold War, were those anon-ymous and coded agents of espionage and counterespionage, moving with stealthy footfall "along those warrenlike corridors of that anonymous build-ing in Whitehall where no one exists even when they're alive,"[6] or, at the end of the day, sitting in those "little reading rooms at the Admiralty, little committees popping up with funny names": JIC, M, Q, 007, etc.[7] As Michael Denning suggests, "the spy novel is in a sense the War novel of the Cold War."[8]

Sir Michael Herman, a former secretary of Whitehall's Joint Intelligence Committee, observed in 1989: "The Cold War was in a special sense an intelligence conflict … Never before in peacetime have the relationships of competing power blocks been so influenced by intelligence assessments."[9] Indeed, the main theater of this war was the office, the conflict's secrets contained in boxes, cabinets, and folders. Some of its greatest works of fiction, their titles so often exploiting the strictness of the definite article, meet and mold this matter of fact. Kingsley Amis's *The James Bond Dossier* (1965) was doubtless an attempt to bind Fleming's agent to the desk while Amis wrote *Colonel Sun* (1968);[10] Adam Hunt's *The Berlin Memorandum* (1965) and Frederick Forsyth's *The Odessa File* (1972) were both reminders that Nazi officers were at the dark heart of postwar Germany; while the best known of the post-Fleming spy novels, Len Deighton's *The Ipcress File* (1962), is presented in the form of a secret dossier. Such novels are not without action in the field, but they are at least as interested in procedural issues – archival research or paper chases – to show the extent to which the life of the spy was one of civil service, both insular and invasive.

The hero of *The Human Factor* (1978), Graham Greene's finest espionage novel, is Maurice Castle, "a dullish man, first class, of course, with files,"[11] and this clerk, it emerges, has committed treason. Greene knew the personal implications of such treachery better than most, having worked on MI6's Iberian desk during the war, directly under the command of Kim Philby, who would be unmasked as "The Third Man" in 1963. Four years after his defection, Philby published his memoirs, with an introduction by Greene, who asked, rhetorically: "who among us has not committed treason to something or someone more important than a country?"[12] Treachery by functionaries is not solely a British phenomenon: in *Harlot's Ghost* (1991), Norman Mailer's immense fictional history of the Cold War, it emerges as part of the job:

> In Intelligence, we look to discover the compartmentalization of the heart. We made an in depth study once in the CIA and learned to our dismay (it was really horror!) that one-third of the men and women who could pass our security clearance were divided enough – handled properly – to be turned into agents of a foreign power.[13]

The possibility of divided loyalty meant that operatives needed to be held tight, in compartments or cells. Greene's central figure, Colonel Daintry, a security officer investigating the identity of a double agent in Castle's section, is necessarily imprisoned in the secrecies imposed by his own work. By way of illustration, his immediate superior, Perceval, shows him a Ben Nicholson canvas, "full of squares of different colour ... yet living so happily together. No clash":

> Perceval pointed at a yellow square. "There's your Section 6. That's your square from now on. You don't need to worry about the blue and the red. All you have to do is pinpoint our man and then tell me. You've no responsibility for what happens in the blue or red squares. In fact not even in the yellow. You just report. No bad conscience. No guilt."[14]

Isolated in his box, the individual agent is insulated against the moral chill of the Cold War, so that "an action has nothing to do with its consequences." Later, Castle is given some information in confidence – "you know how we like to make our little boxes watertight. This has got to be your personal box" – and similarly, when he meets with his Soviet control, he is told: "you know how it is in your own outfit. It's the same in ours. We live in boxes and it's they who choose the box."[15] Beyond the hermetically sealed circle of his immediate contacts – his briefing officer, his mission controller, and his director in the field – the agent has no existence: he is out in the cold.

Greene's choice of name for his double agent is significant: *Castle* implies the Englishman's home – and it is to secure a settled domestic existence for his South African wife that he commits treachery – but also opens the box of chess pieces which are central to the widespread representation of the Cold War as a "game, a military game, a Kriegspiel,"[16] or a stalemate. The chess board is made of sixty-four ruled squares – a world of black and white, of balanced oppositions, of strict rules of engagement, and of predictable strategies. In Fleming's *From Russia with Love* (1956), the SMERSH planner is Kronsteen, a grand master who has all the moves of Bond's end game worked out, while each chapter of Deighton's *Funeral in Berlin* (1964) carries an epigraph from an untitled chess handbook bearing a thematic relevance. Early in this novel, Harry Palmer, the Burnley-born spy, encounters a KGB colonel over a chess set:

"Are you a chess player, English?" he said.
"I prefer games where there's a better chance to cheat," I said.
"I agree with you," said Stok. "The preoccupation with rules doesn't sit well upon the creative mind."
"Like communism?" I said.
Stok picked up a knight. "But the pattern of chess is the pattern of our capitalist world. The world of bishops and castles, and kings and knights."
"Don't look at me," I said. "I'm just a pawn. I'm here in the front rank."[17]

Palmer is right; his moves are limited to the next square and at any moment he might be sacrificed for the sake of the greater game.

Howling spaces

In *Underworld* (1997), Don DeLillo busted open the bunker mentalities of the Cold-War world. At the heart of this vast book is a representation of a paradigm shift that occurred when the war moved from subterranean cells into wide open skies. As she putters about in her Midwest kitchen on October 8, 1957, mom Erica Deming feels a twisted sort of disappointment, a *Weltschmerz*:

> It flew at an amazing rate of speed over the North Pole, *beep beep beep*, passing just above us, evidently, at certain times. She could not understand how this could happen. Were there other surprises coming, things we haven't been told about?[18]

As it happens, the American way of life has been blown open by Sputnik, a 184 lb antennaed metal sphere orbiting at 18,000 miles an hour almost 300 miles overhead – the thin end of a weapon system launched out of Kazakhstan aimed at the values of Middle America. At the time of its blast-off, the satellite was construed by Krushchev as a form of communications technology: its trajectory announced that man could live in a world of simultaneous information, which is to say, a world of resonance in which all data might influence other data, whose center is everywhere and whose margin is nowhere. Within a few months of its launch, work began on an alternative use for the satellite – surveillance – and, within a generation, such technologies, both photographic and acoustic, would Google the planet. From her split-level suburban house, Erica Deming looks out:

> All up and down the curving streets there were young trees and small new box shrubs and a sense of openness, a sense of seeing everything there is to see at a single glance, with nothing shrouded or walled or protected from the glare.[19]

Depicted here, four days after the launch of Sputnik (and in contradistinction to the hitherto closed world of the Cold War) is a new sense of openness; of vulnerability to aerial attack. With the benefit of fifty years' hindsight, the "glare" is not solar, but rather that of the satellite moving across Middle America, looking down intently, omnisciently. Where connectedness and surveillance – the twin tracks of the Sputnik project – intersect can be found the heart of the postwar American novel, as it has attempted to frame the next stage of the superpower conflict; a theater of war played out between technology and paranoia. In particular, the work of Thomas Pynchon, John Barth, and DeLillo involves not so much an elaboration of character and event, as before, but an immersion in complex situations and labyrinthine plots which entail the surveillance of many people simultaneously across a network. As a character in *Underworld* muses: "Everything connected at some undisclosed point down the systems line ... it was a splendid mystery in a way, a source of wonder."[20]

In the same novel, DeLillo's Klara Sax muses: "Power meant something thirty, forty years ago. It was stable, it was focused, it was a tangible thing ... it held us together, the Soviets and us."[21] This is deliberately vague, but it is clear that at some point in the late 1960s, the connection between the two superpowers loosened; the power going down the line failed. The syndrome might have been caused by *détente*, but more likely the power outage occurred because the Cold War had begun to be hijacked by another kind of conflict, one driven by the revolution that saw Mundy and his absolute friend, Sasha, agitating in Berlin against the egregiousness of American foreign policy in Indochina. The French critic Paul Virilio states confidently that the paradigm shift took place in 1969, with the attack by Israeli Special Forces on Beirut airport that destroyed a dozen airliners, set alight hangars and fuel dumps, and wreaked $100 million in damage. "The paratroopers destroyed planes and went home. And these acts of war without a war, the equivalent of terrorist acts by one state against another, haven't stopped since." Effectively, "the art of deterrence, prohibiting political war, favors the upsurge, not of conflicts, *but of acts of war without war*."[22]

In *Mao II* (1991), a sleek, haunted, and ludicrously alert novel about "this new culture, the system of world terror," DeLillo has a grievously blocked writer, Bill Gray, emerge from social withdrawal into a netherworld of hostage-taking and terror to observe: "Beckett is the last writer to shape the way we think and see. After him, the major work involves midair explosions and crumbled buildings. This is the new tragic narrative."[23] For his part, Samuel Beckett grew into a writer in the Resistance and further developed his voice through the Cold War, his fictions following its deepest shapes – operatives contained in darkened rooms and filthy cells, leading ghostly existences on the margins, at the frontiers of life and death, and held fast in routine impasse until nothing more than a final howl in space: "oh all to end."[24] Now DeLillo can depict "true terror" as "a language and a vision": "there is a deep narrative structure to terrorist acts and they infiltrate and alter consciousness in ways that writers used to aspire to."[25] In contrast to Beckett's dying words, DeLillo's dying world, America, then, is "the world's living myth," the postwar United States possessing "a certain mythical quality that terrorists find attractive."[26] In *Mao II*, a New Yorker observes of the World Trade

Center towers: "The size is deadly. But having two of them is like a comment, it's like a dialogue, only I don't know what they're saying."[27]

But Ramzi Yousef knew what the towers were saying, and his halting response came a couple of years later when his ad hoc jihadist group detonated a bomb in the basement of the North Tower, killing six people, injuring a thousand, and causing $300 million in damage. For Virilio, that first attack was, in theory, as significant as the second would be, and for the same reason: the terrorists knew that the World Trade Center was "a teleport ... an economic and communications centre." So, using "the speed of mass communication," Yousef timed the bomb-blast to catch the evening news, and Virilio concluded: "Terrorists were the first to have waged an information war; the explosion only existed because it was simultaneously coupled to a multimedia explosion"[28] – the World Wide Web.

After the subsequent 9/11 attack, DeLillo argued that the World Trade towers were not only an emblem of technology, but "a justification, in a sense, for technology's irresistible will to realize in solid form whatever becomes theoretically allowable."[29] Instead of "possible," which might be expected in the circumstances, "allowable" materializes here as an oddly repressive adjective, suggesting the involvement, as necessary, of higher powers in the technological process. The Cold War was characterized by its dazzling technology, much of which was spun off from weapons research. The computer network, the telecommunications satellite, GPS navigation, and, most notably, the jet airliner, "a symbol of indigenous mobility and zest, and of the galaxy of glittering destinations,"[30] were all derived from the military-industrial complex; hence, DeLillo suggests, "the materials and methods we devise make it possible for us to claim our future ... the systems and networks that change the way we live and think"[31] are only ever products developed after the fact of pure war.

Yet in the days that followed the 9/11 attacks, commentators drew attention to the atavistic nature of the offence, suggesting that, despite their embrace of technology, the suicide bombers "want[ed] to bring back our past."[32] For Martin Amis, the conflicts 9/11 signaled were, as ever, between opposed geographical areas, West and East, but now involved "opposed centuries, or even millennia": "a landscape of ferocious anachronisms: nuclear jihad on the Indian subcontinent; the medieval agonism of Islam; the bronze age blunderings of the Middle East."[33] DeLillo concurs: "The future has yielded to medieval expedience, to the old slow furies of cut-throat experience," with the result that "we have fallen back in time and space,"[34] that vertiginous verb implying both a plummet and regression since the attack on America. Finally, it is the terrorists' modification of branded technologies that scars and scares most: "a score or so of Stanley knives produced two million tons of rubble";[35] Boeing airliners became intercontinental ballistic missiles; and, in subsequent jihadi plots against airspaces, Nike Air sneakers would be packed with high explosive; Coke bottles refilled with hair dye and hydrogen peroxide would be detonated by mobile phones; and a blazing Jeep Cherokee, freighted with gas bottles and petrol cans, would be rammed into an airport concourse in Scotland.

DeLillo observed that, with the fall of the Twin Towers, "there is something empty in the sky. The writer tries to give memory, tenderness and meaning to all that howling space."[36] Some make their excuses and leave be: Jay McInerney's *The Good Life* (2006) opens on 10 September and then jumps forward to the day after the attack; the author felt that "the book would be more powerful leaving that space empty for everyone to fill in."[37] In graphic contrast, Jonathan Safran Foer's *Extremely Loud and Incredibly Close* (2005) furnishes a series of fifteen photographs printed on consecutive pages which, when flicked, reverse the descent of a man who jumped from one of the Twin Towers. In the fiction, this reversal comforts Oskar, the grieving nine-year-old hero who thinks this rising man may have been his father, murdered in the attack; however, it provides scant comfort to the relatives of the towers' 2,750 fallen. Perhaps only DeLillo has provided an adequate fictional complement to the gravity of these events; his *Falling Man* (2007) features passages which record the perspective of one of the hijackers, named Hammad, whom we see first in Hamburg, subsequently in America, and finally on the airliner, lashing out at time. As the plane approaches the tower, we inhabit the hijacker's simulated consciousness, but then, at the instant the Boeing strikes the building, the point of view shifts to that of Keith Neuducker, the corporate lawyer who descends from his office and emerges into the corpse-strewn plaza, where DeLillo now reprises (with some minor variation) the novel's haunting opening sequence: "it was not a street any-more but a world, a time, and a space of falling ash and near night."[38] Other novelists have drawn, in ever-increasing circles, the ramifications of the "war on terror," which spread, in the weeks after 9/11, in an arc encompassing the ancient deserts of Afghanistan, the packed *madrasahs* of Pakistan, and, within eighteen months of the "Planes Operation," the air-conditioned bunkers and spangled palaces of Baathist Iraq.

One of the main architects of the "war on terror," US Secretary of Defense Donald Rumsfeld, famously pronounced at a press briefing in early 2002 that the threat heralded by the 9/11 attacks was indescribably omnipresent:

> The message is: there are known knowns. There are things we know that we know. There are known unknowns. That is to say there are things that we now

know we don't know. But there are also unknown unknowns. There are things we don't know we don't know.[39]

In a curious way, what Martin Amis has called Rumsfield's "haiku like taxonomy of the terrorist threat" tracks the paradigm shift in international relations over the last three decades.[40] The movement from "known knowns," the certainty that certain nations have nuclear weapons, to "known unknowns," the uncertainty about numbers or deployments, is familiar and stable enough to be part of a Cold-War discourse. But lying beyond the cordon are the "unknown unknowns" of the terror cells, the black boxes of conspiracy existing virtually now, beyond the reach of any Defense Department. For perhaps information networks are the true location of Rumsfeld's "unknown unknown": the internet, originally a Cold-War effort to speed up communication between battle groups, now hosts the only truly legitimate writing about the "war on terror" – the military blog – and simultaneously functions as a vehicle of recruitment and logistics for the global jihad, or, at the very least, for dissenting voices such as the "Counter-University" in le Carré's novel. Now, and forever, the "war on terror" is, it seems, an information war, whose scrolling pages howl away across cyberspace to the crack of doom.

NOTES

1. John le Carré, *Absolute Friends* (London: Hodder & Stoughton, 2004), 367.
2. Ibid., 370, 377.
3. George Orwell, "You and the Atom Bomb," *Tribune* (October 19, 1945); rptd in Orwell, *The Complete Works of George Orwell*, ed. Peter Davison, 20 vols. (London: Secker & Warburg, 1986–98), XVII: 321.
4. Orwell, *The Complete Works*, XVII: 320.
5. Orwell, "Toward European Unity," *Partisan Review* (July–August 1947); rptd in Orwell, *The Complete Works*, XIX: 163.
6. Adam Hall, *The Berlin Memorandum* (London: Collins, 1965), 15.
7. Le Carré, *Tinker Tailor Soldier Spy* (London: Hodder & Stoughton, 1974), 28.
8. Michael Denning, *Cover Stories: Narrative and Ideology in the British Spy Thriller* (London: Routledge, 1987), 92.
9. Cited in Peter Hennessy, *The Secret State: Whitehall and the Cold War* (Harmondsworth: Penguin, 2004), 3.
10. *Colonel Sun*, the first "continuation" Bond novel after Fleming's death, was written by Kingsley Amis under the pseudonym Robert Markham.
11. Graham Greene, *The Human Factor* (London: Bodley Head, 1978), 38.
12. Greene, "Foreword," Kim Philby, *My Silent War* (London: McGibbon and Kee, 1967), v–vii: vii.
13. Norman Mailer, *Harlot's Ghost* (London: Abacus, 1992), 13.
14. Greene, *The Human Factor*, 46.
15. Ibid., 65, 146.

16. Paul Virilio and Sylvère Lotringer, *Pure War*, trans. Mark Polizzotti and Brian O'Keeffe (New York: Semiotext(e), 1997), 169.
17. Len Deighton, *Funeral in Berlin* (London: Jonathan Cape, 1964), 43.
18. Don DeLillo, *Underworld* (New York: Scribner, 1997), 518.
19. Ibid., 514.
20. Ibid., 408.
21. Ibid., 76.
22. Virilio and Lotringer, *Pure War*, 32–3.
23. DeLillo, *Mao II* (New York: Scribner, 1991), 157.
24. The final words of Beckett's brief novella *Stirrings Still* (1989), the last work published in his lifetime.
25. Vince Passaro, "Dangerous Don DeLillo," *New York Times Magazine* (May 19, 1991), 36–8: 35.
26. DeLillo, *The Names* (New York: Scribner, 1982), 114.
27. DeLillo, *Mao II*, 39–40.
28. Virilio and Lotringer, *Pure War*, 174.
29. DeLillo, "In the Ruins of the Future: Reflections on Terror and Loss in the Shadow of September," *Harper's* (December 2001) 33–40: 36.
30. Martin Amis, *The Second Plane* (London: Jonathan Cape, 2008), 6.
31. DeLillo, "In the Ruins of the Future," 37.
32. Ibid., 36.
33. Amis, *The Second Plane*, 14.
34. DeLillo, "In the Ruins of the Future," 35.
35. Amis, *The Second Plane*, 4.
36. DeLillo, "In the Ruins of the Future," 36.
37. Quoted at www.usatoday.com/life/books/news/2007-09-10-911-novels_N.htm (accessed January 2009).
38. DeLillo, *Falling Man* (New York: Scribner, 2007), 2.
39. Donald Rumsfield, Defense Department briefing (February 12, 2002), available at www.defenselink.mil/transcripts/transcript.aspx?transcriptid=2636 (accessed January 2009).
40. Amis, *The Second Plane*, 52.

FURTHER READING

David Caute, *The Dancer Defects. The Struggle for Cultural Supremacy during the Cold War* (Oxford University Press, 2005).
Noam Chomsky, *9–11*, (New York: Seven Stories, 2001).
   Power and Terror: Post 9–11 Talks and Interviews (New York: Seven Stories, 2003).
Thomas Friedman, *Longitudes and Attitudes: Exploring the World After September 11* (New York: Farrar Straus Giroux, 2002).
Fred Halliday, "'High and Just Proceedings': Notes Towards an Anthology of The Cold War," *Millennium: Journal of International Studies* 30.3 (2001), 691–707.
   Two Hours that Shook the World: September 11 2001: Causes and Consequences (Basingstoke: Palgrave, 2002).
Ted Honderich, *After the Terror* (Edinburgh University Press, 2002).

Harry G. West *et al.*, *Transparency and Conspiracy: Ethnographies of Suspicion in the New World Order* (Durham, NC: Duke University Press, 2003).

Odd Arne Westad (ed.), *Reviewing the Cold War: Approaches, Interpretations, Theory* (London: Frank Cass, 2000).

Stephen J. Whitfield, *The Culture of the Cold War* (Baltimore, MD: Johns Hopkins University Press, 1991).

INDEX

Cambridge Companions to …

AUTHORS

Ovid edited by Philip Hardie

Harold Pinter edited by Peter Raby
(second edition)

Sylvia Plath edited by Jo Gill

Edgar Allan Poe edited by Kevin J. Hayes

Alexander Pope edited by Pat Rogers

Ezra Pound edited by Ira B. Nadel

Proust edited by Richard Bales

Pushkin edited by Andrew Kahn

Philip Roth edited by Timothy Parrish

Salman Rushdie edited by Abdulrazak Gurnah

Shakespeare edited by Margareta de Grazia and
Stanley Wells

Shakespeare and Popular Culture edited by
Robert Shaughnessy

Shakespeare on Film edited by Russell Jackson
(second edition)

Shakespeare on Stage edited by Stanley Wells and
Sarah Stanton

Shakespearean Comedy edited by
Alexander Leggatt

Shakespeare's History Plays edited by
Michael Hattaway

Shakespeare's Poetry edited by Patrick Cheney

Shakespearean Tragedy edited by
Claire McEachern

George Bernard Shaw edited by
Christopher Innes

Shelley edited by Timothy Morton

Mary Shelley edited by Esther Schor

Sam Shepard edited by Matthew C. Roudané

Spenser edited by Andrew Hadfield

Laurence Sterne edited by Thomas Keymer

Wallace Stevens edited by John N. Serio

Tom Stoppard edited by Katherine E. Kelly

Harriet Beecher Stowe edited by Cindy Weinstein

Jonathan Swift edited by Christopher Fox

Henry David Thoreau edited by Joel Myerson

Tolstoy edited by Donna Tussing Orwin

Mark Twain edited by Forrest G. Robinson

Virgil edited by Charles Martindale

Voltaire edited by Nicholas Cronk

Edith Wharton edited by Millicent Bell

Walt Whitman edited by Ezra Greenspan

Oscar Wilde edited by Peter Raby

Tennessee Williams edited by
Matthew C. Roudané

August Wilson edited by Christopher Bigsby

Mary Wollstonecraft edited by
Claudia L. Johnson

Virginia Woolf edited by Sue Roe and
Susan Sellers

Wordsworth edited by Stephen Gill

W. B. Yeats edited by Marjorie Howes and
John Kelly

Zola edited by Brian Nelson

TOPICS

The Actress edited by Maggie B. Gale and
John Stokes

The African American Novel edited by
Maryemma Graham

The African American Slave Narrative edited by
Audrey A. Fisch

American Modernism edited by
Walter Kalaidjian

American Realism and Naturalism edited by
Donald Pizer

American Travel Writing edited by
Alfred Bendixen and Judith Hamera

American Women Playwrights edited by
Brenda Murphy

Australian Literature edited by Elizabeth Webby

British Romantic Poetry edited by
James Chandler and Maureen N. McLane

British Romanticism edited by Stuart Curran

British Theatre, 1730–1830, edited by
Jane Moody and Daniel O'Quinn

Canadian Literature edited by Eva-Marie Kröller

The Classic Russian Novel edited by Malcolm
V. Jones and Robin Feuer Miller

Contemporary Irish Poetry edited by
Matthew Campbell

Crime Fiction edited by Martin Priestman

The Eighteenth-Century Novel edited by
John Richetti

Eighteenth-Century Poetry edited by
John Sitter

English Literature, 1500–1600 edited by
Arthur F. Kinney

English Literature, 1650–1740 edited by
Steven N. Zwicker

English Literature, 1740–1830 edited by
Thomas Keymer and Jon Mee